More than twenty-eight thousand species
are threatened with extinction.
That is 27 percent of all assessed species.

—International Union for Conservation of Nature (IUCN)

Every Penguin in the World

A Quest to See Them All

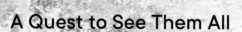

Written and photographed by
CHARLES BERGMAN

SASQUATCH BOOKS
SEATTLE

Printed in China

SASQUATCH BOOKS with colophon is a registered trademark of Penguin Random House LLC

24 23 22 21 20   9 8 7 6 5 4 3 2 1

Editor: Jennifer Worick | Production editor: Jill Saginario | Designer: Tony Ong

Library of Congress Cataloging-in-Publication Data
Names: Bergman, Charles, author.
Title: Every penguin in the world : a quest to see them all / Charles Bergman.
Description: Seattle, WA : Sasquatch Books, [2020] | Includes
    bibliographical references and index.
Identifiers: LCCN 2019022803 (print) | LCCN 2019022804 (ebook) | ISBN
    9781632172662 (hardcover) | ISBN 9781632172679 (ebook)
Subjects: LCSH: Penguins.
Classification: LCC QL696.S473 B4735 2020 (print) | LCC QL696.S473
    (ebook) | DDC 598.47—dc23
LC record available at https://lccn.loc.gov/2019022803
LC ebook record available at https://lccn.loc.gov/2019022804

ISBN: 978-1-63217-266-2

Sasquatch Books
1904 Third Avenue, Suite 710
Seattle, WA 98101

SasquatchBooks.com

Unlabeled photos: pp. ii–iii: Gentoo penguins, Falkland Islands, British Overseas Territory; p. vi: Emperor penguins, Snow Hill Island, Antarctica; p. viii: King penguins, South Georgia Island, British Overseas Territory; pp. xxx–1: Fiordland penguins, South Island, New Zealand; pp. 42–43: Magellanic penguins, Peninsula Valdés, Argentina; pp. 94–95: Gentoo penguins, Falkland Islands, British Overseas Territory; p. 177: Emperor penguins, Snow Hill Island, Antarctica

To Benjamin, Sweet Baby B,
and his new sister, Georgie;
Eric, my genius;
Ian, my wizard;
and Susan, my love

Contents

Foreword

PENGUINS ARE SOME OF THE MOST readily recognizable characters in the cast of species that call the oceans home. People rarely fail to register an emotional response to penguins. Yet, on our watch, these famously flightless birds are not faring well. Penguins are threatened by climate change, fishing pressure, invasive species, habitat loss and pollution, and more. Eleven of the eighteen species alive today are undergoing population declines and ten species are considered to be facing a high risk of extinction in the wild.

Every Penguin in the World is about the emotional connection people have to penguins. Charles and Susan embark upon a pilgrimage that deepens their connection not only to penguins, but to the world, to each other, and to themselves—captured through compelling stories and arresting photographs. This book is a timely reminder that it is often only the beauty that people find in nature that stands between our natural world and its destruction. During my career in conservation, I've been lucky to work with several species on the edge of survival—including the African penguin you'll meet in this book. I would dearly love them to be around long after I am gone. There are reasons to be optimistic: there are successful conservation stories for penguins, and teams of dedicated people working to ensure these beautiful, charismatic species stick around.

The (penguin) species you like best may not go extinct in your lifetime. But someone's favorite might, if we aren't careful. So, we all need to do our bit. If not, the days of pilgrimages to see every penguin in the world will be a thing of the past. Let's make sure that doesn't happen on our watch.

—Richard B. Sherley, PhD, University of Exeter

Introduction

Talking to a Penguin

AT ONCE CUTE AND CLUMSY, penguins are almost certainly the most beloved birds in the world. It's easy to see why. Black and white and upright, they always seem dressed in formal wear, ready for dinner with dignitaries. Their bearing, as they parade past, is striking for its nobility and seriousness of purpose. Yet at any moment, one of the penguins might suddenly slip on the ice and do a face-plant in the snow. Or smack a neighbor with its flipper—slapstick on snow and ice.

This combination of dignity and awkwardness, of self-importance and comic blunder, is both characteristic of penguins and completely relatable. Pride and a pratfall—that's penguins, the beloved clowns at the bottom of the world.

And I have been unable to resist them. Since seeing my first penguins off the red-sand shore of Rábida Island in the Galápagos Islands nearly two decades ago, I've developed a passion for penguins that sometimes veers into a wild and slightly ridiculous obsession. That sighting changed my life. I would not know how much, however, until some years later.

At first my wife, Susan, and I enjoyed going places where we could find penguins in the wild. They were great adventures—often exhilarating, frequently uncomfortable, sometimes dangerous. Often whole species can be found only on one particular set of rocks in lonely stretches of stormy seas.

Southern Rockhopper Penguin, Falkland Islands, British Overseas Territory

The Bounty and Antipodes Islands, a long boat ride east from New Zealand, are the only places to see erect-crested penguins, for example.

King Penguins, Falkland Islands, British Overseas Territory

Another example would be royal penguins, endemic to Macquarie Island, halfway to Antarctica, south of Australia.

And then there is Antarctica itself, inescapably associated with penguins. What is Antarctica but an enormous frozen island, surrounded and isolated at the bottom of the world by a circumpolar sea? It's the only place you can find the magnificent emperor penguins or the very cute Adélie penguin. And for me, the Antarctic Peninsula remains the best place to see the delightful chinstrap penguin, with the black stripe under its chin giving it a distinctive military bearing.

Despite the challenges of bad weather and cold destinations, Susan and I loved it all. We discovered that chasing penguin encounters may involve discomfort and difficulties, but the penguins recompensed every hardship.

To our friends and family, this growing passion for penguins was nearly incomprehensible. While they were going to the beaches of Hawaii, we were headed to places none of them had heard of. Then we told them we were going to find penguins. Suddenly friends would waddle like a penguin, flap their "flippers" like a penguin, even bray like a penguin. The penguins were their own justification.

There came a point, however, when this obsession turned from the thrill of the chase to something more. It grew imperceptibly for us. Some years after seeing my first penguin in the Galápagos Islands, and half a world away on the sub-Antarctic island of South Georgia, we realized that these various adventures were taking shape into something bigger, something we felt compelled to pursue and explore.

We decided to try to see every one of the world's eighteen species of penguins in the wild. At first we resisted the idea, knowing the difficulties and even dangers involved. But we came to feel we had only one option: go for it.

Penguins became our passion and our wild quest. *Every Penguin in the World* tells the story of this pursuit—the adventures we had, what we learned, and how penguins changed us. It is the story of a growing love for and dedication to all the world's penguins.

Why we felt compelled to take on this adventure can best be explained by an encounter I had with a penguin on South Georgia Island. It's a story that suggests the shape or trajectory of our journey. I'll let the penguin explain. Our quest is really our answer to him. It is our response to his call. A distant outpost, South Georgia Island is 900 miles from Argentina, south of the Antarctic Convergence zone, served by no commercial boats or planes. Now inhabited by biologists, South Georgia Island was once the base in the Southern Ocean for whalers, especially Norwegian whalers, at the turn of the twentieth century. Traces of their heyday are scattered everywhere—whale bones, a Lutheran church, ghost towns like Stromness, and whalers' graveyards. Ernest Shackleton began his famous disaster—the voyage of the *Endurance* Expedition—from South Georgia. It came full circle twenty-two months later when he reached Stromness after his ship was crushed by ice in Antarctica and he made his epic journey back. He's buried on the island and his stone marker has become a destination for Antarctic pilgrims under the spell of his 1914 mission.

But South Georgia Island really belongs to the seabirds and the marine mammals. The colonies of birds are incredible, heart-stopping, and deeply moving. They will drop you to your knees in awe. Penguins and albatross breed here. Wandering albatross come to the island only to nest, along with several other beautiful albatross species. The wandering albatross has a wingspan of thirteen feet—incomparable, the longest wings on the planet. Macaroni penguins come ashore in the millions to nest on South Georgia. The headliner among the island's birds, though, is probably the king penguin.

King Penguin,
Macquarie Island,
Australia

King Penguins, South Georgia Island, British Overseas Territory

Traveling the Southern Ocean is always an adventure: frequently exhilarating, rife with dangers, on occasion terrifying. It is the world's only ocean that circles the globe and is a nursery for storms that gather force as they spin unobstructed around this endless sea. There's nothing to slow them down or dissipate their power.

The winds over these waters created the superb wings of the albatross, long and bladed and made for riding the air effortlessly. And the seas enticed penguins to give up flight and live an aquatic life. For those who love wildlife and wild landscapes, South Georgia is a must-see.

I think it is the most beautiful place on earth.

On my first visit to South Georgia Island, we arrived at St. Andrew's Bay for an early landing. Before breakfast, before the sun had even risen, many of us clambered into Zodiacs to go ashore. On the pebbled beach, a light surf made the stones clatter. Rugged and snow-covered mountains ringed the flat sweep of land behind the beach. King penguins gathered in small groups. Some preened themselves after just returning from fishing and bathing in the sea. Others headed into the water.

One group some distance inland was resting along a pool of water from a small stream. The birds, a rare blue sky, and jagged peaks—all were reflected in the water. The scene captured the feel of the island's wild beauty. I dropped to my knees, then flat on my stomach. I inched closer, pulling myself forward with my elbows. I wanted to photograph this stunning scene.

The penguins were unperturbed. They ignored me. I was at their eye level, even lower, and that reduced the sense of threat for them. As I lay there, penguins slowly gathered about and around me, as though I were just another part of the landscape. A part of the colony.

I felt something hitting my rubber boots. I turned to see a very large king penguin. He was poking at them, almost like a woodpecker.

From his size, I guessed it was a male (they are usually larger than females). He moved up and snipped at my pants and gave them a tug. He worked his way up my body until he was standing beside my head, looking down his long, sharp beak at me.

For a fleeting moment I worried that he might try to stab me in the face with his daggered beak. We studied each other

carefully. He was just back from the sea. His white stomach shone with a thin film of seawater and flashed in the sun like a mirror. His back, pewter gray, was flecked with dark specks. Against these basic colors, the accents of vivid orange make king penguins the most beautiful of all penguins.

His "ear patches" reminded me of commas, and the beak, an orange dash. If king penguins could talk, I thought, they can punctuate themselves.

He kept an eye on me while he lifted his head. He pumped his chest like a bellows. And he called out. It sounded like a kazoo.

Over and over again he called, hoarse and throaty.

He kept his eyes directly on me. He was saying something to me. That's when I realized that maybe king penguins do talk in their own way. Because I knew what he was saying. I knew because scientists have figured it out.

South Georgia Island has enormous breeding colonies of king penguins. This one, on Salisbury Plain, can have as many as 200,000 breeding pairs. How do mates find each other in such enormous crowds? How does a baby know its parent?

The answer is one of those wonderful facts we get from science. Each individual of the 200,000 breeding pairs of king penguins in this colony has its own unique sound when it calls. To us they sound alike in an undifferentiated wilderness of huzzahs. To the penguins, each call carries its own unique identity. Each penguin is known by its own call.

The king penguin finished calling, then stood by my head and watched me.

He was expecting me to respond. He was inviting me to announce myself.

The penguin had announced himself, told me who he was. He expected me to say who I was. Nature and animals frequently call us to our truest selves, call us to a response. And response is the root of the word *responsibility*.

That call was a turning point in my life. Our quest for penguins was about to move beyond adventure. I searched for an adequate answer to the question his call posed: Who am I? Particularly in relation to this specific penguin. And what is an adequate response to the king penguin?

One that would be response-able. A response that acknowledged the irresponsibility of humans so far in the catastrophes of endangerment and extinction now sweeping the planet. My career as a writer, photographer, and teacher has been, in many ways, a long quest to answer this double question—who am I, and what is my responsibility?

One of my favorite poems by the great Latin American poet Pablo Neruda is called "Bestiario." It is his *bestiary*, or book of beasts. Neruda describes conversations with a number of animals, including the "exemplary penguins." Toward the end of the poem he makes it clear that he is seeking a new kind of wisdom from the animals. A wisdom we have lost.

He is a seeker and animals are among his chief guides on his journey: "I will not leave this planet without knowing what I came to find. . . . I have to go much farther," he says. "I have to go much closer."

Go farther and get closer. Listen. Animals are talking to us. They are calling us. We have only to learn to listen.

King Penguins,
Falkland Islands,
British Overseas
Territory

AFTER ALMOST TWO DECADES and countless miles, Susan and I completed our quest. By the end, it felt as though we had fulfilled a promise made to ourselves and the king penguin on South Georgia. And maybe to every penguin in the world. The adventures never stopped, and one of the big rewards for us was stories.

We learned enormous amounts about these tough birds. Yet we also came away with a kind of awe about them. That they can live in the harsh conditions that they endure. That their colonies are such overwhelming sights. That we still know so little about their lives at sea, where most of their time is spent. That through them we can see the state of our oceans' health. That they are so beloved, yet so endangered, and virtually all in decline.

Which leads to the largest question, for us, concerning penguins: If we cannot save what we love, and everyone loves penguins, what can we save? This question drove us to learn as much as we could about efforts to save penguins. We felt we had to bear witness to what we were learning, an important part of our answer to the king penguin.

And as we reached out—as we went farther—we could feel ourselves changing. The questions the penguin posed for us—who are we and how do we respond to the call of another creature?—grew in importance for us. These became our big questions on our journey. They turned our quest into a pilgrimage, and us into pilgrims. Seekers of something special and sacred. Seekers of something bigger than us, but which would lift us up and make us bigger as a part of the whole.

How do we answer for ourselves in a response that is also responsible and ethical to the creatures?

A journey of adventure, a quest for knowledge and conservation, a pilgrimage for something sacred and transformative. These are the three parts of our attempt to see every penguin species in the world. The penguins may need to be saved, and yet, unlike us, they do not need to be redeemed.

We met amazing people on our journey. Scientists and conservationists, photographers and birders, guides and

tourists. Some birders had more than 8,000 species ticked off on their lists, and there are just about 9,000 species of birds in the world. Amazing. Susan and I were with one birder on South Georgia when he saw his first king penguin. The man, Mickey, was from northern England. He might have been speaking of all penguins when he said, "That is the most bonny bird of them all."

In trying to learn the lessons that penguins have to teach us, I sometimes skate on thin ice over the troubled waters of anthropomorphism. It's inevitable, if you're looking to interrogate a penguin. They must be the most anthropomorphic birds in the world. With their shining white chests, so bright they might be silver, penguins are living mirrors, reflecting us back to ourselves. They look like little people, with their flippers—or wings—like arms, and their characteristic and charming waddle. Wherever they are going it must require formal wear, because they're always dressed in basic black-and-white tuxedos.

They stand upright. They are irredeemably social, living in colonies of 200,000 or more, and we see in them our social virtues and vices—they're monogamous but cheat, they live side by side and steal from their neighbors—and more.

If they seem clownish, even cartoonish, it's because penguins are also feathered parodies of ourselves. A sudden pratfall or a blast of projectile poop onto a neighbor undermines their swagger and self-importance.

They are our "mini-me," childlike, diminutive versions of ourselves. And like children, they evoke a fondness in us, a parental care and affection.

Yet when we see ourselves in animals, we have to wonder how much of that is really there and how much is projection.

For most biologists, anthropomorphism is so problematic it is avoided at all costs. But surely it has its place and its uses. Anthropomorphism may produce bad science, but it does help us understand our feelings toward animals. If we don't care *about* creatures in an endangered world, how will we care *for* them?

For Susan and me, the feelings the penguins inspired in us changed us over time. Because they are so beloved, they are uniquely capable of teaching us about love for the natural world. They are living lessons in caring for the earth and its creatures, in all their beauty and vulnerability.

And yes, I answered the king penguin as he stood next to me on South Georgia, giving him my best imitation of his call. Throaty, a bit wheezy. I don't know what he thought.

The king penguin gave me a last look and headed inland. Susan and I followed him. Our journey really began with him. He walked into the snow and up to a ridge between rocky outcroppings. We could hear him calling to no one in particular that we could see. Announcing himself to the mountains and the snow, to the blue sky and empty spaces. Declaring himself to the world.

King Penguins, South Georgia Island, British Overseas Territory

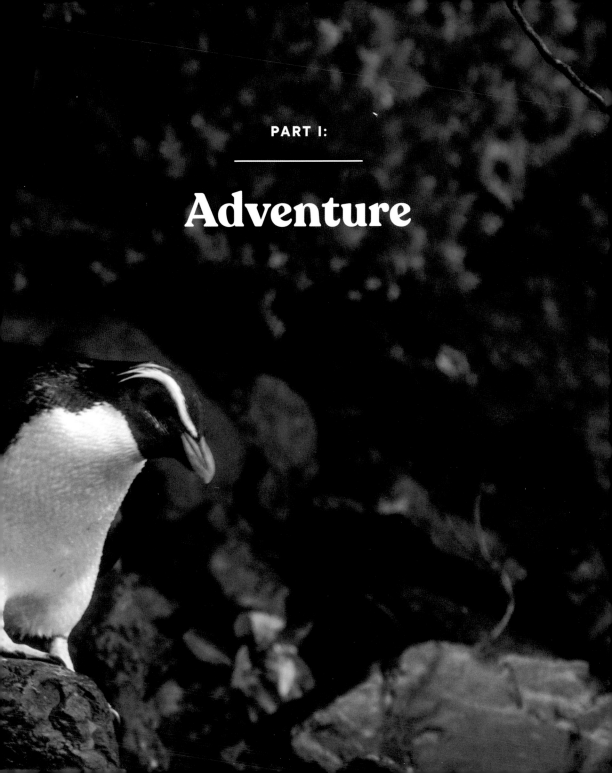

PART I:

Adventure

Mark of the Penguin

Lake Moeraki, New Zealand

43.7333° S, 169.2833° E

"WE'RE GOING TO HAVE TO FIND another way out of here,"
Gerry said. Though standing right beside us, he was shouting
to be heard above the hammering rain. Susan and I were
where he had left us two and a half hours earlier. Perched
on a jumble of rocks, where a penguin path turned from the
rocky shore up a muddy slope into a dense forest, we had not
moved. We had been focused on the Fiordland penguins as
they passed within just a few feet of us.

It had rained the whole time. At first lightly, then gaining
force, and now it was slanted and sleeting. We'd had to put the
camera gear away and were huddled under a small umbrella.
We did not hear Gerry as he came up behind us.

Gerry has a sturdy Celtic frame. Thick calf muscles,
visible because he always hikes in shorts, a testament to his
twenty years of guiding people on hikes in southwestern New
Zealand. With his wife, Anne Saunders, Gerry McSweeney
runs the Lake Moeraki Wilderness Lodge. Gateway to the
South Island's rainforests and fjords, the lodge also protects a
"secret beach" with great views of the local endemic penguin
species. The beach is a bit of protected habitat for penguins.
It's a contradiction but it's true: this species is famous for
being unknown. It may be the world's least studied and most

Erect-Crested
Penguin,
Antipodes Islands,
New Zealand

enigmatic penguin. Gerry holds a PhD in ecology, and he embodies the values of wildlife study and protection. Gerry takes people to see the handsome Fiordland penguins, and his tours are a highlight of the lodge.

That's why Susan and I were here. To see this penguin. Seeing the penguin, it would turn out, was the easy part. The bigger challenge became, how do we get out?

The rainforests and shorelines of southwestern New Zealand are notoriously wet, soaked by heavy rains. But the latest onslaught of rain was unprecedented.

"We can't go back the way we came," Gerry told us. The rains for the last two days had been steady and strong. "The water in the river is so high," he said, "and the currents so strong, I almost got knocked over several times coming back down here to get you."

The path through the forest followed a small river, and crossed it many times as the stream twisted and turned. There was no bridge or boardwalk. Normally you just skipped across the stones or splashed through the shallow water. Now swollen with rainwater and runoff, the river was too deep and dangerous to cross as we followed the path back to the road.

"We need another way," Gerry said. "We'll go through the penguin colony."

Fiordland penguins nest in roots and stumps of trees. It's the only penguin species to nest in forests. This was a chance to see an unusual sight: penguins in a forest. We'd go up the penguin path—which was on the face of a very steep bank over twenty-five feet high—and make our way uphill through the pathless forest. An adventure for sure, with the added virtue of seeing a rare penguin species in its unusual habitat, as well as its distinctive behaviors.

Gerry went first and we scrambled behind.

The rain had soaked the soil on the penguin path, so we simply sank in the mud. The trail was steep, the slope muddy. The bank threatened to slide away below us. "Nope," Gerry said. There would be no scenic or educational escape from the penguin beach.

Gerry motioned us back down to the rocks where we had been sitting.

He looked worried. "Only one choice," he said. "We have to go back the way we came—crossing the river." In other words, we would have to step into a river that, he'd already told us, had nearly pushed him over several times. When he arrived, he described the trail as "impossible." Now we prepared to do the impossible.

On our way back, the river's first crossing would be the most dangerous. It was right beside us, where the water rushed from the forest and crashed through sand and big black rocks into the sea. It was dark with dirt and sand, swollen and deep . . . and angry.

Susan and I did not say a word. We followed Gerry to the riverbank. I remember a penguin sitting amid the rocks in the surf, watching as we prepared to step in.

— — — — — —

Antarctica

82.8628° S, 135.0000° E

ALMOST BY DEFINITION, penguins mean adventure. The penguin of our imagination is associated with distant seas, frozen temperatures, and, above all, ice. That is a formula for adventure. Adventure is how we express the urge to be wild. It's a call to borderlands and edges. It's the call of the wildernesses that surrounds our lives and stalks our dreams, of the space between our comfort zone and the contact zone.

Penguins and Antarctica imply each other, as if they could not exist independently. Antarctica itself is the last great continent for exploration and discovery; it was the twentieth century's landscape of adventure. It's the only continent to be imagined before it was discovered. The ancient Greeks believed that a great continent had to exist in the south to counterbalance the continents in the northern hemisphere. For Dante, the lowest circle of Hell is a frozen empty place—Antarctica.

In fact, we think of it as a kind of negative place, a no-place. It was the only continent uninhabited by humans. No humans, no land mammals, no trees, virtually no plants, no heat. A nowhere of the imagination. It is the great global other—the "anti" continent: "Anti-arctic."

It is still a continent frequently not even included on a modern map—it's simply left off. Formed 35 to 40 million years ago, it is cut off from the rest of the world by the only circumglobal sea: the Southern Ocean. As far as we know, no human set foot on Antarctica until 1821, when crew members of the ship *Cecelia*, with John Davis as captain, did so. For humans it's existed in the imagination more than on a map. And there is something strangely surreal about it when you actually see it—a fairytale place of glittering ice and snow.

One of my students captured this otherworldly, paradoxical nature of Antarctica in a class I teach, in which we literally travel to and study in Antarctica. "Let's pretend we don't exist," Priscilla Middleton said. "Let's pretend we're in Antarctica."

Priscilla was actually quoting a well-known indie rock song—"Wraith Pinned to the Mist" by of Montreal—which somehow did not make her words any less apt. In the early twentieth century, Antarctica was synonymous with adventure. It was the landscape of heroic possibility. The names of the first explorers evoke amazing stories of struggle, death, and heroics of every kind: Robert Falcon Scott, Roald Amundsen, Ernest Shackleton.

These explorers are not distant history. Their adventures in Antarctica are only a century old. When I visit Antarctica, I still feel their presence very strongly. Their huts are still there. They give a tangible thrill to the places. And the scale of

Emperor Penguins,
Snow Hill Island,
Antarctica

everything in Antarctica is so vast in both time and space that I always feel I am among the first to walk there.

I have taught a course on Antarctica for undergraduates at my university six times. They feel what I feel there: humbled and exhilarated at the same time. You feel small and, paradoxically, not insignificant. Small and yet bigger in "the bigness of the whole," as Shackleton put it.

It's life-changing.

At the heart of the adventure of Antarctica are the penguins. They are the "locals," the original inhabitants. And yet—and here's the point—they are and are not creatures of Antarctica. Of the world's eighteen species of penguins, only two live their lives wholly within Antarctica: the emperor and the Adélie.

Many live in temperate parts of the globe—think of African and Magellanic and Humboldt penguins.

Yes, they are creatures of Antarctica. But not really, since most do not live there. One species lives on the equator—the Galápagos penguin.

Yes, they are creatures of the southern hemisphere. But one species can be found about half a mile across the equator in the northern hemisphere—again, the Galápagos penguin.

Yes, they are creatures of ice. But some live in deserts— the Humboldt penguin, for example.

Yes, they are creatures of remote and distant places. But some live in and near cities—the little penguin, for example, is easily seen in Melbourne, Australia, as well as in harbors in New Zealand.

They resist our categories. Yes, they are birds. They have wings, which are more like flippers. Plus, they do not fly. Or more precisely, they only fly in water.

Yes, they seem cuddly and dear, as if we could take them home for pets. But they are feisty and strong and cranky and tough enough to live out winters in the Southern Ocean.

Yes, we love them more than any other bird. And yet, they are among the most endangered family of birds in the world.

What I love about penguins is this ability to contradict our sweeping stereotypes. They challenge us to think of them in new ways. This is the penguin I love—the penguin as living paradox. It's the creature of both black and white. Paradox has a long history as a way of learning and thinking. My PhD dissertation in Renaissance literature was about paradox. It shakes up complacency and forces new ideas.

That's my hope for penguins. That through my crazy quest to see them all, they can help me find new ways to think about my relations with wild creatures and what it will take to save them.

For the first two days of our stay, Gerry had refused to take us to the penguin beach. "Too much rain," he said flatly. "Too dangerous."

When we came for lunch on the third day, however, he had changed his mind. The rain had been light all morning. There was a window of opportunity. "We leave right away."

I looked at Susan knowingly. "The honeymooners," I said.

At dinner the night before, we met two newlyweds from New York. They had come here on their honeymoon largely to see the penguins. They had only one more day—today—to do so. They were young and eager and impossible to deny.

Gerry relented.

I was thrilled. We were the coincidental beneficiaries of their success with Gerry.

Plus, guiding visitors to this private and secret penguin beach is a mainstay of Lake Moeraki Wilderness Lodge's business. Within an hour we were on a narrow path through the rainforest leading to the penguin beach. Heavy with moss, green with gigantic tree ferns, the forest was hushed and sparkling wet. We crossed the stream at a number of points. We leapt from stone to stone and splashed across. The water wasn't deep, and our decision seemed vindicated.

Half an hour later, we emerged from the forest onto a high sand dune overlooking a rocky shoreline. The stream slid out of the forest and around the sand dune, now a small river as it cut a path through the sand and into the Tasman Sea.

"Let me introduce you to number eleven." Gerry smiled. We had explained to him that we were on a quest to see every penguin species.

We were face-to-face with a Fiordland penguin.

"You can stay here," Gerry said. "But I recommend a spot across the stream. The penguins will pass right by you there and it's great."

A quick slosh through the river—noticeably deeper here on the beach—and we were set up by the penguins. Gerry said goodbye, promising to be back in about two and a half hours to gather us up and guide us out.

We watched Gerry leave with the honeymooners, who wanted to see sea lions as well. He had pulled out his yellow rain jacket, and the three disappeared along the beach. Susan and I turned to the penguins in a soft gray rain.

Even before Gerry and the honeymooners left, the penguins were hopping up the rocky beach toward us. It is a strange feeling—a modern conundrum—to be very close to rare birds, difficult creatures to see. And yet when you find them in the right spot, they can feel abundant. Even while you know they are not.

These penguins shuffled right up to us, stopped, and began preening before hopping up the muddy bank to their nests. For the next two and a half sodden hours, these penguins were our world.

Before the brush with disaster.

THE MAORIS CALL THIS PENGUIN "TAWAKI," which is both easier and more elegant than the cumbersome English name. The Tawaki or Fiordland penguin is a small and rare member of the famous group of "crested penguins." This group of penguins is beloved for the jaunty yellow crests. The rockhoppers, macaronis, royals, erect-crested, Fiordland, and Snares penguins each sports its own unique and jaunty crest. The Fiordland looks very much like the Snares penguin, which is endemic to Snares Island just south of the third-largest New Zealand island, Stewart. The Snares penguin is a small crested penguin, just about eighteen inches tall, and there is something delicate, even fragile, in its general appearance. Its crest, for example, is swept back and elegant, a pale straw color.

The classification of Fiordland and Snares as two separate species dates from the 1950s, but it seems an unresolved issue among experts. A third species of crested penguin in New Zealand is the erect-crested penguin on the Bounty Islands.

A handsome penguin, it is also apparently closely related to the Fiordland and Snares penguins. It too has been considered by some experts as basically no more distinct than a subspecies.

We saw the Snares penguin at Snares Island in gale-force winds. Our sighting was good enough to identify the penguin, but weather conditions prohibited photography.

Nevertheless, the Fiordland, Snares, and erect-crested for now seem safe as three distinct species. Fiordland and Snares are listed as vulnerable to extinction by the International Union for Conservation of Nature (IUCN); the erect-crested is listed as endangered.

Another penguin species in New Zealand is also endangered and has a fascinating taxonomic story. The strangely beautiful yellow-eyed penguin is found mainly on the sub-Antarctic Auckland Islands, which is where Susan and I would see them. There are a few on New Zealand's South Island, too. Apparently there was once another species of penguin, very closely related to the yellow-eyed, which occupied the mainland of South Island, while the yellow-eyed lived on the other islands. When this other species was harvested to extinction about 500 years ago (as it is thought), the yellow-eyed penguin was able to gain its own toehold on the mainland.

Penguins often seem fragile, sweet, even huggable. They bring out a feeling of protectiveness in us. Surely it's a big part of why we love them and feel tender toward them. It's another mistaken notion; the paradox is that these sweet birds are tough as nails.

The Fiordland is a temperate-climate species that spends six months per year somewhere in the Tasman Sea. No one had any idea where they go until recently. With satellite transmitters on a few penguins, scientists learned that they swim some 4,250 miles to feeding grounds. They swim on average 50 miles per day for six months.

Which suggests another key feature in the mystique of penguins. There is so much about them that we just do not know, and so much of what we do know is limited and partial. They swim from the ocean depths to live among us for a time. And the Fiordland is one of the most mysterious. It nests on one of New Zealand's main islands. But its colonies are loose, not densely packed, and in remote forests. These penguins are shy and retiring. And if you'll allow an oxymoron, they are famous for being little-known.

Population numbers are fiercely disputed, but one estimate is about 2,500 pairs—one of the very rarest of penguins.

These penguins before us would leave land in just a couple of weeks, by early December, and not be back again until June.

And for all the wild, sweeping, and stark landscapes of their lives, there's something intimate about the Fiordland penguin. Many penguins are monogamous or nearly so. Some practice "serial monogamy"—or fidelity for a season. The Fiordland is faithful to its nest site, but not necessarily to mates.

As we watched the penguins come out of the stormy sea and climb into the forest, the rain gathered force through the afternoon. We hardly noticed. The penguins held our attention. The species is unique in another way too, one that is discernible only at very close range, and only when the penguins are excited.

They have a series of white stripes, small but distinct, on their black cheeks. These stripes help to distinguish the

Fiordland from the closely related Snares penguin. We looked carefully and could see the markings easily. It seemed right that this penguin with a Maori name, Tawaki, also seems to have a tattoo. The markings look like signs of belonging, as if they are members of a tribe.

——— —— —— —— ——

BEFORE GERRY RETURNED for us on the penguin beach, Susan and I sat for about an hour in the rain. We'd put the camera gear away to protect it, and huddled under my small umbrella. We watched the penguins at close range and enjoyed their company. The rain fell hard, we got close to stay warm, and we waited. The penguins approached us, curiosity overcoming shyness.

It was a miserable afternoon, and we were happy. Happy to be there. Happy to share the adventure together. Happy because, well, it's hard to be unhappy in the company of penguins.

I never imagined that penguins would become a defining adventure of my life. It's hard to know what suddenly makes you realize the depth of feeling you may have for something. In my case, I have always chosen the wild side of life. I love pathless landscapes, rare animals, distant adventures. I love animals and I have always pushed the edges of my comfort zones.

It was no surprise that seeing a penguin in the wild would be a great moment in my life.

The key to my devotion to penguins, though, is Susan. Her love for animals is profound. It stretches from her childhood and a baby robin she nursed to health as a little girl in Seattle. While I may love the wild side of travel a bit

Galápagos Penguin,
Galápagos Islands,
Ecuador

more than she—I've slept in some of the strangest and most rudimentary of places, and I've taken some pretty rugged excursions on assignment for magazines—our passion for animals is a deep connection between us.

At some point, we realized that our adventures with penguins were more than fun excursions to see various species. We began to see that our relationship itself was marked and inflected by our love for penguins, and the things we did for that love.

A guide from New Zealand once gave me perhaps the best definition of an adventure that I've heard. He makes a living helping people have adventures, so he's had time and a reason to think about it. "An adventure," Cameron Walker said, "is when you embark upon a journey where the outcome is unknown."

I look back at Susan and me sitting in the rain with rare penguins, under our little umbrella. I remember us just as we were about to step into the river, holding hands. She is incredibly brave, and she is strong in the clutch. I love that about her. And I realize our relationship is itself an adventure that has grown through the years. Penguins have been part of our deepening love. They are part of who we are as a couple and they define our ongoing adventure together.

Galápagos Penguin,
Galápagos Islands,
Ecuador

Bartolomé Island, Galápagos Islands

0.2850° S, 90.5490° W

WHEN I SAW MY FIRST PENGUIN, I had no idea it would have such an impact on Susan and me. But I did know it could change lives.

My first penguin was not in Antarctica. It was not in the far south, like Tierra del Fuego. I saw my first penguin very close to the equator. In fact, though penguins are almost entirely birds of the southern hemisphere, I saw mine half a mile north of the equator, in the northern hemisphere. It was

Adventure

a Galápagos penguin, seen near Bartolomé in the Galápagos Islands. This penguin was breaking all rules and stereotypes.

That same day, I took my students snorkeling from the beach near the huge stone column at Bartolomé. At this iconic landmark of the islands, a pointed pillar of stone sticks out of the water like a leaning tower. Whalers and sailors of another era called the islands "Las Encantadas": the Enchanted Isles. In the stark volcanic islands, they saw the mysterious and otherworldly habitations of sorcerers and wizards and giants.

We might also want to add penguins to that list.

Jessica Darling and I were snorkeling along the rocks near the beach of Bartolomé. We were startled to discover a small penguin standing on the rocks just above the water. The water was shallow enough that we could stand and study the penguin, which more or less ignored us.

The Galápagos species is small, its features indistinct, like a smudged version of the Magellanic penguin. It is in a group of "banded penguins," —the Galápagos, Humboldt, Magellanic, and African penguins. The Galápagos penguins survive so far north because of the cold water carried by the Humboldt Current from the far south and up the west coast of South America.

In the volcanic landscape of the Galápagos Islands, straddling the equator, nothing could have seemed more out of place, more anomalous, than a penguin.

Jessica and I were just two or three feet away from one of them.

Then it dove into the water. Though awkward on land, it was graceful and elegant underwater. It did not so much swim as glide effortlessly. Jessica and I swam with it to the jutting obelisk of stone at Bartolomé. A quick beat of its wings, and it was gone.

An art major, Jessica could barely contain herself. Her eyes were huge, and she was trying to suppress laughter. Later, on the boat, she drew the penguin. She gave that drawing to me, and I still have it more than fifteen years later. It was a life-changing moment for us both, a landmark on paths we were just discovering.

"One of the highlight experiences of my life," Jessica told me recently, when I spoke to her about the "penguin quest" Susan and I had committed to. She's now a mom and busy with life. "I think of that penguin often."

It amazes me how such moments of close encounter stay with us, take up residence inside of us. They may even serve as points of orientation and meaning as we find our way through life. For myself, I had no idea yet where that penguin would take me.

⸻

Lake Moeraki, New Zealand

ADVENTURE IS ALSO AN UNINVITED GUEST who comes to you in the company of disaster. Adventure inevitably has connotations of loss of control and even failure: adventure is what you have on a journey when something goes wrong.

On the edge of the river that cut across the penguin beach, we were definitely facing danger and disaster. We wove arms and hands to form a human chain: Gerry upriver, Susan in the middle, me downriver. Gerry shouted final instructions.

"Don't let go at all costs," he said. "Don't fall down. Shuffle your feet. Do not let your feet leave the bottom. If you get knocked down, the next stop is the Tasman Sea and Tasmania."

The river was now some thirty-five feet across. It was muddy brown, swollen, scary.

"I've never in twenty-five years seen it like this," Gerry said. I did not find that comment helpful. But I did not blame him in any way. Quite the opposite; our safety depended on him and his experience. It was that I had no words for this moment, just a last look at the penguin watching us.

"Be tough and hold on," Gerry said, and stepped in. Then Susan.

At moments like this, when I must act but know the outcome is in doubt, I have the sense of handing myself over

Galápagos Penguins,
Galápagos Islands,
Ecuador

to the fates. I summon as much courage as I can muster, and step in with a sense of defiance and resignation.

For Susan, I felt unalloyed admiration.

I was at first shocked by how deep the river had gotten. Only two and a half hours prior, it had barely covered our ankles. Now it was up to our thighs. The deeper it got as we crossed, the more powerful were the currents. The water was incredibly strong and unrelenting.

We were like three chained convicts shuffling to freedom.

It got deeper. Halfway across, it crested at our waists.

That's when I felt my feet being shoved downstream by the current. I was losing my footing.

"I'm going down," I yelled.

"Get to your feet," Gerry screamed.

"You're pulling me down, too," Susan yelled.

We each kept saying the same words. Nothing anyone said helped me. Telling me not to lose my footing was useless advice—like telling a major league pitcher with control issues to throw strikes. If he could, he would. I was not trying to lose my footing. I could not stand, and I did not want to drag Susan down. But I could not let go of her, or I would surely have been swept downriver.

The next ten minutes exist in my memory somewhere between a blur and a blank. I know I went down, and I went down hard. I dragged Susan down with me. I know that because what I next remember is that I had grabbed her jacket. She was downriver and I was not going to let go for anything. I feared she would be swept away.

The water was shallower. But with my thirty-five-pound camera pack on, I could not get up. Susan was on her hands and knees. Every time she tried to stand, the current knocked her off her feet. I could not see Gerry anywhere.

The first words I remember were Susan's.

"Let me go," Susan was screaming at me.

We were both down, struggling to get up. She was on her knees and upright; I was on my butt and completely down. I had gone under. I realized we were pinned against the sandbank on the other side of the river. To this day, I don't know exactly how we got there. The currents must have pushed us there. Both Susan and I were disoriented. It took some seconds—it felt like a long time—to realize where we were, and that we had almost made it across the river. In practical terms, it meant I could let go of Susan. In fact, I was holding her down, and she wanted to get up and out of the river.

Gerry was on the sandbank. He helped us crawl out of the river and onto the sand, where we collapsed. We were okay. Soaked and shaken, but okay. I felt a pain on my backside but ignored it to focus on getting out. Though my camera pack had gone completely underwater with me, it was waterproof and sealed. Not a drop inside on the gear.

We were lucky. We could easily have been driven by the force of the river's surge out to sea. Perhaps our tenacity, our refusal to let each other go, saved us from that frightening fate.

Gerry was already thinking ahead.

"There are four more crossings," he said. "I don't know how we can do that."

I looked over at the penguin. It was still there, on the rocks. None of this was life-or-death for the penguin. Quite the opposite. Rain and storms and strong currents were normal for the penguin. And if it had any ideas for us, it

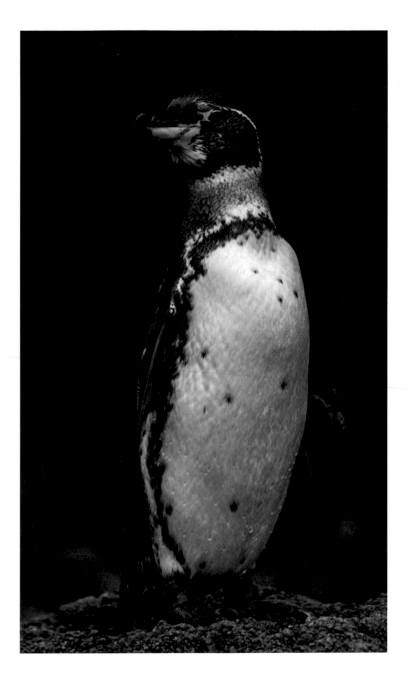

wasn't telling. From the penguin's point of view, we must have looked pitiful and inept.

For just a minute, I hated that damn penguin.

━━ ━━ ━━ ━━ ━━

South Georgia Island

54.4296° S, 36.5879° W

THE NEARLY DISASTROUS RIVER CROSSING in New Zealand was not my first near-death experience in the wild. I almost drowned on ice floes on Baffin Island in the High Arctic; I've had a gun put to my head while looking for endangered parrots in the forests of Puerto Rico. And I was involved in a Zodiac misadventure on South Georgia Island.

Zodiacs are crucial for finding, seeing, and photographing penguins. Made famous by Jacques Cousteau, they are essentially enormous inner tubes shaped like a boat. Supposedly they are unsinkable.

We put two Zodiacs to the test. It was not a brush with death so much as a slightly scary thrill ride that could have gone bad.

Zodiacs are the method of choice to get people off expedition ships and onto shore in wild and remote places. Our Zodiac adventure came on South Georgia Island.

We had spent a beautiful afternoon on shore. I was excited because I'd just watched an elephant seal give birth. I'd seen the whole thing. But I knew something was seriously wrong when the expedition leader, Ted Cheeseman, rounded us up before our scheduled time. He said that the seas had changed. The ocean swells were breaking higher and higher at the bar

of the natural harbor where we had off-loaded. Too high, and they could break over the Zodiac and perhaps spill us all.

We had to leave now, or risk getting trapped on shore for the night.

Susan and I were the last passengers in the last Zodiac.

Ted was our Zodiac driver. We listened intently.

Two Zodiacs remained: ours with the last passengers, and another, driven by Rod Planck, with the last guides. We would cross the bar first, then the guides. Ted briefed us on what to expect. Our goal was to get up and over the swells before they would break over and on top of us. Ted said we had to charge hard at the wave, then back off on the power as we crested, to bring the Zodiac back down.

Power and timing are everything. As instructed, we all held tightly to ropes and hunkered down. "We'll almost certainly grab air," Ted said.

We waited for the right wave. We could see everyone on the big ship, gathered on the rear deck. They were all watching the drama unfolding in the final two Zodiacs.

Ted gunned the outboard. We surged forward. The wave broke as our Zodiac powered over it, above the white water. The pontoons were completely out of the water. We literally went airborne.

Ted throttled back, the Zodiac's nose dropped, and we splashed back on the sea. We cheered him in our Zodiac as he steered us back to the ship. We watched from the stern as the guides' Zodiac approached the bar. They idled in place, waiting for a small swell. Rod, the driver, sensed his chance and the Zodiac charged the wave. They made it over as the wave broke under them.

Black-Browed
Albatross,
Falkland Islands,
British Overseas
Territory

Still going full throttle, the Zodiac did not return to water. We watched, astonished, as it went completely vertical. The transom in the rear was several feet out of the water. Clinging to ropes, the guides dangled like festoons from the Zodiac. On the ship, everyone gasped.

The Zodiac did not flip, though it came as close as possible without going over. It simply dropped down and popped into position. Miraculously, no one fell out of the Zodiac.

Rod Planck is a terrific photographer, an excellent birder, and an experienced Antarctic guide. He had a habit of dressing entirely in black, which made him a bit formidable. I thought of him as the Johnny Cash of South Georgia. After that, with Susan, I began to give him nicknames.

Rod prepare-to-walk-the-Planck.

Or Rod, prepare-to-meet-your-maker, Planck.

Since everyone made it back to the ship safely, the jokes came fast and furious. No one had seen a Zodiac go vertical like that before, and the video of the Zodiac went viral among expedition ships in the Southern Ocean. Both of these Zodiacs did that day what neither Zodiacs nor penguins are supposed to do.

They flew.

Lake Moeraki, New Zealand

GERRY MADE AN EXECUTIVE DECISION. "We can't do all those crossings," he said. I could see his mind at work. "We're going to cut one or two out," he announced. "We're trailblazing through the colony."

After every one of these intense experiences, veering out of control and toward disaster and even death, I have had the same feeling afterward: I was hyperclear, seeing the world sharply and vividly, as if reality had become high definition.

As we hiked up from the beach, the moss in the rainforest was so thick and lush that when we stumbled and fell, it was almost fun. We pushed through underbrush. We scrambled over logs. Our clothes were soaked, we were tired to the bone. And often we could not even see Gerry. He was up ahead, out of sight, finding a path through the forest for us.

Susan was exemplary through this ordeal. She likes to say she comes from tough farm stock. She never once complained, never protested or showed signs of breaking down in exhaustion.

"I always knew we'd make it out," she said later. "Don't waste energy talking. Just keep goin'."

Two more crossings—deep, but narrow. Gerry stood in the middle of the stream each time, took my camera pack, and lobbed it onto the far side. The moss was so thick it landed with barely a sound. Then we crossed. The water was above our waists. But we could hold on to branches, so we felt no real danger.

The most memorable moment came when we walked past a Fiordland penguin standing outside his nest in a tree trunk. It reminded both Susan and me of a Hobbit at the gate to Middle-earth. We were on some kind of passage in this adventure, crossing into new worlds. It was not clear yet, though, what that passage was.

Steeple Jason Island, Falkland Islands

51.0338° S, 61.2205° W

ONCE, ADVENTURES WERE PART OF A JOURNEY that heroes had to overcome to get back home. Now we seek adventures to escape from home. Or to make home more meaningful. Odysseus fought a Cyclops and resisted the songs of the Sirens in order to return home. The Romantic poets flipped the script. They loved the wild, the unruly, the adventure on a mountain top, "peak" experiences and sublime moments of earthly awe.

The goal was not to find your way home, but to have intense feelings in wild spaces. Thinkers like Alexander von Humboldt sought experiences of what he called the sublime: peak experiences charged with feeling.

The search for penguins inevitably took us places that staggered us with wonder. Perhaps the most powerful feelings I've had among wild animals came on the Falkland Islands. These islands are largely undiscovered by ecotourists but are a wildlife treasure. They are superb for penguins. And the greatest natural spectacle I've ever seen was on Steeple Jason Island—a nesting colony of about 150,000 pairs of black-browed albatross.

Steeple Jason is part of a group of small islands in the far west of the Falkland Islands. The albatross colony is on the main island, which is only 3 square miles. It's accessible only by boat, has no human inhabitants (except the occasional scientist), and is a tricky landing even in the best conditions. Susan and I landed on a gray day. We shuffled carefully from the Zodiac to slippery rocks and then onto a grassy shoreline. We had to hike through tall, thick tussock grass. But we emerged onto the edge of the colony.

It was heart-stopping and moving. At first we felt overwhelmed by the sheer size and scope of the colony. Birds—big birds—crowded every inch of the sloping land between the base of the island's peak and the shoreline. This is the largest colony of its kind in the world. More than 70 percent of the world's black-browed albatross nest right here.

They construct nests of mud, which look like stove pipes, and lay their eggs in the cup on top. Southern rockhopper penguins nest among them but can easily be overlooked because the albatross steal the show.

Penguins and albatross bear an unlikely yin-and-yang relationship. The Southern Ocean enticed penguins to quit flying and turned their wings into flippers. This same ocean and its storms enticed albatross to do the opposite: they grew perfect wings and became superb creatures of flight. The wings are long and bladed, up to thirteen feet in wandering albatross. They are made to glide on the stormy winds of the Southern Ocean. A bird may go round and round, chalking up a million miles. They are so comfortable on a glide that their heart rate is lower than at rest on land. When we arrived, albatross were everywhere: taking off and landing, skimming above our heads, flying by at eye level.

I kept waiting for an albatross to run into me. To graze me with a wing tip. One never did. But they cruised by me, close enough to touch.

I kept waiting for an albatross to lift me up on those incomparable wings. How often, I confess, has my heart

seemed to fly with the albatross. How often have they taken me for a thrilling ride.

I love these birds, which teach the unforgettable lesson of the necessity of wonder.

Chatham Island, New Zealand
43.9967° S. 176.5229° W

THREE DAYS AFTER NEARLY DROWNING in the river next to the Fiordland crested penguins, Susan convinced me to see a doctor. We had boarded an expedition ship on Chatham Island, about 170 miles west of New Zealand's main islands. The itinerary of the ship would take us to the outlying sub-Antarctic islands that include the Antipodes, Bounty, Campbell, Macquarie, Auckland, and Snares Islands. We hoped to see five species of penguins.

But during the time between the river calamity and leaving Chatham on the expedition ship, Susan grew increasingly alarmed by the bruise that had spread relentlessly on my backside. It was larger than any bruise I'd ever seen or had. It extended from my knee on my left leg, up my thigh, across my butt, and up into my back. What's more, it was sickeningly ugly—black and purple and olive.

We made an appointment with the ship's doctor.

When I dropped my pants, the doctor audibly gasped. "I've never seen anything like that before," she said.

When I lost my footing in the river, the force of the currents must have slammed me against the submerged rocks. I had noticed the pain almost immediately as we hiked through the forest, up from the penguin beach. But I'd had other things on my mind. The doctor called it a "violent bruise," and there was nothing to do but monitor it and expect it to fade on its own.

When I photograph animals, my goal is always to try to enter their world, to get a sense of how they might see things. It's an exercise in empathy and dedication. Photography is especially good at enabling us to see the world from an animal's point of view. It's one of the reasons I love photography. But this was going too far, getting too literal, almost joining them at sea.

I remember looking at the bruise and thinking this was ridiculous.

Still, it is the nature of our passion for something—wild animals, penguins, sixteenth-century literature, whatever you love—that we must give ourselves over to it, and a price will be paid. Demands will be made. It will grab hold of us, test us, shake us, and perhaps nearly drown us. It's the price of a passionate devotion. Susan and I paid the price for our joint goal of seeing all eighteen species of penguins.

I came out of the Fiordland penguin adventure feeling bruised and exhilarated. I felt marked by the experience. The penguin quest was stamping us in ways we were only just beginning to grasp. I thought of the chevron markings that were like tattoos on the faces of the Fiordland penguins.

"The penguins did this to me," I told Susan, as we left the doctor on the ship. "The penguins tattooed my ass."

PART II:

Science and Extreme Conservation

Ten for Ten

Robben Island, South Africa

33.8076° S, 18.3712° E

A BACK-PORCH EMERGENCY INTERVENTION. Susan held the penguin chick in her gloved hands, just under the flippers. Barely eight inches tall and about a month old, it was cute as only penguin chicks are—like a small child in fluffy pajamas.

Except that it was skinny, perhaps terminally skinny. Its sternum looked like it might break through the skin and down. It was so tired it barely squirmed. Richard Sherley slid a plastic feeding tube down the chick's throat. It did not protest. It seemed beyond caring.

A penguin chick on life support.

It was a startling introduction to the African penguin. Susan and I had just arrived on Robben Island, 13 kilometers on a ferry from Cape Town across Table Bay in South Africa. It was our first day as Earthwatch volunteers on the research and conservation project with these penguins. Additionally, I was on assignment for a major US magazine to write a story on these struggling penguins.

Unless you're a penguin biologist, you're not likely to think of penguins when you hear the name Robben Island. Many people are surprised to learn that there are native penguins in Africa. In fact, Africa and penguins seem like an oxymoron: blazing Africa and frigid penguins. But there are

Southern Rockhopper Penguins, Falkland Islands, British Overseas Territory thousands of penguins on Robben Island. It's the last best stronghold of Africa's only penguin.

And like this hapless chick, they have not been doing well.

Thousands of tourists come to Robben Island every year, taking the ferry, riding tour buses, and visiting the infamous prison that dominates the island. For several decades this prison housed about 1,500 political prisoners. One of the twentieth century's great heroes, Nelson Mandela, spent eighteen years here. Now the prison is sacred to his memory, and to the memory of all those who were imprisoned for the crime of opposing apartheid.

The island has always been a sad place for outcasts and the marginalized. The political prison was preceded in the nineteenth century by a leper colony. The penguins represent another kind of marginalized population—an endangered species.

I knew very well coming here that the African penguin was one of the most endangered animals in Africa, and one of the most endangered birds in the world. And while it's true that people love penguins, there's something very disturbing about seeing a beloved creature and a beloved species on life support.

The scientific name for the African penguin is *Spheniscus demersus*, which means "diving wedge." It refers to the penguin's diving ability when chasing fish. It might as well refer to its population crash over the last century.

"I hate to say it," Richard Sherley said as he hydrated the baby through the plastic tube. "But this species is on the way out. Unless something serious changes."

Sherley has a PhD in marine ecology and conservation biology, and teaches at University of Exeter. He has dark hair, red cheeks, and a surprising frankness.

While we were tending to the young chick at the Earthwatch house, Mario Leshoro walked up with a cardboard box. Born in Johannesburg, he came to Robben Island in the 1990s, fell in love with penguins, and knows the island like few others. In his box was another chick, this one older, bigger, but also dangerously skinny.

Sherley pulled out a graph that showed typical growth rates for chicks. He marked the weights of these chicks on the graph. They were all in the bottom 5 percent of weight for their age. "If we did not intervene," Sherley said, "they would never fledge."

We gave them triage, and Sherley arranged for them to be ferried to a seabird rehab center in Cape Town. I made a note to myself to visit them when we left the island. To see what happened to them.

It's not just the prison that casts a long shadow across the island. Another is the shadow of extinction. I was here to find out how a beloved bird could be so endangered, and what "serious change" was needed to prevent its extinction. The prison is a sad story that leads to hope. I wanted to find out if this penguin's sad story could lead to hope as well.

——— ——— ——— ——— ———

How many species of penguins are there really? How do we know? What difference does it make?

The species question, as I've come to call it, stalked our quest. If you intend to see every species, you've got to know somehow what a species is and how many there are. On the docks for the ferry to Robben Island—before starting work with the penguins—I realized that we may not actually know how many species of penguins there are.

Les Underhill met us on the docks as we were preparing to board for the ride to Robben Island. Underhill began working with the penguins on the island in 1990. He came to the island to band birds and wound up creating a project whose goals are both to study and to save Africa's penguin. The first major project was to band all the penguins on the island. "We have breeding data that dates back almost three decades," he said. Modern science runs on data. Underhill is a mathematician and helped develop the field of statistical ecology. "We put statistics into biology," he said.

Banding is the low-tech way, the old-school way, of generating data. For birds it has been enormously valuable in understanding migrations and movement patterns.

"We were not going to lose these penguins," Underhill said.

The entire enterprise of saving birds—penguins, in this case—from extinction is predicated on the notion of species. We identify endangered species and we recover species. It is fundamental to our understanding of the loss of wildlife.

Yet in the case of the African penguin, Underhill pointed out, the species question is still open, at least for a number of researchers. The African penguin is currently considered one of four species in the genus *Spheniscus*. The other three are Magellanic, Humboldt, and Galápagos penguins. African and Magellanic penguins are very similar, as are Humboldt and Galápagos penguins.

"*Spheniscus* are very close," he said. "They're all jackass penguins—all make the same braying sound."

They look similar as well, with white bellies, a long, arcing black stripe on the chest, white on the head, and pink at the base of the beak.

Most significantly, according to the biologists who wrote the accounts of the Magellanic, Humboldt, and Galápagos penguins in *Penguins: Natural History and Conservation*, these species "interbreed readily in captivity," and share similar genetic material. All these factors contribute to an uncertainty about their status as separate species.

However, if the African penguin were to lose its status as a separate species, if it were to become officially a subspecies, the consequences could be the nail in the coffin of Africa's penguins. Resources for recovery of endangered species—especially funding, but also incentives for experts to invest their energy and attention—are allocated primarily and almost exclusively to particular species.

As it is now, according to Underhill, "the African penguin may be gone in the next fifty years." What little hope it has would likely be snuffed if it were to lose its status as a separate species.

The taxonomic status and the conservation status of several other penguins is similarly fluid, particularly in this genus. They inhabit the temperate climates of Africa and South America, which brings them into competition and sometimes outright conflict with people.

As a rising star among penguin biologists, Tom Hart explained the situation to me during a fierce storm in the Drake Passage on a Russian icebreaker. This was during our trip to a colony of emperor penguins, the subject of the narrative in Pilgrimage (page 95).

His case is compelling.

We met at dinner the first night on the ship. He's young—in his thirties—and fair. Strong frame. Outdoorsy, as you'd expect. He's a researcher at Oxford University, where he directs the Penguin Watch program. Hart is certain that the conventional and current taxonomy of penguins will change. And he uses genetics to make his case. We sat across from each other, with the boat swaying wildly, pummeled by waves. When I mentioned to him that my wife and I were on a quest to see every penguin species in the world, he looked at me, gave a friendly smile, and said, "Too bad."

"Why too bad?" I asked.

"I hate to ruin your quest," he responded, tongue mostly in cheek.

"Me too," I replied. "How would you?"

Northern Rockhopper
Penguins, Tristan da
Cunha Archipelago,
British Overseas Territory

"Because I bet you don't know how many species there are."

"Well, is this a trick question?" I asked. He was friendly and conversational, with an air of imperturbable confidence associated with professors—dons—from Oxford and Cambridge. "There are now eighteen recognized species," I said. "There were seventeen, but the rockhopper was split recently into two: southern rockhopper in the Falkland Islands, and northern rockhopper in some very remote islands in the Atlantic and Indian Oceans."

When Susan and I began chasing penguins—before it had become a quest—the official number was seventeen. The split made the idea of seeing all eighteen much more difficult, because the northern rockhopper is extremely difficult to get to. They are on the Tristan da Cunha archipelago halfway between Cape Town and Rio de Janeiro. No commercial ships make routine calls. When we asked in Cape Town about getting there, one person suggested a fishing boat.

Hart had made a huge splash recently, reported by newspapers around the world. His team discovered an enormous colony of Adélie penguins. Hard to believe, but 1.5 million penguins had been previously overlooked and undocumented. It speaks to how much we have yet to learn about the world. He found them on the Danger Islands—the name seems perfectly suited to the discovery—a scattering of rocky islands at the tip of the Antarctic Peninsula. For his PhD, he tracked macaroni penguins at sea to study foraging behavior. Penguin Watch uses time-lapse cameras to monitor wildlife in remote places and is changing the way scientists monitor polar regions.

As we ate our dinner on the ship, the seas of the Drake Passage were growing more violent. The ship was tossing wretchedly. A whole wall of plates crashed to the floor in the kitchen. The boat was lurching side to side. Passengers were making for their cabins, clinging with both hands to railings.

Macaroni Penguins, South Georgia Island, British Overseas Territory

"How many do you think there are?" I took the bait.

"There will be another rockhopper split," he said, referring to the eastern rockhopper on the outer islands of New Zealand. This split was widely rumored already. Susan and I were prepared for it, making sure we'd seen the subspecies while we were there.

The captain came on the speaker system and told us we were taking twenty-one-foot waves broadside to starboard. Winds were now approaching 75 miles per hour. We were going to veer into the wind and waves, he told us. He reminded everyone to take care, and hold on for safety, always: "One hand for the ship."

"Gentoos?" I asked. Rumors were blowing around Antarctica that the penguin with the white "turban" on its head might actually be split into three species.

"Yep, three: Antarctic, South American, New Zealand."

The real news for me, the biggest surprise, had to do with two species I love. The macaroni penguin, with huge populations on South Georgia Island, and the royal penguin, endemic to Macquarie Island, are, according to Tom Hart, one species. Half a world apart, they share similar yellow crests that look as though they are combed backwards. The macaroni has a black face (usually), the royal a white face (mostly). Hart says that genetics reveal them as one species.

One of the women tending tables—a friendly Russian lady—mistimed her step and handhold. It was her first time on a ship to Antarctica. The boat swung suddenly upward, after rolling to thirty-five degrees on its side. The force

launched her off her feet. She flew a meter or two and landed on her stomach on a nearby table. Luckily, she was all right. But we were all a bit shaken by it.

In my journal, while taking notes as Hart spoke during dinner, I did some quick reckoning with Tom Hart's species list. I came up with twenty.

That did not address the *Spheniscus* penguins either.

On yet a different expedition to the sub-Antarctic islands around New Zealand, the expedition leader, Adam Walleyn, suggested that part of the difficulty is we are not entirely sure anymore how to define a species. "The concept has gotten

Southern Rockhopper Penguins, Falkland Islands, British Overseas Territory more difficult. It used to be simple. The defining boundary for a species was breeding or not. No longer."

The boundaries between species have grown more fluid, contested, and I might even say wilder.

"Choose your own number of penguin species," Walleyn said.

The flying waitress pretty much cleared the dining room. Your cabin and your bunk were the safest places to be. The ship, an icebreaker, was not made for such seas. It sacrificed keel and stability for flat-bottomed ramming power. The rock and roll, pitch and lurch, were not for the faint of heart or weak of stomach. Dinner was literally a movable feast.

Hart told me he was planning a penguin trip to the largely unexplored South Sandwich Islands, and I got excited to join him. Who knew what was left to discover on such remote islands? Hart publishes frequently on penguin genetics and speciation, and two of his recent papers on this topic are listed in the Select Bibliography (see page 184). He clearly has a passion for wildlife in extreme environments and is working to conserve the creatures, like penguins, who live in these challenging parts of the planet.

We were among the last in the dining room. I assured him he had not ruined Susan's and my quest—that we had been carefully observing all the subspecies that might become species. If the number went to twenty, we would have seen them. For us, the point was not the number. The point was the fulfillment of a difficult commitment and the homage to penguins implied in it.

I returned to our cabin two decks above. The ship was still rolling to thirty-five degrees, which is almost halfway from upright to the water. I held on with both hands, waiting for the ship to begin to right itself, before lurching to the next secure handhold. However many species there might be, the world of penguins was a lot less stable than I had thought going into our project.

Luckily, I never get seasick.

— — — — —

Early morning on Robben Island, and we were doing every volunteer's favorite job: weighing and measuring penguin chicks. Richard Sherley did the difficult task. He plunged into a thorn bush that protected a penguin burrow—in this case, a shallow scrape the size of a kitchen sink. He somehow emerged with a fairly large chick.

The adult African penguins are handsome in their way. But when it comes to charismatic good looks, they can't compete with the penguin superstars like rockhopper or king or emperor. The African penguin chicks, however, are pretty much irresistible, with a strong cute factor. Fluffy down covers them everywhere: gray above, white on tummy. They look like cuddly store-bought stuffed animals.

Sherley handed the penguin chick to Susan, who was beside herself with joy. She held it firmly beneath the flippers. "It's muscular," she said. "It is not cuddly. It's more like a very strong and struggling Jack Russell terrier."

The chick was still quite young, recently hatched, all downy and cute. The chicks grow quickly. At about one month they join a crèche, or nursery of other chicks, while both parents go fishing. Speed of growth depends a lot on food supply. Between two to four months, they emerge into the feathers of their juvenile plumage, a pewter-blue color. The juveniles are called "baby blues."

We slipped the chick into a green bag to weigh it. We measured beak and flippers. Sherley examined the bird carefully. The information generated by these exams—the data—is invaluable in determining growth patterns.

As he held it, he warned us to be careful. "A penguin has four weapons. Their beak gives a sharp bite. The flippers deliver a real whack. The claws scratch hard and can infect. And if you survive these, there's always the poop."

Southern
Rockhopper
Penguins, Falkland
Islands, British
Overseas Territory

He paused. "A shooting stream of hot fish soup."

It was struggling in Sherley's grasp. Behind us, just across the road, was the main entrance to the prison that dominates the island. This baby was born across the road from its front door. I looked hard at the chick. It made its appearance in this world after a century of declines for the African penguin. In the twentieth century, the numbers traced a steady and steep decline: very rough estimates put the population at about 1.5 million in the 1930s to about 60,000 now. The first decade of this century saw troubling new collapses.

It's not just African penguins. This baby may well have represented the state of every penguin in the world: strong, tough birds with a fragile hold on survival. As Richard Sherley told me, "Of the eighteen species alive today, eleven are undergoing population declines and ten are considered to be facing a high risk of extinction in the wild."

Even species that seem abundant show signs of being vulnerable. The Magellanic penguin, close relative to the African penguin, is still abundant in South America. But scientists do have concerns. Since 1987, they have shown a steady decline. The IUCN Red List lists the decline at 30 percent ("near threatened").

The Humboldt penguin of northern Chile and Peru is also in trouble, officially listed as vulnerable by the IUCN. Since the 1930s they have been in decline, which intensified after the El Niño of 1982–83. Perhaps only 40,000 remain.

The Galápagos penguin is likely the rarest penguin of them all. There may be as few as 1,500 left, about half of what there were in the 1970s. It is the embodiment of the officially endangered penguin.

Certainly, much of the appeal of penguins is that they are so improbable. We're unlikely to imagine a penguin if we have not seen one. Even more unthinkable is that we might lose them.

It's a biting and bitter paradox. The most beloved group of birds in the world is also among the most endangered.

And yet, here was the future in the form of this chick. Richard let it go. It scurried back to its thorn bush.

"You know," Susan said to me, "this is our tenth species of penguin."

"On our tenth wedding anniversary," I replied. "That's ten for ten."

It was then, just outside the infamous prison, that we were inspired to try to see every species of penguin in the world—in the wild. And to spread the word about their conservation.

Weighing and measuring and holding the chicks was one of the great wildlife experiences of my own wild life. I felt more connected to the penguins, to Susan, and even to myself.

That night, I woke from a wonderful dream. I woke Susan up, I think because I was talking. She turned on the light. "You're dreaming," she said.

"I know. It's one of my best dreams ever."

"What was it?"

"I dreamed I was at the White House. Or at least some big official function. The Obamas were there."

Susan laughed.

It made sense to dream of them. This was 2013, and Barack Obama was traveling in Africa. Michelle Obama was visiting Robben Island the week after we were leaving. They were the talk all over Africa.

"Yeah, and Michelle Obama asked me to dance."

Macaroni Penguins,
South Georgia
Island, British
Overseas Territory

"What was the dance?" Susan asked.

"A polka," I said. Susan laughed harder.

"And what was she wearing?" Susan asked.

"A polka-dot dress." Now we both laughed.

"Okay," I said, "turn the lights out. I want to go back to my dream. I want to go back to Michelle."

Bear with me a moment. I love *A Midsummer Night's Dream*, Shakespeare's most magical play. One of the central characters, Nick Bottom, is, as his name suggests, something of an ass. Yet he has the dream of a lifetime. He dreams the fairy queen has fallen in love with him. He's transported to

her world. He is the only human in the play to see the fairy queen. He glimpses a new level of life and is transformed by his dream of wonders.

This was my day of wonders.

Perhaps that's the first answer to finding hope in a dark time. Follow the love.

El Pedral, Argentina

42.9648° S, 64.3943° W

IT WAS MY SECRET BEACH. For three days, I had it all to myself. Wild surf, no other people, and a steeply pebbled shore. A southern right whale had just cruised by, perhaps 100 feet from shore. Sea lions patrolled the coast, hoping to snatch a negligent penguin. And Magellanic penguins returned to their nests after a day of working the seas for fish. The surf receded and black penguins appeared.

They are the wild foam's wild heart.

I was lying on the first steep incline of the shore up from the sea, amazed at how easy it was to not be me. I was trying to get out of myself and let this be about the penguins. The world's not all about us—that's the first principle in a conservationist's ethic.

It had not been difficult. For three days I let these Magellanic penguins be the story. It was all about them. After they preened on the edge of the surf, they moved up the beach in twos and threes. It was hard to get solid footing in the deep pebbles, and the penguins slid backwards and tumbled.

Several times the penguins noticed me lying near them. They walked up to me, poked me, leaned in, and looked closely.

"Look for me here," Pablo Neruda wrote about his own beach in Chile, "between the stones and the ocean."

I was pretty sure the penguins thought I was either a log tossed onto the shore, or a large stone that had just appeared. In any event, they soon ignored me, which was what I most wanted. If I was patient enough, the penguins would show me how they wanted me to see them.

Almost by luck, I managed to find this undiscovered beach, El Pedral. The name refers to the stones, *piedras*. I'd driven due east out of Puerto Madryn, Argentina. It's a classic

Magellanic
Penguins, Peninsula
Valdés, Argentina

Patagonian road in Argentina: flat, dusty, straight—
60 kilometers without a turn. The road ends at a steep bluff
above the ocean—Punta Ninfa. Below, long, lunkish elephant
seals lounged on the ocean beach.

A few kilometers before the dead end, an inconspicuous
padlocked gate guarded the dirt track to an old Argentine
estancia, or ranch from another era. Wood floors, old photos,
large rooms—the house is capped by a peaked turret top,
which symbolizes the *hotel de campo* (the country lodge).

A small track led to a parking spot where I left the rental
car. Two kilometers through the colony led to the beach where
the bay met the ocean.

Ten years ago, this colony did not exist. Magellanic
penguins have been coming here and digging burrows for
their nests. Other locations are growing too, notably Estancia
San Lorenzo. It's becoming one of the largest colonies in
Argentina, at 150,000 pairs.

The penguins are on the move and they are coming from
the famous colony at Punta Tombo, where Dee Boersma of the
University of Washington has been studying them for forty
years. At its peak, it was an enormous colony of half a million
Magellanic penguins.

African and Magellanic penguins both have the horseshoe
round stripe on their white chests. Both have a blush of pink
on their faces. Both have spots on their chests, and each
individual has its own unique number and placement of spots
on its chest. Each penguin is identifiable as an individual.

The Magellanic has a second black stripe on its throat.

These penguins are not penguin royalty, if you will. The
emperor, king, and royal penguins—these are all beautiful

and arresting. But these banded species have no flash, no penguin bling.

Yet I love them. I love their diligence and their purposefulness as they come and go to the seas—their daily commute—to catch fish. They strike me as noble for their work ethic. They seem so earnest, as though nothing could be more important than the task at hand.

These are the penguin working class, the proletariat penguins.

Because they reveal to us the conditions of the seas, Boersma calls penguins "marine sentinels." These two *Spheniscus* penguins were the first penguins seen by European explorers, who likened them to flightless geese and slaughtered thousands of them for food. Since then, human pressure has been unrelenting: egg collectors, guano collectors, oil spills, ballast and petroleum discharges, and persistent conflicts with fisheries.

These are old-school environmental problems. They are not easy to solve, but they are identifiable, localized, and susceptible to compromise and solution. You can get your head around them. After four decades, Boersma has amassed enormous amounts of data and has had success at negotiating changes in shipping lanes and fishing practices to benefit penguins.

In Cape Town, biologists and managers created marine reserves where fishing is not allowed, after research showed that intensive fishing near colonies contributed to the collapse of penguin populations in the early 2000s—a collapse from which they have not yet recovered.

These are solutions of policy and practice, supported by careful science.

The penguins at El Pedral point to a new wave of issues and challenges. These problems are global, hard to understand, and not easily solved. The oceans themselves seem to be changing: water quality, ocean acidification, water temperatures, El Niño, current direction, climate change or variation. These are systemic problems, harder to see and comprehend. And they defy national borders.

In Argentina, the growing Pedral colony shows that penguins on are the move. It appears the penguins are following their prey, establishing colonies near the changing centers of the schooling anchovies.

It's a penguin mystery. In *Penguins in the Desert*, a book on his research on Magellanic penguins as a graduate student of Boersma, Eric Wagner quotes her as saying, "We don't know how they make their decisions."

African penguins' main prey are anchovies and sardines. These fish have recently changed their principal location some 250 miles to the east. What exactly is going on is still a mystery. Sherley and others suspect there are basic changes in the Benguela Current that comes to Africa from the south. In any event, the penguins are tied to Table Bay, where their chicks are. There are not nesting islands in the new locations of anchovies. Penguins cannot migrate with their prey.

The new environmental problems are hard to think about—they're abstract, systemic, and frightening. Combine that with political incompetence, lack of resolve, and willful refusal to listen to the science, and it's easy to see why people grow demoralized. It's easy to see why people slide into despair or denial.

"It's that the problems are everywhere and nowhere," Susan once said to me.

In the face of such problems it's easy to feel small and insignificant and powerless. Which is why you have to know what feeds your soul. What will help you find your way. For me, it has always been the animals themselves. If I let myself enter their world, I feel small in another way. At El Pedral I was alone for days and had plenty of company. It was humbling to be with them like that. They made me feel connected to a world bigger than me. "Only connect," E. M. Forster famously wrote in *Howards End* more than a century ago. These two words could easily be a conservationist's

mantra, a guiding principle in reforming our relations with the earth and its creatures.

It's one of the remarkable things about Antarctica. Or penguins. You can feel overwhelmed in a positive way. In a way that evokes love and reverence.

Penguins are one of the best antidotes for despair that I know. They are living lessons in caring for the planet and its creatures, in all their beauty and vulnerability.

African Penguins, Boulders Beach, South Africa

Science and Extreme Conservation

Robben Island, South Africa

33.8076° S. 18.3712° E

ONE OF THE BIGGEST REVELATIONS of our penguin quest has been how interconnected and entwined our lives are with theirs. They may live in another hemisphere, in the far south. But we are increasingly stitched to them. Partly this is a function of the current global nature of life and the far-reaching environmental issues that has generated.

It is also because penguins have entered our hearts and affected our imaginations.

And, Susan and I grew increasingly aware that our own relationship was marked by our love of penguins. This was a discovery that gradually emerged into our awareness as we went about our volunteer duties with the biologists. Every day, Susan and I counted penguins going to sea and returning at night. We weighed and measured baby penguins. We collected trash from the beaches. We counted molting penguins, apparently the best way to get reliable numbers on penguin populations. We counted wading birds on the island.

We even helped Sherley put a satellite tracking device on an adult penguin. By mapping the penguin's movements in Table Bay, biologists and managers could get a better understanding of the intersections of penguins and human fisheries.

Penguins nest in the shadow of the prison. In the predawn hours, as we were on our way to our work sites for the day, we would see penguins in lines commuting to the sea, moving past the prison in single file.

It was impossible not to think of Mandela as we watched the penguins stream past the prison.

The prison dominates the island, a reminder of the fight against racism. It is now a museum and a World Heritage Site. It is also a monument to courage. It was on this island, working in the quarries, that Mandela's idea of national reconciliation was developed.

Mandela often worked with others on the beaches of Robben Island, collecting seaweed to be sold to Japan. In his book *Long Walk to Freedom*, Mandela wrote that prisoners often "laughed at the colony of penguins," so comical as they marched to the sea. They reminded him of a "brigade of clumsy, flat-footed soldiers" as they passed the prisoners. The penguins gave the prisoners relief from the drudgery of prison life, offering comedy and consolation.

It is one of the great unremarked ironies of conservation: this prison, once an instrument of racism, now offers a de facto sanctuary for this last remnant of African penguins.

Like Mandela, we too found consolation and pleasure in the daily rhythms of the penguins.

Susan put it this way: "The birds fill your heart. I could spend days watching and being in their presence. They have such important lives and business to do. They work really hard for their chicks, and in their lives, too. I love watching them, how they come in from the sea, their chests so pretty, and they soak up the sun and their eyes go to half-mast and they are enjoying it. It's all one of my favorite things ever."

Penguins and prisons: In both epic and intimate ways, penguins are woven into the fabric of our lives. In the great historical sweep of a nation and its heroes, and in the private

African Penguin and
the Author, Boulders
Beach, South Africa

Photo by Susan Mann

dedication of a married couple trying to make a difference,
penguins console and inspire us.

The colony of penguins on Robben Island illustrates
better than any other in the world the many ways our lives
are implicated in theirs. We imagine penguins as remote and
distant, but what we do matters to them and their future.
Perhaps even more, who we are matters to them. They tangle in
our histories, charge our imaginations, and light up our lives.

These penguins call us to a deeper resolve and
commitment to do what we can on their behalf. If we cannot
save penguins—cannot save what everybody loves—what can
we save?

Antarctic Sound

63.3333° S, 56.7500° W

BIRDING IS LIKE LEARNING to see. Spot a lovely bird, figure out what it is, and you have an unforgettable memory. You have been rewarded for your attention to the world.

It can also make a genuine contribution to science. Birders advance the understanding of bird distribution and migration.

My first sighting of an emperor penguin was an experience of pure birding.

The emperor is the iconic penguin. It is what people think of when they think of penguins. In movies and documentaries, it is the defining image of a penguin. Large, striking head plumage with "ears" like a rising sun, stomach washed with creamy gold—this species is "the perfect penguin," as one photographer called it in the title of her book. Plus, it is the species with the most endearing chicks.

The emperor penguin is synonymous with Antarctica.

It is the essence of penguin. It is "penguin-icity," if you will.

Since emperor penguins are creatures of the Antarctic deep south, they are a challenge to see. They nest farther south than any other bird in the world, famously nesting and raising chicks in the Antarctic winter and on sea ice far from shore. The usual strategy is to sign on to an expedition dedicated to visiting a colony. It's expensive, requires icebreaker ships and helicopters and hiking, and offers no guarantee that weather and ice conditions will cooperate. On our penguin expeditions, we've talked to many birders who spent a small fortune to visit a colony and then could not get

Adélie Penguins,
Paulet Island,
Antarctica

off the ship—could not see the penguins they had come so far and spent so much to see.

Susan and I developed another strategy. I borrowed techniques I've used to find other difficult species.

Interviewing guides and other experts on Antarctic birds, I learned that it is sometimes possible to see emperor penguins as they sit on icebergs drifting through the Antarctic Sound—the passage at the northern tip of the Antarctic Peninsula. About 100 miles south of the Antarctic Sound in the Weddell Sea is Snow Hill Island, home to the world's northernmost colony of emperor penguins. Occasionally— rarely, really—juvenile emperors are stranded on a chunk of ice in the spring breakup, drifting forlornly on currents until they decide to swim.

On one of our visits to Antarctica, we decided to try to find one of these drifting emperor juveniles moving west through the Antarctic Sound.

Emperor Penguins, Susan Mann, and Author, Snow Hill Island, Antarctica

Photo by Jude Tasker

Science and Extreme Conservation

I taught a study-away course at my university for many years that focused on environmental literature and Antarctica. It included a two-week expedition to the Antarctic Peninsula, and ten days in Argentine Patagonia. I told my students that if any of them could see an emperor penguin, and show that penguin to me, I would give that student an A for the course. The result was an avid interest in learning where to find emperor penguins and how to identify them.

Our ship, the *Ushuaia*, agreed to try to pass through the Antarctic Sound in January, if ice conditions allowed. We entered the sound from the south on the eastern side of the peninsula, after visits to Paradise Harbor and Palmer Research Station. As the ship navigated through a mass of drifting ice, we made our way to the bridge to watch. Susan and I arrived on the bridge to find several highly motivated students.

No one, including the guides on the ship, gave us any chance of seeing an emperor penguin. Truth to tell, some of the guides even thought we were deluded. They watched on the bridge with a friendly but slightly dismissive interest.

There were hundreds, even thousands of little Adélie penguins standing picturesquely on icebergs. Hundreds more porpoised through the water ahead of the ship. Just before reaching Esperanza base, the Argentine station on the Peninsula, we noted a penguin clearly bigger than the Adélies. It was alone, hunch-backed, drifting on a piece of ice the size of a yacht. Amazingly, the ice drifted right next to us on the starboard side.

I ran through the diagnostic list: size, indistinct "ear patches" forming on its head. That narrowed it to either king or emperor. Next, the beak: An emperor beak is slightly curved downward; a king's is straight. This one was decurved! And finally—yes!—black feet.

Photographs confirmed it: emperor penguin. We sent the record and our notes and photos to Aves Argentinas-Asociación Ornitológica del Plata—the country's main organization for the study and conservation of birds. The record was officially accepted. We had made our own genuine contribution to polar science with this piece of data.

For several of the students, it was an experience they will never forget. The juvenile emperor penguin taught them a new way to see, a new way of recognizing another life in the world. It's a bit like you're seeing for the first time. You realize the world is full of other creatures and everything changes for you.

As much as I loved the sighting, I still wanted to see an emperor colony—a fervent desire that was to be fulfilled almost as an ultimate climax to our penguin quest. I longed to see the gorgeous adults and their incomparable chicks.

Although this was not a sighting of an emperor at its most beautiful or endearing, we felt no apologies. We were proud of this sighting and all that went into it. As we watched the lonely young emperor drift out of sight behind us, lost again in the ice, we danced across the upper deck of the ship.

Northern Rockhopper Penguins, Tristan da Cunha Archipelago, British Overseas Territory

Cape Town, South Africa

33.9249° S, 18.4241° E

ABOUT TWO DOZEN adult penguins darted around the swimming pool. Two young penguins looked at us through the window of a pet carrier. Before I could see any baby penguins inside, an adult penguin with a spectacular crest of thick yellow feathers marched up to us.

African Penguin,
Robben Island,
South Africa

She rocked back on her heels and looked up at me.

"Meet Rocky," Nola Parsons said. "She's our resident northern rockhopper. I should warn you, Rocky thinks she's the Queen of the Rehab."

At that point in time, Susan and I had not yet seen a northern rockhopper penguin. Nor had we come to the rehab center with any idea we'd see one. We had come to see the emaciated penguins we had shipped over from Robben Island.

Nola Parsons was the chief veterinarian for the Southern African Foundation for the Conservation of Coastal Birds (SANCCOB). It's a mouthful. The organization takes in seabirds of all kinds in South Africa. Rocky was one of about 1,500 penguins that show up at SANCCOB every year. By the time they get to SANCCOB, they're in bad shape, often near death. Rocky had been found on a beach to the east. Her feet were swollen, she was starving, and she had several infections.

"That was four years ago," Parsons said. "Now she rules the rehab."

Rocky had come over to inspect us, since we were new to SANCCOB. Parsons assured her we were okay. We turned back to the baby penguins. Rocky left. "She's going to the laundry room." Parsons smiled. "She likes the heat from the dryers."

Inside the pen, the two baby penguins that had shocked us on the first day on Robben Island had been growing up. Now about seventeen days later, they had put on weight, lost their down, and were "baby blue" African penguins. Once near death, they looked great. They looked fully recovered.

During the ten days we were working on Robben Island, we rescued about one seabird per day, including a cormorant, two Cape gannets, and two Hartlaub's gulls—handsome seabirds with delicate black beaks and legs. They're endemic, endangered, and the seventh-rarest gulls in the world.

We sent five penguins over to SANCCOB for more complete veterinary treatment.

"These two penguins are doing fine," Parsons said. "The other three were too far gone." They were beyond help. I was happy to see two of the penguins obviously doing very well.

"Let's go see what Rocky is doing," she said.

We found Rocky near a dryer in use.

She was special and she owned it. Why she would like the laundry room was a mystery, since she came from the cold climate of the South Atlantic. "It's crazy," Parsons said, "but she loves to be warm and cozy."

"Rocky's got the 'wow factor,'" Parsons said. "She mesmerizes people. She's friendly and fun and kids can get close to her. Even touch her."

With her charisma, Rocky was named the official "ambassador penguin" for Cape Town. She visits schools, greets kids who come to SANCCOB, and serves as a representative of the hundreds of seabird species in jeopardy worldwide. "Seabirds are in trouble," Parsons explained. "All around the world. We stress conservation issues. Rocky makes them real for people."

Parsons believes that through Rocky people get a feel for the "invisible lives" in the sea.

The recovery of at least two of our penguin chicks, plus the unexpected encounter with Rocky—once near death and now the star of the rehab center—made a huge impact on Susan and me. Perhaps we are entering a new and more frightening time for us and the planet.

Perhaps the situation is extreme and requires a new kind of conservation, an extreme conservation, to go along with traditional conservation strategies. Rocky illustrates what I mean by this. Situations are so dire for many species that biologists, veterinarians, and volunteers now increasingly intervene to save them one creature at a time. I think of Richard Sherley on Robben Island giving triage to a starving chick. I think too of the people at SANCCOB who saved Rocky and the two chicks we sent there. Every penguin matters.

And perhaps as well this requires a new summons of courage in the face of great problems and long odds. The need is enormous. In addition to penguins, SANCCOB takes in all the other seabirds in the area as well.

But successes are possible. The rehab center in Cape Town shows what people can do. I have been active in environmental organizations. Most recently I have served on the board of a bird sanctuary near my home, as well as chairing the board of the Indonesian Parrot Project. Volunteers are the front line of the conservation battles.

Volunteers make places like SANCCOB work. It's the number-one thing most of us can do to make a difference.

Earthwatch also offers ways to volunteer.

Perhaps you are young, like my students. When I've taken them to Isla Martillo, in the Beagle Channel, to work with Dr. Andrea Raya Rey and her research project on Magellanic penguins, a number of students have been inspired to dedicate themselves to wildlife. Or to geology or oceanography. And they can become scientists whose research can lead to changes in policy and practice on a large scale.

Most of us, however, may not work professionally in conservation. But our contributions are valuable. In addition to volunteering on science projects, there is the crucial matter of supporting scientists and science in research and fact-based recommendations.

The truth is, the problems facing us are huge, and there may be debate about specifics, but in the bigger picture, we know what we need to do. It's not really a mystery and everyone can help: Support science and conservation efforts, reduce our ecological footprint, know the sources of our food (including fish from the Southern Ocean), and be sure it is sustainable. Join an organization that reflects your values. Read, speak up, vote.

Make a sanctuary of your yard, as Susan and I have done.

Volunteer.

If you're unsure where to start, consult the Resources in this book (see page 187). The range of opportunities is vast.

"The volunteers love Rocky," Parsons said. "We find her therapeutic."

Policy, practice, and personal psychology.

African Penguins,
Robben Island,
South Africa

Or think of it as engaging with the world on several levels: Head, hands, and heart.

Thinking, doing, being.

Your involvement will change you, especially if you work to bring your values and how you live into closer alignment. Listen to the experts. But listen to the creatures, too. Listen to the penguins. You might find your ideas about the creatures will change. You might find that they will point you toward a deepening bond with creatures in ways you had not imagined before.

Take Rocky, for example.

Parsons lifted Rocky and we all went into a larger room. I sat on the floor to take notes. Parsons held Rocky close and rubbed her forehead and chin. Rocky settled in. Her eyes began to close. She seemed headed for a rockhopper reverie.

Parsons has red hair. Rocky's big shock of yellow head feathers looked like long blond hair. "I sometimes get the urge to braid her feathers." Parsons laughed.

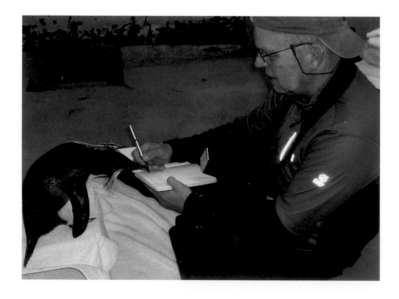

Northern Rockhopper Penguin and Author, Cape Town, South Africa

Photo by Susan Mann

"Rocky thinks she's a person," Parsons said. "She has her up days and her down days. She's more like us than most people think. She's an individual, and when people see that it makes a huge difference."

She set Rocky down. The penguin strutted up to me, stuck her dark orange beak in my journal, and shoved my pen around with her beak. It was funny. Rocky settled into my lap. She nipped the pen. She snipped a page. I half expected her to write me a note in my journal. She really did want her nose in everything.

Rocky then waddled to a small stool covered with a towel. She hopped up. The stool was set there just for Rocky and she loved it. It was a throne for the Rehab Queen.

Her big personality gave her a swagger that was undeniable. Perhaps, I remember thinking, this is the "serious change" Sherley was talking about. Perhaps what we need is a new way of thinking about these penguins, and animals more generally.

In Rocky's "personality," I glimpsed something new in penguins. This wild and outrageous pursuit of penguins was morphing into something I had not imagined.

What began as adventures was becoming more like an ongoing conversation with penguins. I was looking for something from them. A new way of thinking about them? Perhaps something from the heart?

They were taking Susan and me someplace and we had to follow.

I've always been a seeker, and this was feeling more and more like a journey of the heart. I felt increasingly like a pilgrim of penguins.

PART III:

Pilgrimage

A Pilgrim among Penguins

Snow Hill Island, Antarctica

64.4667° S, 57.2000° W

"THIS CANNOT BE HAPPENING," I said to myself. "Please, not here."

Susan had just come and gone. She was with our friends Andrew and Jude. They had moved ahead, into the center of a group of penguins.

"They're very close," she told me. "Including the chicks. There are lots of them and they're active and super cute."

She would be just 100 yards away.

"Come find us."

As she left, I gathered my camera gear. I had been sitting in the snow after struggling to walk. I couldn't, not even take a few steps. The pain was too great. For all practical purposes, 100 yards might as well have been 100 miles.

Standing was no better. The pain built until I had to sit back on the snow.

This is not good, I thought. *I'm here in the colony, surrounded by penguins, and I can barely watch them.*

I could hardly see through the pain.

I tried not to think about the list of obvious consequences, but they were pressing on me: how would I get back to the

Emperor Penguins,
Snow Hill Island,
Antarctica

ship, how was I going to photograph, and, worst of all, would I be able to get back to this colony of penguins?

This was the culminating trip of our penguin quest. By now, though, this journey had taken on a life of its own. As our encounters with penguins accumulated and our passion for them deepened, our penguin quest had become more to us than a list of species to check off. We still enjoyed the challenge of seeing penguins, of course, and learning about them. But our encounters had taken on personal meaning for us.

One measure of how much these penguins had come to mean to us was that, strictly speaking, we had completed our quest. We had seen an emperor penguin already—the juvenile on the iceberg drifting through the Antarctic Sound. But this day promised the penguin experience we had long dreamed of having—observing a *colony* of emperors.

Along the way, we began to think of ourselves not just as having a series of adventures, and not even as a couple on a quest. We had begun to think of ourselves as pilgrims of penguins. And this trip—to a colony of emperor penguins with chicks at Snow Hill Island in Antarctica—was like the holy grail.

All life is sacred. This planet of ours remains the only place in the universe that we know of that supports life. And these penguins, emperor penguins, live as close to the great mystery of life as any creature may be able to get. Fossils were discovered on a neighbor island to Snow Hill—Seymour Island—of a prehistoric penguin that lived about 60 million years ago among dinosaurs, was six feet tall, and is among the oldest bird fossils we have.

Edward Wilson, the ornithologist on Robert Falcon Scott's doomed expedition to the South Pole, made his

own wild pilgrimage in the name of science to collect an egg at an emperor colony in 1911, believing it might be the missing link between dinosaurs and birds—the embodiment of an evolutionary mystery. He was wrong. Nevertheless, Gerald Mayr, paleontologist and curator of ornithology at the Senckenberg Research Institute in Germany, believes they are useful in understanding the origins of birds. It's easy to appreciate how penguins are associated with the still-mysterious origins of species—which Charles Darwin unforgettably called "the mystery of mysteries."

Emperor penguins are the tallest living penguins at three and a half feet. Beyond an impressive size, though, these penguins lead lives that seem impossible, almost incomprehensible. Where other birds abandon Antarctica in the winter, emperor penguins turn into it. What's more, they choose winter in Antarctica to breed, lay eggs, incubate, and raise their chicks. Temperatures are consistently between twenty degrees below zero and fifty degrees below zero, with ferocious winds. They do not go to land and do not make nests. Rather, they form their colonies on sea ice. While females leave to feed at sea, the males incubate the eggs—for about 115 days of darkness and fasting. They will eat nothing and lose 40 percent of their weight. They tuck the egg inside their feathers, held on top of their feet. And males stand upright the whole time.

These birds are a marvel. A living mystery in their own right.

Emperor penguins are the only birds in the world to live entirely in Antarctica.

They are the only birds to breed in the Antarctic winter.

They are the only birds in the world that may never set foot on land during their lives. The Snow Hill colony, for example, is on sea ice some distance from the actual island.

King Penguins, Falkland Islands, British Territory Overseas

No explanations can effectively exhaust the awe that these birds inspire. Then there is their diving ability. They can dive up to 1,800 feet and stay down for twenty-two minutes. To do this, before diving, they increase their heart rate from their normal rate of 100 beats per minute (bpm) to 200, for oxygen loading. During a dive, the rate drops to 20 bpm, to conserve oxygen.

This trip to see emperor penguins had become a spiritual journey for both Susan and me. I did not just want to see them. I wanted to "see them with the eyes of the heart," as the Sufis say about pilgrimages. Sufism has been called the mysticism of Islam. Pilgrimages in this tradition are an outer journey and invoke an inner journey, the goal of which is to find the divine that resides in all things, according to Laleh Bakhtiar in *Sufi: Expressions of the Mystic Quest*. I wanted to live in the presence of these unlikely creatures and let them stir in me a sense of awakened wonder.

I had gotten to the colony, but I could feel my hopes and dreams for this journey slipping away.

— — — — — —

SUSAN HAD TOLD ME to join her farther into the colony, only 100 yards away. But the pain in my lower back, hip, and right leg stopped me in my tracks. My thighs knotted up in cramps and spasms. Electric pain shot through my lower back and hips.

Each step was painful as weight punished the raw nerves in my back.

A Pilgrim among Penguins

If I was not able to walk 100 yards to find Susan, I could not think how I would walk the mile and a half from the colony to the base camp at the end of the day. Somehow I'd managed to get to the colony, but in doing so had reinjured my back.

The rules and requirements for the expedition were explicit. We were all responsible for getting ourselves on foot to the colony. No sleds to the rescue. To get here, we had taken a Russian icebreaker from Ushuaia, Tierra del Fuego, across the Drake Passage—the crossing took three days in the teeth of a hellacious gale. After a very rough passage, we passed through the Antarctic Sound at the tip of the Antarctic Peninsula and burst into the Weddell Sea in glorious sunshine. The icebreaker smashed through ice for a full day, exhilarating to watch. The bow rode up and over the ice, dropping down on it in thunderous crashes. The ice cracked ahead of us as well. Breaks shot out through the ice like jagged lightning bolts in sharp, piercing tones like gunshots. We plowed through ice for 100 miles, to about 6 miles off Snow Hill Island, on the east side of the Antarctic Peninsula.

That's when the two helicopters came out. Early in the morning helicopters shuttled us, six at a time, to a base camp on the sea ice, located about a mile and a half from the colony. We hiked this final distance. The point was to disturb the penguins as little as possible.

It was an easy hike. Under normal circumstances, I am fit and active. I exercise daily, enjoy hiking, and can trek for gorillas and chimpanzees and penguins without problems. In this case, shortly before our expedition to the penguins on Snow Hill Island, I had injured my lower back working in our garden. My fourth and fifth lumbar vertebrae crunched the sciatic nerve, which runs from spine to hip and all the way down to the ankle. I suffered angry nerves and contracting muscles that were intense. Physical therapy helped and prepared me for this Antarctic mile and a half.

Emperor Penguins, Snow Hill Island, Antarctica

I made it to the colony. The pain was building. By the time I got up to join Susan, it had become too much. I could not get to her. Could not send a message.

I could only wait for her to return, which I knew she'd do.

I managed to shuffle to a protruding slab of ice and sat down to wait.

After about twenty minutes, I saw her walking toward me.

"Why aren't you coming?" she said. "You're missing the penguins."

"I can't walk. No kidding."

Her brown eyes stared at me.

"Wait here, I'll be right back." With that, she was gone.

I was virtually paralyzed by pain. The ice was almost blindingly beautiful, glittering under a full Antarctic sun. The sun lit up the ice from within, glowing in shades of blue and turquoise and azure. Huge icebergs were frozen in the ice all around the colony, providing protection for the penguins from the wind. Like the icebergs, I felt stuck in place, caught in arrested motion.

I wanted to tell Susan I was going nowhere, but she was already gone.

Macquarie Island, Australia

54.6208° S, 158.8556° E

SOMETIMES WE THINK BEST with the heart.

It's a lesson I had been learning from the penguins we encountered through the southern hemisphere. I found myself searching for something from them, and for a long time I was not sure what it was. And I knew there was a purpose for me in these wild trips to some of the most remote places on the planet.

I had the growing sense that penguins had something they wanted to teach me. I often had the sense that they were calling to me, not in words, but in the way music moves us without words. The penguins had become our guides as well as our goal in travel. I felt that I was on an inner journey as well—that the deeper I went into the lives of penguins, the deeper I went into myself.

Let me give an example.

Macquarie Island is an Australian territory about halfway to Antarctica. It is uncommonly beautiful and the only place to see the curious and charming royal penguin. The island also supports huge colonies of king penguins.

They are close relatives to emperor penguins and have similar plumage. The king penguin is almost as large and sports even more emphatic accents of orange on its "ear patches," beak, and chest. On a visit to the Macquarie Island Station at Buckles Bay on the north end of the island, Susan and I sat on the beach near the boardwalk and watched one particular pair of king penguins.

They were obviously courting. As penguins do, they would assume poses in which they would mirror each other. These poses are stunning to watch. One of the pair will, say, lift its head, point its beak to the sky, and hold the pose. The other will do the same, mirroring its partner. After a minute or two, they will break and move to another pose. It is ritualized behavior. Frans de Waal, the well-known primatologist, calls such mirroring in animals the biological origins of empathy.

This pair moved into a later stage of courtship, close to mating, in which the male gently wraps his neck around his partner's. They will "embrace" in this way over and over.

Photos of these postures suggest a startling tenderness and intimacy.

Then this pair did something I had not seen before and have not seen since. They began walking down the beach, stopping occasionally to pose again. What was moving to us was that they walked flipper to flipper. They were like human lovers on a romantic stroll, holding hands. This was not accidental. They resumed "flipper-holding" after each pose, making sure their flippers touched as they walked.

The photograph I took of them is one of my favorite images. The body language of these penguins is eloquent. The suggestion of an emotional bond is inescapable.

Yet the official biological explanation of penguin courtship focuses on rote and automatic behaviors—driven by hormone and instinct and chemical impulse. One biologist named David Campbell, in a book I otherwise love, describes such courtship displays as "hard-wired and unvarying." He even speaks of the "robotic penguins."

I don't dispute the behaviorist explanation. This is not about epistemological politics, if you'll pardon a big phrase. I just think this description is spectacularly unfair. A robotic explanation may, ironically, do little to make anyone care for penguins. Why would one care about a robot? Why save a creature that is nothing but hormones, or worse, that is essentially a machine? We are only likely to save what we care about. The mechanistic explanation may avoid anthropomorphism, but at what cost to both us and the penguins? It cuts the heart of the mystery from their lives, as it would do to ours. What it leaves out, of course, is feelings. The question is, in behaviors like "hugging" or "hand-holding" that are so recognizable to us, do penguins also feel?

King Penguins,
Macquarie Island,
Australia

What would I believe? Viewing these two king penguins was an important stage in my deepening sense of penguins. They might as well have extended an invitation to walk with them, hand-in-hand. They did not look like robots walking on the beach. It's a vexed question—believe the dominant paradigm of animals, as mechanisms, and doubt the evidence of your own eyes? Would I have the courage to believe my own lying eyes?

Emperor Penguin,
Snow Hill Island,
Antarctica

Snow Hill Island, Antarctica

SUSAN WAS BACK in fifteen minutes. She had taken charge
of the situation, which is her way. She had convinced the
expedition leaders to haul my gear back on one of their sleds—
essentially, to make an exception to the rules. But I would have
to walk back to the base camp. No exceptions there.

Andrew and Jude had come over too. We met four years
earlier on our expedition to the sub-Antarctic islands of
New Zealand. They too were on a quest to see all eighteen
species of penguins. They too love photography. We seemed

destined to become good friends. We have since traveled often together—finding new species of penguins, trekking with chimpanzees in Uganda, tracking jaguars and macaws in the Pantanal of Brazil.

And now, to an emperor penguin colony in Antarctica.

Andrew said he'd walk with me, to help if needed, to keep me company at least. He's an uncommonly thoughtful man. His background is human resources, as is Susan's. He's developed a unique perspective linking human behavior in workplaces to natural behavior of other big-brain animals such as chimpanzees, which he applies to the workplace. His training program for companies is called "Hardwired Humans." When Jane Goodall tours Australia, where Andrew and Jude live, Dr. Goodall and Andrew often talk jointly to business audiences about our social natures.

As we started the walk, the expedition leader, Ted Cheeseman, approached me. Susan and I had traveled with him to South Georgia before. We admire him. He looked me in the face, aware that this was going to be an ordeal. He handed me two walking sticks.

"Stay strong," he said.

What followed was the worst mile and a half of my life. I had never felt such intense pain. Andrew and I barely exchanged a word. But I was deeply grateful for his company. I counted my steps. Ten steps—that was how far I could go before being stopped by the pain. I could not stand. I had to drop to my knees.

Andrew waited. With the walking sticks, I pulled myself back to my feet and did it again. And I kept repeating Ted's words to myself: "Stay strong."

It was my silent mantra.

I might as well have crawled on my knees back to the base camp. It took over an hour and a half to walk one and a half miles—a distance I would normally walk easily in fifteen to twenty minutes.

When we got to the base camp, a helicopter arrived for the 6-mile jump back to the ship. Nobody mentioned my struggles. There was nothing to be said. I was relieved to return to the ship. But it was impossible to imagine repeating that agonizing walk to the colony and back tomorrow.

We all knew what was at stake—how could I possibly make tomorrow's visit to the colony?

- - - - -

Bartolomé Island, Galápagos Islands
0.2843° S, 90.5506° W

SUSAN HAD A PILGRIM'S HEART long before I met her. The penguin has been a creature with which she feels a deep—and even spiritual—connection. Like most people, she loved them. And, like most people, she had never seen a penguin in the wild. On one of the study tours I led to the Galápagos Islands for students at my university, Susan came along. The Galápagos penguin was the animal she most wanted to see.

She had strong reasons. A year before her first trip to the Galápagos, she had discovered a lump in her breast. It turned out to be an aggressive form of cancer, stage three. A mastectomy and six months of chemotherapy and radiation treatment followed.

"Through my treatment," she said later, "one of the things that kept me going, that I looked forward to, was going to

the Galápagos with you and your students. I wanted to see a penguin in the wild. That was my chance."

One year after her diagnosis, she was on a boat in the Galápagos. She was still recovering physically and emotionally. Her hair had not grown back yet, but fuzz was coming in. Our last stop after seven days on a boat was at Bartolomé. I told her there were usually penguins here.

Susan went snorkeling.

"In my head, I was saying to the penguins, 'please come to me,'" she told me. "I swam and swam, looking underwater."

When she stopped and raised her head out of the water, she finally saw her penguin on the lava rocks about twenty feet away.

"It was looking right at me!"

She swam up to it. They looked at each other. She thanked the penguin for its beauty, and she felt its "penguin strength."

"I love their spunky personalities," she said, "and their hardiness."

She returned to the boat with a full heart, feeling energized. That was her first penguin pilgrimage, fifteen years ago.

She is still cancer-free.

I would not say the penguin healed her. Nor would Susan. She would say it is part of a larger picture of health, in the spirit of gratitude and a full heart that help us to heal.

My first experience as a pilgrim was, by contrast, accidental and almost comical.

While teaching at the University of Oviedo, I lived in Asturias on the north coast of Spain. Easter weekend, we took the students one province away to Galicia and Santiago de Compostela. It has been renowned since the Middle Ages as one of the great pilgrim destinations in Europe. Called simply the "Camino," or the Way, this pilgrimage is sacred to St. James, one of the Apostles.

We attended vespers, or evensong, on Good Friday. It was an incredible experience. We all crowded into the church's nave. Several priests lowered a huge brass container that reminded me of the space capsules used to shoot men into space.

It was a censer—the "Botafumeiro" in Spanish—that hung from the nave ceiling on a thick hempen rope. After lighting the incense, they swung the Botafumeiro down the cathedral nave. Smoke billowed into the cathedral and the censer flew from one end of the church to the other. The cathedral filled with smoke. People inside thrilled to the sight, exhilarated by the censer flying down the length of the cathedral.

A priest welcomed the pilgrims to this Good Friday moment. "Your prayers are like this smoke, rising to heaven," he said. "The hearts of pilgrims, too, are like the smoke. They too are rising to heaven."

I was aware I was not one of the *peregrinos*—that is, pilgrims—crowding inside the church. But I also knew I felt my own heart rising to the heavens with the incense and censer. I wanted to shout, "I feel it too, I feel it."

I had gone into the cathedral on Good Friday like a tourist. I came out changed a bit. I would not say I had become a pilgrim all at once then. This was my first sense of what a pilgrimage means. I don't necessarily mean a Christian pilgrim, but a modern pilgrim on a journey of spiritual discovery. I could see clearly that a pilgrimage is a journey the heart makes out of hope—hope to be healed, hope to be whole, hope to be changed.

Snow Hill Island, Antarctica

BACK ON THE RUSSIAN ICEBREAKER, after my aborted first visit to the emperor penguins, I made lots of new friends. Of course, most of the ninety passengers on the ship had seen me struggle on the path back from the colony. Many of them approached me at dinner to express their empathy for what I was going through. Many had suffered back pain as well.

A woman who called herself a healer offered to "lay hands on me."

A neurosurgeon gave me what amounted to a private consultation. She surprised me when she offered an amazingly detailed diagnosis of my condition. She told me that I was a good candidate for surgery.

A well-known photographer told me he'd had similar back problems and showed me stretches that he does every morning.

Susan and I lingered over dinner with Andrew and Jude.

Gentoo Penguins, Falkland Islands, British Overseas Territory

"I was worried for you today," Andrew said. "You were marooned on the outskirts of the colony. I know how much this trip means to you."

He offered to carry my camera gear the next day, to make it easier for me on the hike.

In a previous career, Jude had been a pharmacist. She had a big job with "big pharma," working for Pfizer. In what was tantamount to a spiritual transformation, she left that career. She rejected the vision of the medical model, as she says, "renouncing the dogma of medicine and health that relies on drugs." Instead, she has become a counselor.

It's part of her life journey, she says. She now focuses on the way our own mindsets and attitudes contribute to holding us back. Her practice is called "Breaking the Iceberg," and

Gentoo Penguin, Falkland Islands, British Overseas Territory penguins have played a big role in what she calls her own "spiritual journey to learn who I truly am."

With penguins, she can be "present in nature, still, transfixed."

Jude encouraged me to think positively about the next day.

We said good night at our cabin doors, which were side by side.

"Somehow I've got to get to the colony tomorrow," I said. But it was not at all clear how I would do it.

"Our bodies are designed to heal themselves," Jude said. "So allow for and expect a miraculous recovery."

"Do you have any extra miracles lying around in your cabin?" I asked. "I can't find one anywhere in ours. Can I borrow one?"

I lay on my bunk that night, waiting for sleep.

And yes, hoping for a miracle.

- - - - -

Falkland Islands
51.7962° S, 59.5236° W

A QUEST IS NOT about answers. It is about the questions that compel us. I have come to think of a pilgrimage as travel motivated by and dedicated to an inner longing, to some felt need or lack, directed to a goal that signifies something personal. A quest to find a beast is among the most ancient of narratives, in which animals give meaning to an inner journey. Susan and I had come to this colony of emperor penguins because many other penguins had offered us glimpses of deeper questions that inspired us. If we could more clearly see "heart" and feelings and spirit in penguins, perhaps we could grow in our heart and feelings as well.

Gentoo Penguins, Port Lockroy, Antarctica

I love gentoo penguins for their playfulness, especially in the water. One time, in the Falkland Islands, I watched them playing in the waves and found myself again wondering what they must be feeling. The interesting thing was that their play definitely made me feel strong emotions of exhilaration and happiness.

Gentoos are common penguins. That is to say, there are lots of them and you can see them pretty easily. I think they are handsome penguins, but they are not flashy or flamboyant. They are your basic black and white. They are distinguished by a white "turban" across their black head that led early explorers to call them gentoos. The term is thought to derive from the mid–nineteenth century *gentoo* in India's English, for a Hindu. Since turbans have nothing to do with Hindu religion but are more a cultural product of India, the name is a case of cultural misappropriation. But it has stuck.

The gentoo penguin's only colorful features are bright orange beaks and feet. What makes this penguin so delightful, though, is a playfulness that is infinitely entertaining. Gentoos are a joy to watch as they play in the surf. I watched one pair of gentoos in the almost clear water of Carcass Island in the Falklands. They were simply rolling and tumbling in the surf, catching wave after wave.

On another occasion in the Falklands, I watched groups of gentoos riding waves. As a big wave rose and started to break, a gentoo blasted out of the water like a torpedo, catching air. Below it, in the water, the dark shapes of three more penguins were just visible surfing as well. Some hopped out of the surf

Pilgrimage

and "water-skied" to shore. Others porpoised together farther offshore, in what looked like synchronized swimming.

The most common theory to explain play in animals is that through play, the young learn skills they will need as adults. One biologist, Lynda Sharpe, writing in *Scientific American* after years of studying play in meerkats, concluded that no compelling evidence has been produced for any of the theories about play. She argues that play remains one of the great enigmas of animal behavior. And at any rate, the theory about young animals does not explain why adult animals play. What are these adult penguins doing? Are they playing in the surf, as they certainly appear to be doing? What are they doing when they are playing? Could these penguins be enjoying themselves as much as I enjoy watching them?

There is another behavior that is common to penguins. One evening on nearby Saunders Island in the Falklands, I watched as an amazing sunset began to develop. I decided to photograph a group of gentoo penguins under a blazingly beautiful sky. They had been watching the sunset. As I walked behind them, though, they turned to watch me—as interested in me as I was in them.

And then one lifted its head, pointed its orange beak to the sky, pumped its chest like a bellows, and screamed out a loud call. It's provocatively named an "ecstasy call," or an "ecstatic display song." Researchers at the University of Turin identified two related "songs" in African penguins. The first, the "ecstatic display song," is sung by single penguins during mating season. The second is the "mutual display song," sung by partners to each other.

Edward Wilson of Robert Falcon Scott's expedition to the South Pole was the first to use the term "ecstasy call" a century ago. The term has stuck, even among biologists, for whom such obvious attributions of intense emotion are normally anathema.

And it raises the obvious question, what do the penguins feel when they make these calls? What do the penguins feel as they ride the surf into shore, over and over again? And why does it raise in our own hearts an undeniable exhilaration to behold it?

When one penguin begins its ecstasy call, the effect is often contagious. It sweeps through the colony, unmusical and loud and insistent. It's usually likened to a loud bray. I think it sounds like an asthmatic duck. It's a sound you won't forget. It's harsh and jagged, one of the defining sounds of the Antarctic wild.

It's the sound you hear, and it's also a sound you feel as you hear it—an exhilarating sense of your heart leaping to life in your chest. It will linger in your memory for years.

That evening, the gentoo penguins were in full throat, an ecstasy chorus under a fiery sky. It felt like the penguin equivalent of howling at the moon.

Snow Hill Island, Antarctica

THE FOLLOWING MORNING OFF SNOW HILL ISLAND, our group was called first to the helicopters for the ride to base camp on the ice. I had already been up for hours by then. Sunrise was at four in the morning. It seemed to morph the ice all around the ship into lava, a cauldron of molten reds and yellows.

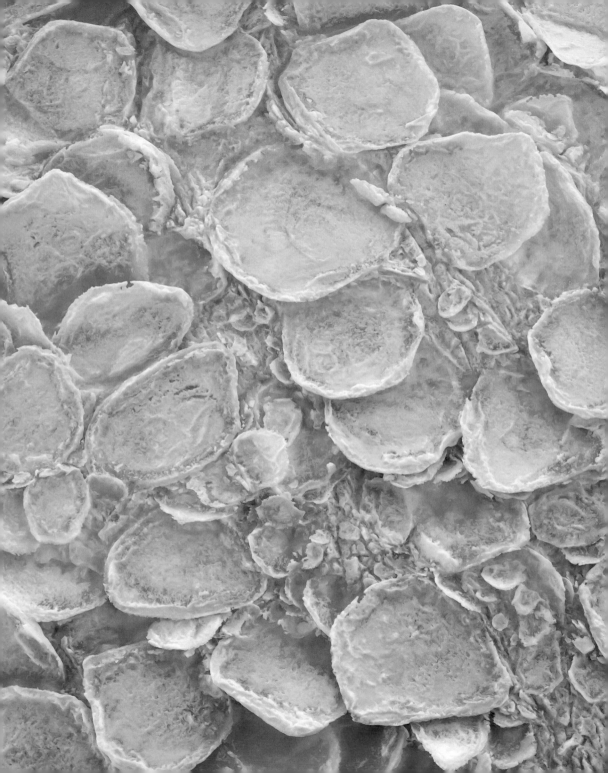

The helicopter lifted off the helipad into another day of clear blue skies and warm temperatures—hovering between thirty degrees F to thirty-five degrees F. A week earlier, temperatures at the colony were a windy twenty degrees below zero with low visibility. We knew how lucky we were with the weather.

"How do you feel?" Jude asked.

"Good enough to give it a try," I said. "I'll tell you when we get to the ice. When I start hiking."

The entire expedition to the emperor penguins off Snow Hill Island was an adventure on a grand scale, made up of countless minor adventures. The helicopter rides to and from the base camp on the fast ice were themselves highlights of the whole trip. We were five or six people per helicopter,

Emperor Penguins, Snow Hill Island, Antarctica

plus gear. Two Russian pilots flew the choppers. We hummed over the colony at a high enough altitude to avoid bothering the penguins, but low enough to navigate by sight.

And what a sight it was—an almost visionary landscape of white snow and ice, with blue sky, blue seas, and dreamy shades of blue glowing inside the ice. Huge icebergs were frozen in place by the winter sea ice. In the distance, Snow Hill Island revealed flanks of dark earth, perhaps a mile or two from the colony. We were going to land on what is called "fast ice"—sea ice that is attached to the shore or land. The penguin colony was on this fast ice.

The emperor penguins could be made out as we approached our landing site—small black shapes against a blinding and boundless white. They were the only living things to see. It was lonely and gorgeous and thrilling.

We dropped softly onto the ice, obscured from the colony behind an iceberg the size of a football stadium. The four of us gathered by the tent, put on our gear, and turned to the colony.

"Moment of truth," I said.

We set out on the path. I was counting my steps. I got to thirty and had to take a rest. But I did not have to go to my knees.

"It's much better," I told Andrew. "I don't know why. But I think I'll make it to the colony."

Susan and Jude walked ahead.

As we approached the colony, Andrew and I were joined by three adult emperor penguins tobogganing home. We entered the colony in procession. They stood up, regal birds entering home territory, escorts for Andrew and me. The emperors looked less comfortable walking than tobogganing. They waddled. I limped.

We caught up with Susan and Jude, who watched us arrive. "You look better," Jude said.

"I don't know what happened, but I feel much better. It's not perfect. But I'm much improved."

"Looks like you got your miracle," Jude said.

"It feels like a miracle," I said. "My penguin miracle."

The colony was its usual cacophony of wheezing adults and chirping chicks. The chicks were very active. Small groups were on the move, making their way across the ice to other subcolonies. Many chicks wandered alone or in groups of two and three. One group of three stopped near me, came in close. One of the young penguins stepped forward, looking at me. It was close enough to touch. It bobbed its head, first forward toward its chest, then bouncing up and stretching back so it was looking up and backward. It's the head bob the chicks make when they give their high, almost whistled call.

Then it fell forward, lay on its stomach, and ate ice.

I lifted my head, stretched my arms, flapped, and called out to the whole colony—the best version of an ecstasy call I could render.

━ ━ ━ ━ ━

TUCKED INSIDE THE WEDDELL SEA on the east side of the Antarctic Peninsula, the emperor penguin colony on Snow Hill Island was only discovered in the 1990s. It's the northernmost colony of emperor penguins in the world. Its location just south of the Antarctic Sound makes it the only colony regularly visited by Antarctic cruise ships or expedition ships for tourists.

It is still largely inaccessible and protected by the winter ice covering the Weddell Sea. The only reliable way to approach Snow Hill is on an icebreaker with a hull specifically made for smashing through the ice. We spent a full day crashing through the ice. The island was once famous for a party of the Swedish Antarctic Expedition (1901–03), who spent two winters stranded on Snow Hill. Ernest Shackleton had hoped to land there and utilize the hut used by the Swedish expedition, but strong currents carried Shackleton and his men past Snow Hill and the whole peninsula.

Now the island is better known for its emperor penguins. It's one of about fifty-five known colonies of emperor penguins in Antarctica, with an estimated global population of 238,000 pairs. The colony at Snow Hill has varied in size over the years. Currently its population is estimated at 4,000 pairs. When we were there in October 2018, there seemed to be at least as many chicks!

However amazing their life history, wedded to Antarctica and its ferocious winters, their isolation in Antarctica has served emperor penguins very well in one important regard. They are emperors of a remote empire of ice, protected by the stormy moat of the Southern Ocean. The first colony of emperor penguins was not discovered until 1902. Protected by their isolation and the elements, they have remained largely unaffected by human intrusions and human pressures.

The International Union for Conservation of Nature (IUCN) lists the emperors' status as the relatively benign "near threatened." That is already changing. Colonies in the west are showing signs of decline. Most notably, the colony that was filmed for the Oscar-winning documentary *March of the Penguins* is in serious danger. Two threats will shape the

future for these spectacular penguins. They feed on a variety of fish and a small crustacean called krill, which is crucial for penguins as well as seals and whales. Krill is the foundation of the Antarctic food chain. It is the tiny creature that supports the largest creatures on the planet—the whales. Krill are also the most numerous animals on the planet.

In one of the on-board lectures, called "License to Krill," Adrian Boyle warned that a serious threat to emperor penguins is coming in the form of a growing commercial fishery in krill. One of its principle centers is around the Antarctic Peninsula and the Weddell Sea. The situation concerning krill in Antarctica is difficult to determine. Adrian Boyle, for example, offered statistics of a very dramatic

Emperor Penguins,
Snow Hill Island,
Antarctica

and alarming decline in krill. Other experts say there is no documented decline in krill yet. Richard Sherley, who studies African penguins on Robben Island, told me, "I don't think there is any evidence of a decline in krill abundance. At least, there is an ongoing debate about this."

There is definitely a potential for a big decline as fisheries increasingly turn their attention to krill. New technologies such as "suction" harvesting by huge trawlers make it possible to clean the ice of krill. It's like taking an enormous vacuum cleaner and "hoovering" the habitat clean. Given the global history of overfishing, it is entirely likely that we could deplete the food base of the oceans.

Amazingly, its main markets are animal feed, 45 percent; nutritional supplements, 45 percent; and human food, 10 percent. "I don't think people taking the supplements realize that they're taking food from penguins," Adrian told me.

"Or the impact they may be having on the populations of whales and penguins," Tom Hart, the Oxford University penguinologist, added. "We need to change that."

The decline in krill overlaps with the even bigger threat of global warming for penguins. As ocean temperatures rise, sea ice contracts. At a key stage of their lives, krill require sea ice. And of course, emperor penguins need the sea ice for their colonies and raising their chicks. The young penguins must be developed enough with juvenile feathers replacing down before the sea ice melts. Currently, mortality of emperor chicks in the first year is already high, at about 40 percent.

As Tom Hart put it, "I think people would be pretty surprised at how many penguin species are declining. And, the importance of krill to penguins."

The world has shrunk. Even emperor penguins, once protected by inaccessibility, are tangled up in human lives. Few people realize how their actions have an impact on creatures like penguins. The reach of our daily lives is largely invisible to us, but it extends all the way to Antarctica through the fish we eat, the way we feed our pets, even the omega-3 nutritional supplements that use krill oil.

Our lives aren't inseparable anymore.

—— —— —— —— ——

FOR TWO DAYS AT SNOW HILL I lived my penguin miracle. I could make it to the colony, move among the subcolonies, and move among the penguins. I am still not sure what changed in regards to my back issue. It's not like I felt no pain. I had to pace myself. But the weather was wonderful—above freezing with sun shining through soft clouds—and we were able to spend full ten-hour days in the colony.

Much of the time I photographed penguins. My goal was to let them show me what they wanted me to see about them, how they wanted to be seen. Photography helps us enter into the world of animals, and my job is to be patient enough to wait for them to reveal themselves.

My reward is often startling to me.

At Snow Hill I had two especially powerful moments with the emperor penguins. Both involved the chicks. I knew going down there that the chicks were cute. Nothing prepared me for just how cute they really are. With their gray-fluff bodies, white faces, and black "helmets," they are by far the cutest penguin chicks. They must be some of the cutest babies in the whole world.

The chicks stole the show. They formed crèches, or nurseries. Some crèches were small, just three or four babies. Some were quite large, with more than fifty babies. The crèche had a life of its own, a dynamic sense of multiple energies and personalities roiling around. Often an adult babysitter tried to manage the crèche, and it was entertaining to watch. A chick or two might wander outside the crèche, and the adult would round them up, bring them back. The chicks were surprisingly well-behaved, except that they had a super-abundance of energy. The energy would build, and they would press against the margins of the group.

Then *boom*, there was a breakout and a stream of chicks would pour out, heading for another colony. The adult would follow in pursuit—sometimes bringing them back, sometimes not. Sometimes the chicks made it to a new subcolony.

I found one crèche especially engaging. A group of eight chicks had successfully escaped and was making its way up an icy slope toward a new subcolony. They headed roughly in one direction, but each chick moved at its own pace. They came upon a scooped dip in the snow, which they apparently found irresistible.

They stopped and the last one bumped into the one in front of it and fell down. They were looking every which way, disorganized. They squeezed tightly into a group.

Then all but one looked in the same direction. That one craned its neck to look straight at me. That was the instant. I took that picture of the group as it came together.

The colony was made up of countless stories happening all over the place. The narratives felt immediately and easily recognizable to me.

The evidence increasingly points to the probability that birds feel in ways we might—that seeing ourselves in them is not always projection. Tim Birkhead, a well-known ornithologist, writes in *Bird Sense: What It's Like to Be a Bird*, "In humans, consciousness integrates the different senses." That is to say, we make a story out of the information we gather through our senses. "I have no doubt that the senses of birds are integrated as well, and that this creates feelings. . . .

The more we find out, the more likely it seems that birds do have feelings."

Noah Strycker is also an ornithologist. He extends the idea to penguins. In *The Thing with Feathers*, he writes, "Penguins may be emotionally similar to us . . . Birds have feelings, just like us. Penguins have feelings."

Jude put it more simply: "The chicks seem to enjoy cuddling together."

All of us have felt such wonderful moments, when an image we see resonates inside. You not only see, but you feel it in the way your heart thrills to the scene. In such moments, my heart opens and I feel myself in the contact zone with another creature. This is the space where change happens. New realities emerge as I see with new eyes and animals take on a new depth. And at the same time, I feel myself transformed.

These are the moments with penguins I have come to love. I am born and reborn again and again in being with the animals I love.

I have only to let myself go and live the feeling.

Here at the culmination of our penguin quest, what I saw in this crèche of penguin chicks spoke directly to my own wayward and wandering heart. I have often felt like an adult orphan. What these penguin chicks in their tight group stirred in me was a longing that is one of the most basic feelings of my life. The longing to belong.

It's not just me who needs a lesson in belonging. Our culture as a whole has this to learn, still: how to connect with the earth we live on and call home, and how to take our place with and among the creatures for whom this is also home.

Gypsy and pilgrim, I felt in these penguin chicks and in this colony of emperor penguins what it meant to come home and, with that, just a little bit more I like I belonged.

— — — — — —

THAT SUDDEN MOMENT when the crèche formed reminded me of another class of students. We had come back from Antarctica, had seen lots of penguins, and had even volunteered in helping a biologist measure and weigh baby Magellanic penguins. Then we had traveled to El Chaltén, in Patagonia. We hiked in the afternoon to the camp just before the steep rock climb to Laguna de los Tres—where the rockface of Fitz Roy begins.

We were going to get up in the early morning darkness and hike to the lagoon for the sunrise. Spectacular.

But the evening was really cold. We ate our camp dinner standing up in a loose group, shivering. And one of the students said, "Let's make a crèche." They huddled together like penguin chicks in a tight group. And it helped them keep warm at the campground at the base of the Fitz Roy massif. After that, the crèche became part of our identity as a group. To this day, we see each other and say, "Remember the crèche?" And we laugh and recall huddling like penguin chicks at night in Patagonia. Sometimes you don't have to memorize something to learn it by heart. You just have to let yourself live what you love.

LET ME END WITH ONE FINAL STORY about every penguin in the world.

On my last day in the emperor penguin colony at Snow Hill Island, I watched a young chick, perhaps a month and a half old, looking for its parents. The chicks must get lost a lot as they wander among the subcolonies while their parents are fishing.

This chick was alone. It passed through the colony, approaching each adult it could find that was unclaimed by another chick. It stood before the adults, begging. The begging of chicks is a constant noise in the colony. The chicks drop their chin and beak into their chest, then throw their

Northern
Rockhopper
Penguin, Tristan
da Cunha Islands,
British Overseas
Territory

head back, and it bobs up and down, giving a high-pitched and insistent "chee, chee."

The adults looked at the chick carefully, and, concluding it was not theirs, moved on. One or two actually pushed the chick away with their flippers. The chick sat on the ice, looking rejected and forlorn. Then it approached another adult.

After about ten tries it found what was obviously its parent. Actually, I think the parent recognized the call of its own chick and then found it. The chick quit begging. It turned around and backed into the stomach and chest of its parent. I was surprised at how the chick settled into its parent's feathers as if onto a soft pillow, sinking in.

It quit begging. It didn't seem interested in food. The parent leaned forward and with astonishing tenderness examined its chick. I will never forget the adult. Its breast feathers were washed in a rich yellow. The sun-orange of the "ear patches" and the line of orange on its long beak showed in subtle blotches. The shades of yellow and orange seemed to glow. Really glow. One eye gleamed from its black penguin face.

The chick looked at me, contentment written all over its face. The chick might as well have been offering up a summary of my own story of a pilgrim among penguins.

For me, the chick might as well have been every penguin in the world.

The Journey of Our Lives

Gough Island

40.3186° S, 9.9353° W

FOURTEEN DAYS AT SEA. Our goal was in sight. And conditions were deteriorating by the minute. Winds were picking up, whipping whitecaps on the sea. A dangerous ten-foot swell was coming at us broadside.

It was early morning, but there would be no sunrise today—just low clouds obscuring the horizon and a building gale.

The captain pulled us into a more or less protected position on the lee side of Gough Island. It's one of the most remote islands in the world. Halfway between Cape Town, South Africa, and Rio de Janeiro, Brazil, it's an extremely difficult place to get to, and going ashore is prohibited.

Six hermitted and hardy souls staff a weather station on this far-flung outpost. They may be alone, but they do not lack company. Gough is one of the most important islands in the world for nesting seabirds. At least twenty-four species breed on the island, totaling about 8 million birds. They

Southern Rockhopper Penguin (Albino), Falkland Islands, British Overseas Territory

include a number of rare and beautiful species: the critically endangered Tristan albatross, the striking Atlantic yellow-nosed albatross, the elegant sooty albatross. It is the only place in the world—this single island—where the magnificent spectacled petrel breeds.

For the really serious global birders on board—and there were probably ten of them with lists of 7,000 to 9,000 species—the big prize was a tiny, nondescript bird called the Gough bunting, found here and only here.

And one bird is found here that all of us wanted to see. It may be the most difficult-to-see penguin in the world, not just because the location is remote, but also because few ships ever visit. The northern rockhopper may be the coolest penguin most people have never heard of. For Susan and me, this was the final species of our penguin quest.

Number eighteen.

The species did not even exist when Susan and I began looking for every species of penguin. It did not suddenly evolve in the last few decades, as if evolution kicked into overdrive to fashion a new species of penguin. Rather, you might say the northern rockhopper had just been created by humans.

About 80 percent of the world's population of this species lives here, in the Tristan da Cunha archipelago, which includes Gough Island. The rest are found on two even less visited islands of the Indian Ocean, Amsterdam and St. Paul Islands.

According to BirdLife International, a paper in 2006 argued that the southern and northern rockhoppers should be split. Put differently, one of the subspecies of the rockhoppers should be acknowledged as a distinct species.

Why? The penguins in the north are smaller overall and have a spectacular bushy crest that sets them apart from southern rockhoppers. In terms of behavior, the timing of nesting is different. And DNA tests suggest the two populations diverged about 680,000 years ago.

BirdLife International, the unofficial arbiter of these things, accepted the split. So too has the IUCN, officially listing the northern rockhopper as endangered. The IUCN estimates the population at about 240,000 pairs. Population trends are not well known, but are certainly declining.

This isolated penguin was the main reason most of us were on this ship, whose itinerary would take us from Ushuaia, Tierra del Fuego, to South Georgia Island, and then to visit all the islands as we headed north up the middle of the Atlantic Ocean to the Cape Verde Islands. Five weeks on the ship, and this was the morning we'd really signed up for.

The stern deck gradually filled with passengers. Everyone was hoping for a good view of the penguins. But conditions were conspiring against us. The light was bad, the tossing boat on this rough sea rendered binoculars useless, and a slanting rain and thick air further ruined visibility. We could barely make out the island, much less the penguins. Though we could not land on Gough, the plan was to cruise the shoreline in Zodiacs for close views of the birds. But the deteriorating weather threatened to make Zodiac rides too dangerous. The captain and guides would not lower the Zodiacs into the water if the risks were too great.

For Susan and me, the northern rockhopper penguin had come to mean much more than number eighteen. A few years earlier, a doctor's visit had changed my life. It gave me deeply personal reasons for wanting to see this final species.

We watched as one Zodiac with the expedition leader, Sebastian, and one guide, Adam, left the ship and made toward shore. They were checking out conditions for us. They banged and bumped over the whitecaps.

Our chances, such as they were, rode in that Zodiac.

Steilacoom, Washington

47.1698° N, 122.6026° W

WE ARE ALL JUST one doctor's visit away from our own mortality. As the years accumulate, appointments with my doctor begin to feel less routine and more like a crap shoot. You never know what news might be in store. I have friends and family who seem healthy, then get suddenly sick, even die unexpectedly—felled by a heart attack at home, or taken by a rare cancer way too young. Another is fine one day and learns the next she has a brain tumor. Even Susan has had the doctor's visit where she learned she had cancer.

A few years before the ocean odyssey to Gough Island, with our penguin quest in full swing, a shake in my left hand sent me to a neurologist for a consultation. The doctor put me through a series of simple tests for coordination, balance, and short-term memory. Susan was beside me as I went through my paces. My memory was good: I remember every detail of that office and those tests.

The doctor had a lot to say that August afternoon, but I really heard only two words that changed my life.

"Parkinson's disease."

The moment is seared in my memory. I suspect this is true for anyone who has gone through their own life-changing diagnosis.

Susan and I stopped on the way home at our favorite Mexican restaurant. Comfort food and two big margaritas. We had done the same thing after Susan's diagnosis—it's the beginning of the process of coming to terms with this new

Zodiac with
Students and Minke
Whale,
Paradise Bay,
Antarctica

reality in our lives. I have always been active and healthy.
Never even been hospitalized. I did not go through denial,
but this did not fit with my self-image. One thing is true
about Parkinson's: everyone has their own trajectory with the
disease. It's also true that everyone has to find their own path
into a suddenly complicated future.

Surprisingly, for me at least, this doctor's visit turned
into one of my life's great clarifying moments. I don't really
care for the military and bellicose metaphors often used with
serious diseases: battling cancer, fighting for his life. Nor do
I believe in giving in. Acquiescence is not my style. After a
period of stunned disorientation, I began to get my legs back

underneath me. I threw myself into research about the disease and what I could do about it. It was not a battle for me. I wanted renewed immersion in life. I wanted to be born again, not in body, but in an embrace of life. I know we can't make time stand still, but I also know we can make time fly. I began with some sobering soul-searching. What quickly became clear to me was that a diagnosis of Parkinson's was not the worst thing I might have heard from my doctor. It is not what anyone wants to hear, of course. But it is not the worst news, not by a long shot. A diagnosis of Parkinson's is not a death sentence, like some forms of cancer. Parkinson's will not kill you. I might easily have twenty or thirty more years to live.

No, not a death sentence. It is, I realized, a life sentence.

One immediate response for me was to return to the penguin quest with renewed energy and enthusiasm. Life

Magellanic Penguins,
Peninsula Valdés,
Argentina

became suddenly much more meaningful to me. I did not get depressed—maybe I only brushed against depression a bit. Instead, my passion for penguins and my passion for life coalesced. Animals had helped me before through dark times in my life. Perhaps they could help me again.

———— ——— —— —— ——

Gough Island

IT GOT ROWDY AND FUN ON THE STERN as we waited for the Zodiac to return from its reconnaissance. Desire to see the penguins was intense and people were lively and talkative. With Susan and Andrew and Jude, I started a tongue-in-cheek chant, fashioned after the chants at political protests.

"What do we want?" I asked.

"Penguins!" Susan and Jude and Andrew demanded.

"When do we want them?" I asked.

"Now!" We all laughed.

The Zodiac returned. Over the PA system, the expedition leader, Sebastian, called us to the main lounge for a briefing. We crowded into the room. Everyone came to hear if we could board the Zodiacs or not.

After a rundown on the weather—winds over 30 miles per hour, heavy rain, another front closing in on us—he described conditions in the Zodiac. Whitecaps made the ride bumpy. Swells made the gangway for getting into the Zodiacs a challenge, potentially dangerous.

Finally, he rounded to the point.

"Conditions," he said, "are extremely marginal."

"How many still want to get into Zodiacs?" he asked.

Virtually every hand in the lounge went up.

The birders were already thinking about extending their time in the Zodiacs. They asked a series of questions. How long will we be out? Could we stay out longer? They hoped for a sighting on the cliffs of the Gough bunting, which was possible.

I couldn't really blame them. They probably would never be here again. It was likely their only chance to see this species. I probably would have stayed out with them. In fact, one of the big surprises to me is how much I enjoyed hanging out with the world birders on all these voyages to remote islands with rare endemic species. They spent every possible minute at sea on deck, watching. And arguing, I might add, about the finer points of seabird identification. They were extremely knowledgeable and happily shared their knowledge with me.

But the expedition leader did not need that now. It was easy to see the stress on his face. Letting us go was a tough decision. The birders' questions just added more anxiety. "Let's see what it's like out there first," he said, with remarkable forbearance.

Susan and I hurried to our cabin to get our stuff.

As we were heading out, we heard the expedition leader telling everyone to dress warmly and wear rain gear. "Please," he implored, "take care."

Steilacoom, Washington

As you might expect, I read voraciously after my diagnosis—to learn more about the disease, what my life might look like, what research was underway. Susan and I also went to workshops and conferences. And I interviewed neurologists and a naturopath. I was especially interested in developments that would help minimize the progression of the disease and control its symptoms. In one interview with a neurologist, I described my obsession with penguins. I told him about our travels, including the trip we were planning to Gough Island for the northern rockhopper.

Would this diagnosis inhibit our travels before we could finish our list of eighteen penguins?

"Do your traveling now," the doctor said. "Because you won't be able to travel in ten years."

It was sensible advice, certainly. I'd seen friends who were planning big things for their retirement suddenly struck down before they ever fulfilled any of their plans. Don't wait. Do what you love to do. Do it now.

But the response also riled me a bit, got me feisty. It felt like a built-in assumption that I would inevitably be a victim and I might as well give in to that now. But I was not then and am not now willing to concede anything to the disease. After the initial shock of the diagnosis wore off, I got really clear about one thing: I would live as vigorously as possible for as long as possible. I'd already learned some people are "slow progressors." That will be me! That *is* me!

I cannot tell you where it came from, exactly, but I felt an intense clarity of purpose. I had penguins to see. What do we want? Penguins! When do we want them? Now!

Penguins and Parkinson's: If life is a journey, penguins had become a huge part of the journey of my life. They presented a model for me of lives lived in the extremes of hardship and challenge. They survive in some of the harshest and most miserable conditions on the planet. I wanted to emulate them. I wanted their charm, their playfulness, their tenderness and intimacies with their chicks and mates, their intensity of purpose, their toughness in harsh circumstances.

I would live like a penguin in all their fullness of life.

This was clearly part of the deepening of our penguin quest into a pilgrimage. Parkinson's no doubt played a role in changing our quest into "a spiritual journey to see all eighteen penguin species," as I put it to Susan.

One of the psychological challenges with Parkinson's is that it steals your life from you. Your body gets hijacked, bit by bit, and you can lose yourself in the process. Penguins were for me an antidote to that loss. They were my way of reclaiming myself. With them I've been learning a new way of speaking about my life. Of telling a new story to myself, about myself. Our lives are made of stories. Through stories we tell about ourselves, we find our lives and learn to inhabit them. In giving me stories, penguins gave me a life of renewed passion and deepening purpose.

I thanked the doctor for seeing me. I told the doctor that I certainly would do as much of what I loved as possible. I had more penguins to see.

"No travel in ten years?" I asked the doctor. "Would you like to bet on that? Watch me!"

Gough Island

SWELLS COMING AT THE BOAT can make the step into the
Zodiac a dangerous thrill. When it's your turn, you walk down
some rickety stairs slung over the side of the ship, stand on a
small platform, and prepare to step from gangway to Zodiac.
It requires timing—to step onto the pontoon as it is coming
up with a wave. And it requires decisiveness. It's two steps,
really: one, onto the Zodiac pontoon; and two, into the Zodiac.

And a firm grasp of the arm of the crew member there
to help.

After stepping gingerly into the Zodiac, bucking on
the swells, we were bobbing toward the shoreline and the
penguins. A pelting rain came at us sideways as we rode
the surge near the rocky shore, just before the waves broke.
Penguins lined the cliffs, watching us. Dozens of penguins
were in the water in small groups, hanging about the Zodiac.

Without question, northern rockhoppers have the
most stunning crest of any penguin species. The southern
rockhopper is wonderful and elegant, but its crest is tame by
comparison. The northern rockhoppers have a spectacular,
luxuriant shock of golden feathers on their heads, much
thicker and much longer than any other penguin. The plumes
of their crests thrashed wildly on their heads in the wind,
slapping their faces and hiding their eyes. They peeked out
from behind their flailing feathers like shaggy dogs.

Susan commented on how full and thick their crests were,
even wet.

Jude said, "Northern rockhoppers never have a bad hair day."
Their crests were wild, outrageous even, and wonderful. I
might use the same language for our penguin quest as a whole.

Susan and I beamed at each other. Number eighteen. Check!

Soaking wet, hypothermia a real possibility, people's
cameras breaking down in the rain—this was a miserable
experience, and we were completely happy.

And I might use the same language to apply to my
Parkinson's. A miserable thing to be handed. And yet, strangely
and ironically, I've never been so happy in my life as I am now.
What's most important to me has been made clearer by the
Parkinson's: Concede nothing. Love intensely. Do your stretches
and exercises. Don't worry. Be grateful for all you've been given.

When a creature presents itself to us, reveals itself, it is like a gift that nature gives to whatever longing we carry inside of us. Here at the end of our quest, after eighteen species of penguins, Susan and I shared a sense that we'd been rewarded with so much by these creatures. Memories and stories, yes, and also a kind of strength. There is a mythological Greek character, famous for battling Hercules, named Antaeus, son of Poseidon and Gaia. As long as he touched the earth, he was strong and could not be defeated.

Black-Browed Albatross, Falkland Islands, British Overseas Territory

I HAVE GAINED STRENGTH from my contact with animals.
Penguins in particular, because I have had such a long
and sustained conversation with them. In the Zodiac, I felt
wave after wave of gratitude—an emotion that is one of the
foundations of happiness. And I've gained strength from
other animals of the far south, creatures I have not described
in these stories but who have profoundly changed me as well.

Minke Whale,
Paradise Bay,
Antarctica

Several penguin species are not storied here, and especially the southern rockhoppers. Their tenderness toward their mates in intimate gestures was deeply moving.

- The royal penguins of Macquarie Island approached us with wide-eyed friendliness and unfeigned curiosity.

- An elephant seal on South Georgia Island gave birth just a few feet from me. I cannot forget the intensity in her eyes when she turned around and saw her baby, black and bleating and still wet.

- A "weaner" elephant seal, about 250 pounds, just kept coming closer and closer to me on South Georgia Island. They are called "weaners" because the moms simply abandon their babies to fend for themselves—that's how they are weaned. This weaner crawled right on top of me to cuddle. Its eyes were enormous, its face adorable.

- The minke whales of Paradise Bay in Antarctica have blessed us several times, coming right next to our Zodiacs, spyhopping to study us, as we studied them. I watched one rise through the clear water, coming up to the surface directly below a Zodiac carrying several of my students, and it seemed a perfect image of the way animal strength and animal power rise to us in the depths. It was an encounter we'll remember for a lifetime.

- The four humpbacks we saw in Iceberg Alley were feeding all around our Zodiacs, so close. Each time they surfaced to breathe, their whooshes drifted over us like murmurs

King Penguins, Falkland Islands, British Overseas Territory

Sunset, Penola
Strait, Antarctica

from another world. And the students, so moved by it all, shouted, "We love college," over and over.

- A rufous-legged owl in the beech forest of Tierra del Fuego, two nights after my mother died, answered Marcelo de Cruz's call. It came right up to us, in the early hours of night, as we stood in the forest. Marcelo de Cruz told me to be wrapped in the wings of an owl and she would take care of me. And I later learned my mother had been painting a watercolor of an owl for me as a gift before she died. "The owl in the forest was your mother," Susan said. That ungiven gift is the best thing my mother never gave me.

- The wandering albatross in the Drake Passage are deeply in tune to the wind and waves, and my heart seemed to fly as they swooped and glided and soared, as if invisibly connected to the sea by the wind. Albatross prove that nature lives inside of us, as well as outside.

- The black-browed albatross nesting on Saunders Island exchanged duties on the nest, incubating a single egg. I was touched by their "dance" as they strengthened their bond, even as they prepared to separate again. Birds of salt spray and stormy oceans, yet so tender and intimate at the nest, with a mate they will keep for life.

The sunset in Penola Strait, Antarctic Peninsula, lasted over three hours, turning incandescent. In fact, the sun never quite set but skimmed the horizon at about one in the morning and started to rise again. The students with me on that trip will know immediately which sunset I mean.

None of us will ever forget that one, the most beautiful sunset of our lives.

Finally, I remember the king penguin on South Georgia Island who came up and announced himself to me. I am bound to that penguin in gratitude and love. This book and these photos are my answer to your call.

Suddenly, an announcement from the captain to the Zodiacs. Time to return to the ship. The weather was worsening. Winds at 40 miles per hour were on their way. The Zodiac turned to leave. One penguin lifted its flipper. Pink feet, pink bill, and bright-red eyes.

It is hard to be miserable in the company of penguins. It's hard not to feel happy in their presence. Susan calls this feeling "the penguin glow." The red eyes of the northern rockhopper glowed as we said goodbye to number eighteen.

We carry that glow with us now. We will never let it go.

First Sightings

All Eighteen Penguin Species

Listed here are the eighteen species of penguins along with the locations and dates on which my wife, Susan Mann, and I saw them. The scientific name and conservation status for each species comes from BirdLife International.

Galápagos Penguin
- *Spheniscus mendiculus*
- Endangered
- Rábida Island, Galápagos Islands, Ecuador
- January 24, 2003

Magellanic Penguin
- *Spheniscus magellanicus*
- Near threatened
- Magdalena Island, Tierra del Fuego, Chile
- December 2, 2005

Gentoo Penguin
- *Pygoscelis papua*
- Least concern
- Drake Passage, Antarctica
- January 9, 2006

Chinstrap Penguin
- *Pygoscelis antarcticus*
- Least concern
- Half Moon Island, Antarctica
- January 10, 2006

Macaroni Penguin
- *Eudyptes chrysolophus*
- Vulnerable
- Half Moon Island, Antarctica
- January 10, 2006

Adélie Penguin
- *Pygoscelis adeliae*
- Least concern
- Torgerson Island, Antarctica
- January 11, 2006

King Penguin

- *Aptenodytes patagonicus*
- Least concern
- South Georgia Island, British Overseas Territory
- October 20, 2009

Southern Rockhopper Penguin

- *Eudyptes chrysocome*
- Vulnerable
- Sea Lion Island, Falkland Islands/Las Malvinas, British Overseas Territory
- November 3, 2009

Emperor Penguin

- *Aptenodytes fosteri*
- Near threatened
- Antarctic Sound, Antarctica
- January 15, 2010

African Penguin

- *Spheniscus demersus*
- Endangered
- Robben Island, South Africa
- June 10, 2011

Fiordland Penguin

- *Eudyptes pachyrhynchus*
- Vulnerable
- South Island, New Zealand
- November 21, 2014

Erect-Crested Penguin

- *Eudyptes sclateri*
- Endangered
- Antipodes Island, New Zealand
- November 29, 2014

Royal Penguin

- *Eudyptes schlegeli*
- Near threatened
- Macquarie Island, Australia
- December 4, 2014

Yellow-Eyed Penguin

- *Megadyptes antipodes*
- Endangered
- Auckland Island, New Zealand
- December 7, 2014

Snares Penguin*

- *Eudyptes robustus*
- Vulnerable
- Snares Islands, New Zealand
- December 9, 2014

Little Penguin

- *Eudyptula minor*
- Least concern
- Stewart Island, New Zealand
- December 13, 2014

Humboldt Penguin

- *Spheniscus humboldti*
- Vulnerable
- Islas Ballestas, Peru
- January 30, 2015

Northern Rockhopper Penguin

- *Eudyptes moseleyi*
- Endangered
- Tristan da Cunha Islands, British Overseas Territory
- April 8, 2017

Photograph not included in this book due to poor weather conditions during sighting.

Acknowledgments

EVERY PENGUIN IN THE WORLD has been a joy to research and to write. A large part of that joy has come through the people who taught me, worked with me, and helped me. I have many to acknowledge and thank.

Scientists and researchers studying penguins have been gracious with their time and knowledge. This is not a book of science, but it is grounded in science. Perhaps my greatest debt in this regard is to Andrea Raya Rey, who studies Magellanic and rockhopper penguins in Tierra del Fuego. During our visits to Isla Martillo, where she studies a colony of Magellanic penguins, she gave us the opportunity to study penguins in the field and taught us the importance of penguin conservation. Richard Sherley in Cape Town, Tom Hart in Oxford, and Ted Cheeseman in California embodied for me the value of science and conservation. To Dee Boersma, one of the great scientists of penguins, thank you for a memorable afternoon in your living room in Seattle, talking about your research and the importance of penguin conservation.

None of the travel for this book, as well as much of the information, would have been possible without the excellent guides who showed me the way. Foremost among them is Marcelo Martinez of Patagonia Travel Adventures. We have shared countless dusty miles as well as amazing hikes in Patagonia, his natal home. I am grateful for our friendship—for the laughter, the maté, and all the wonderful stories of growing up in Rio Gallegos. Elsa Prado, his wife, organized all of our complicated itineraries. Carina Benente of Peninsula Valdés told me of El Pedral, one of the great places I have visited in Patagonia. Marcelo de Cruz is probably the foremost birder in Tierra del Fuego and opened the doors for me to work with Magellanic penguins. I'll never forget his words: "You must be wrapped in the wings of the owl. She will take care of you in this moment."

Among the other guides I've traveled with, I especially want to thank Monika Schillat, Agustin Ullmann, Rod Planck, and Adam Walleyn. I have traveled with Quark Expeditions, Heritage Expeditions, and Oceanwide Expeditions, among others, and they have all been wonderful. I need to extend a special and personal thank-you to Ute Hohn-Bowen of Antarpply Expeditions and the ship *Ushuaia*—she went out of her way to help me on many of my trips to Antarctica, South Georgia, and the Falklands, and I'm deeply indebted. It's been a pleasure working with her and the terrific staff. The *Ushuaia* changed my life.

To Pacific Lutheran University, where I have taught for several decades: I cannot hope to express my gratitude for the ethos of vocation that enabled an English professor to follow his passions into environmental literature and writing. Combined with the university's emphasis on global education, I found myself doing what in graduate school I would never have imagined: leading classes of fifteen or so students to great natural destinations around the world. We made the bold decision to take students to Antarctica. We are one of the first, if not the very first, colleges or universities in the country to have an undergraduate class actually study in Antarctica. I am certain we were the first to study Samuel

Taylor Coleridge's "Rime of the Ancient Mariner" in the Drake Passage, while albatross circled our ship. I am grateful to President Loren Anderson and MaryAnn Anderson for their vision and support for our bold venture. I am deeply grateful to the Wang Center for Global Education at PLU for all the excellent work that goes into making these life-changing courses possible. To Janet Elaine Guthrie (Rasmussen), Neal Sobania, and Tamara Williams, executive directors of the Wang Center; and Charry Benston, Megan Grover, and Rosemary Raynolds, who provided incredible logistical support—this book and many of the experiences in it would not have been possible without you.

I have loved traveling to the Galápagos, Patagonia, Australia, and, of course, Antarctica with students at Pacific Lutheran University. I speak here only of the places where we saw penguins (I have taken students many other places worldwide). To those veterans, especially of Antarctica— more than 100 students—my great thanks. We shared experiences that create bonds for a lifetime: the best sunset of our lives, the humpbacks in Iceberg Alley right beside the Zodiacs, the minke whales of Paradise Bay, our first penguin sightings, the leopard seal at the Zodiac, helping to weigh and measure penguin chicks, and more. I wish I could list all of the students. I hope they know how much they have meant to me and what a joy it has been to share the wonders of Antarctica with them. Hold on to the "penguin glow."

My agent, Elizabeth Wales, is a delight to work with. I am grateful for her faith in me. Without her, *Every Penguin in the World* may never have been written. And I love her sense of humor.

Matt Mendenhall, editor at *BirdWatching* magazine, and Laura Helmuth, at *Smithsonian* and *Slate*, commissioned articles on penguins which led to this book. I'm deeply grateful to both.

I am indebted to Sasquatch Books' publisher Gary Luke for recognizing the value of a book that is equal parts text and images, stories and photos. Editorial director Jennifer Worick has been a pleasure to work with, for her sensitivity to language and her grasp of the larger vision of the book.

They found their way into this book, but I have to mention Jude Tasker and Andrew O'Keeffe, our penguin buddies. They live in Sydney, Australia. We met on a Heritage Expedition to the sub-Antarctic islands of New Zealand. We have traveled together often, including the expedition for penguin number eighteen. Thank you for reading drafts of this book, and for the great conversations and friendship.

Dan Morgan, a friend since graduate school at the University of Minnesota, read this book in drafts as well. I benefited from his great sensitivity to narration and language.

Finally, to my family—my sons and their wives, Ian and Kristina, and Eric and Catherine. I am so lucky to have such great men for sons, as well as wonderful daughters-in-law. Eric read drafts of this book, and Ian and I traveled to Antarctica together.

And to my grandkids, Benjamin and Georgie, a big thanks for bringing so much joy to us all. They embody the joy of returning home to Seattle after our long and wild travels.

Finally, to Susan, my companion throughout this penguin journey. This book is a gift especially to you. With love.

Gentoo Penguins,
Cuverville Island,
Antarctica

Select Bibliography

Ackerman, Diane. "White Lanterns." *The Moon by Whale Light.* New York: Vintage, 1991. 181–240.

Ackerman, Jennifer. *The Genius of Birds.* New York: Penguin Press, 2006.

Ainley, David G. *The Adélie Penguin: Bellwether of Climate Change.* New York: Columbia University Press, 2002.

Atwater, Richard and Florence. *Mr. Popper's Penguins.* Boston: Little, Brown and Co., 1938.

Bakhtiar, Laleh. *Sufi: Expressions of the Mystic Quest.* New York: Thames and Hudson, 1987 [1976].

Barham, Peter J. et al. "The Efficacy of Hand-Rearing Penguin Chicks: Evidence from African Penguins (*Spheniscus demersus*) Orphaned in the Treasure Oil Spill in 2000." *Bird Conservation International,* 18, no 2 (2008): 144–152.

Bergman, Charles. "Make Way for the African Penguins." *Smithsonian,* May 2012.

———. "Mothers and Other Creatures." *Mothers and Other Creatures: A bioStories Anthology.* 2015, 8–16.

———. *Orion's Legacy: A Cultural History of Man as Hunter.* New York: Dutton, 1996.

———. "The Penguin Quest: A Search for all 18 Species." *BirdWatching,* December 2018.

———. *A Penguin Told Me a Secret.* New York: Xlibris, 2016.

———. *Red Delta: Fighting for Life at the End of the Colorado River.* Golden, CO: Fulcrum Publishing, 2002.

———. *Wild Echoes: Encounters with the Most Endangered Animals in North America.* New York: McGraw-Hill, 1990.

BirdLife International."Rockhopper Penguins: A Plan for Research and Conservation Action to Investigate and Address Population Changes. Proceedings of an International Workshop." Great Britain: BirdLife International, 2010.

Birkhead, Tim. *Bird Sense: What It's Like to Be a Bird.* New York: Walker and Company, 2012.

Boersma, P. Dee. "Penguins as Marine Sentinels." *BioScience,* 58, no 7 (July/August 2008): 597–607.

———. "Population Trends of the Galápagos Penguin: Impacts of El Niño and La Niña." *The Condor: Ornithological Applications,* 100, no 2 (1998): 245–253.

Boothe, Joan N. *The Storied Ice: Exploration, Discovery, and Adventure in Antarctica's Peninsula Region.* Berkeley, California: Regent Press, 2011.

Borboroglu, Pablo Garcia and P. Dee Boersma, eds. *Penguins: Natural History and Conservation.* Seattle: University of Washington Press, 2013.

Campbell, David G. *The Crystal Desert: Summers in Antarctica.* New York: Houghton Mifflin, 1992.

Chatwin, Bruce. *In Patagonia.* New York: Penguin, 1977.

Cherry-Garrard, Apsley. *The Worst Journey in the World.* New York: Carroll and Graf, 1989 [1922].

Clucas, Gemma V. et al. "Comparative Population Genomics Reveals Key Barriers to Dispersal in Southern Ocean Penguins." *Molecular Ecology,* 27, no 23 (2018), 4680–97.

Cole, Theresa L. et al. "Mitogenomes Uncover Extinct Penguin Taxa and Reveal Island Formation as a Key Driver of Speciation." *Molecular Biology and Evolution*, 36, no 4 (2019): 784–97.

Cousineau, Phil. *The Art of Pilgrimage: The Seeker's Guide to Making Travel Sacred*. San Francisco: Conari Press, 2012.

Crawford, R. J. M. et al. "Collapse of South Africa's Penguins in the Early 21st Century." *African Journal of Marine Science*, 33, no 1 (2011): 139–156.

Dann, Peter, Ian Norman, and Pauline Reilly, eds. *The Penguins: Ecology and Management*. Chipping Norton, NSW: Surrey Beatty and Sons, 1995.

Davis, Lloyd Spencer. *Penguins: Smithsonian Q & A*. New York: HarperCollins, 2007.

de Waal, Frans. *The Age of Empathy: Nature's Lessons for a Kinder Society*. New York: Three Rivers Press, 2009.

Flood, Sue and Michael Palin. *Emperor: The Perfect Penguin*. Woodbridge, England: ACC Art Books, 2018.

Forster, E. M. *Howards End*. New York: Barnes and Noble, 2003 [1910].

Fothergill, Alastair. *Life in the Freezer: A Natural History of the Antarctic*. London: BBC Books, 1993.

France, Anatole. *Penguin Island*. New York: Modern Library, 1933 [1909].

Fraser, W. R. and D. L. Patterson. "Human Disturbance and Long-Term Changes in Adélie Penguin Populations: A Natural Experiment at Palmer Station, Antarctic Peninsula." *Antarctic Communities: Species, Structure and Survival*. Cambridge: Cambridge University Press, 1997, 445–52.

Fraser, W. R., W. Z. Trivelpiece, D. G. Ainley, and S. G. Trivelpiece. "Increases in Antarctic Penguin Populations: Reduced Competition with Whales or a Loss of Sea Ice Due to Environmental Warming?" *Polar Biology*, 11, no 8 (1992): 525–31.

Gilpin, Daniel. *Animal Families: Penguins*. Danbury, CT: Grolier Educational, 2001.

Gorman, James. *The Total Penguin*. New York: Prentice Hall, 1990.

Gosnell, Mariana. "The Ice Nursery." *Orion*, September/October 2005.

Haraway, Donna J. *When Species Meet*. Minneapolis: University of Minnesota Press, 2008.

Harrowfield, David L. *Call of the Ice: Fifty Years of New Zealand in Antarctica*. Auckland, NZ: David Bateman, 2007.

Hart, Tom et al. "Comparative Population Genomics Reveals Key Barriers to Dispersal in Southern Ocean Penguins." *Molecular Ecology*, 27 (2018), 4680–97.

———. "Mitogenomes Uncover Extinct Penguin Taxa and Reveal Island Formation as a Key Driver of Speciation." *Molecular Biology and Evolution*, 36, no 4 (2019): 784–97.

Hatherton, Trevor. *Antarctica: A New Zealand Antarctic Society Survey*. New York: Praeger, 1965.

Hooper, Meredith. *The Ferocious Summer: Palmer's Penguins and the Warming of Antarctica*. London: Profile Books, 2007.

Jouventin, P., R. J. Cuthbert, and R. Ottvall. "Genetic Isolation and Divergence in Sexual Traits: Evidence for the Northern Rockhopper *Eudyptes Moseleyi* Being a Sibling Species." *Molecular Ecology*, 15, no 11 (2006): 3413–23.

Kearton, Cherry. *The Island of Penguins*. New York: Robert McBride and Co., 1931.

Lanting, Frans and Christine Eckstrom. *Penguin*. Cologne, Germany: Taschen, 1999.

Line, Les. "The Shrinking World of Penguins." *National Wildlife* (August 2007). Online. https://www.nwf.org/en/Magazines/National-Wildlife/2007/The-Shrinking-World-of-Penguins

Lynch, Wayne. *Penguins of the World*. Buffalo, New York: Firefly, 2007.

McGonigal, David and Dr. Lynn Woodworth. *Antarctica: The Blue Continent*. New South Wales, Australia: Global Book Publishing Pty. Ltd., 2002

Meduna, Veronika. *Secrets of the Ice: Antarctica's Clues to Climate, the Universe, and the Limits of Life*. New Haven: Yale University Press, 2012.

Momatiuk, Yva and John Eastcott. "Penguins at the Edge." *Defenders*, Summer 2009.

Montaigne, Fen. "Signs from Earth: No Room to Run." *National Geographic*, September 2004.

Moore, Kathleen Dean. "The Truth of the Barnacles: Rachel Carson and the Moral Significance of Wonder." *Environmental Ethics*, 27, no 3 (2005): 265–277.

Murphy, Robert Cushman. *Logbook for Grace*. New York: Time-Life Books, 1965 [1947].

Naveen, Ron. *Waiting to Fly: My Escapades with the Penguins of Antarctica*. New York: William Morrow and Company, 1999.

Neruda, Pablo. *Neruda: Selected Poems, A Bilingual Edition*. Nathaniel Tarn, ed. New York: Houghton Mifflin, 1990.

Östling, Brutus and Susanne Åkesson. *Penguins*. New York: HarperCollins, 2007.

Peterson, Roger Tory. *Penguins*. New York: Houghton Mifflin, 1979.

Pigafetta, Antonio. *Magellan's Voyage: A Narrative Account of the First Circumnavigation*. Trans. R. A. Skelton. New York: Dover, 1994 [1969].

Ramel, Gordon. "Spheniscidae—Penguins." *Earthlife Web*. Online. www.earthlife.net/birds/spheniscidae.html

Schafer, Kevin. *Penguin Planet: Their World, Our World*. Hopkins, MN: Northword, 2000.

Simpson, George Gaylord. *Penguins: Past and Present Here and There*, New Haven, CT: Yale University Press, 1976.

Stonehouse, Bernard, ed. *The Biology of Penguins*. Baltimore: University Park Press, 1975.

Strycker, Noah. *Among Penguins: A Bird Man in Antarctica*. Corvallis, OR: Oregon State University Press, 2011.

———. *The Thing with Feathers: The Surprising Lives of Birds and What They Reveal about Being Human*. New York: Riverhead Books, 2014.

Sumption, Jonathan. *The Age of Pilgrimage: The Medieval Journey to God*. Mahwah, NJ: HiddenSpring Books, 2003 [1975].

Swan, Erin Pembrey, et al. *Penguins: From Emperors to Macaronis (Animals in Order)*. New York: Franklin Watts, 2003.

Wagner, Eric. *Penguins in the Desert*. Corvallis, OR: Oregon State University Press, 2018.

Whittington, Phil. *The Adventures of Peter the Penguin*. 2nd ed. Cape Town: University of Cape Town, Avian Demography Unit, 2011 [2001].

Wines, Michael. "Dinner Disappears, and African Penguins Pay the Price." *New York Times*, June 4, 2007.

Williams, Tony D. *The Penguins*. New York: Oxford University Press, 1995.

Yoon, Carol K. "Penguins in Trouble Worldwide." *New York Times*, June 26, 2001.

Young, Euan. *Skua and Penguin: Predator and Prey*. Cambridge, MA: Cambridge University Press, 1994.

Resources

Make a Difference

How can you help penguins, marine life, and oceans through your daily actions? Some of the ways that each of us can make a difference are:

- Calculate and reduce your ecological footprint at FootprintCalculator.org.

- Cut down your use of plastic. Use paper or metal straws, and glass or metal containers for food storage.

- Eat less or no meat. Eat low on the food chain.

- Vote for politicians who support the science of climate change and take actions to address it now.

- Eliminate or reduce the use of pesticides and fertilizers in your yard. Buy organic.

- Advocate for creating and expanding marine reserves.

- Be curious. Continue to learn more about the natural world and how we can care for wild animals and the planet.

- Shop smart. Be conscious about the efficient use of all resources: reduce, reuse, and recycle.

- Reduce fossil fuel use. Walk, bicycle, carpool, and use public transportation.

- Use your voice. Speak up on behalf of the planet and its inhabitants—including wild creatures.

- Conserve water. Let your lawn go brown in the summer. Plant water-efficient gardens.

- Get rid of trash properly. Volunteer for a beach cleanup.

King Penguins,
South Georgia
Island, British
Territory Overseas

Volunteer and Donate

There are many ways to help penguins directly and indirectly. To volunteer with penguins and support local and international organizations, check zoos and aquaria, wildlife sanctuaries, and conservation groups. These organizations provide opportunities to donate, "adopt" penguins, name penguins, and more.

BirdLife International
Penguin.BirdLife.org

Earthwatch Institute (volunteer expeditions)

- African Penguins:
  Earthwatch.org/Expeditions/
  South-African-Penguins

- Magellanic Penguins:
  Earthwatch.org/Expeditions/
  Trailing-Penguins-in-Patagonia

International Penguin Conservation Work Group
Penguins.cl

Ocean Conservancy
OceanConservancy.org

Oceana International
Oceana.org

Sea Legacy
SeaLegacy.org

Southern African Foundation for the Conservation of Coastal Birds (SANCCOB)
SANCCOB.co.za/volunteer

World Wildlife Fund
WorldWildlife.org

Recommended Research Organizations

I hope you're inspired to learn more about penguins and help them. The scientific literature on penguins, Antarctica, the Southern Ocean, and other places that penguins inhabit is voluminous. Rather than list all the papers I have consulted, I share links here to organizations that offer information and databases of published research that can be easily accessed.

If you do a search on the internet, thousands of websites from around the world will pop up on penguins in some way. The list of sites here provides a number of excellent resources. It is not exhaustive but will provide you with an excellent place to begin.

Antarctica and Southern Ocean Coalition
ASOC.org

Antarctica New Zealand
AntarcticaNZ.govt.nz

Australian Government, Department of the Environment and Energy, Australian Antarctic Division
Antarctica.gov.au

BirdLife International: Data Zone
(provides extensive information on many topics)
DataZone.Birdlife.org

Birdlife International
(lists each penguin species' threat level)
Birdlife.org/list-penguin-species

British Antarctic Survey
BAC.ac.uk

Center for Ecosystem Sentinels
EcosystemSentinels.org

Commission for the Conservation of Antarctic Marine Living Resources
CCAMLR.org

Defenders of Wildlife
Defenders.org

Environmental Working Group
EWG.org

Global Penguin Society
GlobalPenguinSociety.org

Happywhale
Happywhale.com

International Fund for Animal Welfare
IFAW.org

International Union for Conservation of Nature, Penguin Specialist Group
IUCN.org/commissions/ssc-groups/birds/penguin

Monterey Bay Aquarium: Seafood Watch Program
SeafoodWatch.org

National Science Foundation, Office of Polar Programs
NSF.gov

Penguin Watch
PenguinWatch.org

Public Broadcasting Service (PBS): Nature (series)
PBS.org/wnet/nature

Scientific Committee on Antarctic Research (SCAR)
SCAR.org

Scott Polar Research Institute
SPRI.cam.ac.uk

About the Author

A writer and photographer, CHARLES BERGMAN has lived nearly his whole life in the Pacific Northwest. He's a longtime teacher of English at Pacific Lutheran University. He's the author of four books, including *Wild Echoes: Encounters with the Most Endangered Animals in North America*. He's written extensively on wildlife and animals in national magazines, including *Audubon*, *Natural History*, and *National Geographic*. His article on wildlife trafficking in Latin America was the cover story in *Smithsonian* magazine. His work springs from a wild dedication to the earth and its creatures. His writing and photography have won several awards, including the Washington State Book Award, Southwest Book Award, IBPA Benjamin Franklin Award, and he was a PEN America Literary Award finalist. He has a particular love for the southern hemisphere and has completed two Fulbright Fellowships, one in Mexico and one in Ecuador. He has taught study tours in Antarctica six times.

Photo by Susan Mann

Come Sing, Jimmy Jo

BOOKS BY KATHERINE PATERSON

Angels & Other Strangers
Bridge to Terabithia
The Crane Wife (translator)
Gates of Excellence
The Great Gilly Hopkins
Jacob Have I Loved
The Master Puppeteer
Of Nightingales That Weep
Rebels of the Heavenly Kingdom
The Sign of the Chrysanthemum

KATHERINE PATERSON

Come Sing,
Jimmy Jo

LODESTAR BOOKS   E. P. DUTTON   NEW YORK

The author and publisher gratefully acknowledge permission to quote
from "Will the Circle Be Unbroken?" on pages 145 and 197. "Will the
Circle Be Unbroken?" by A.P. Carter. Copyright 1935 by Peer
International Corporation. Copyright renewed. Used by permission. All
rights reserved.

LIBRARY OF CONGRESS CATALOGING IN PUBLICATION DATA

Paterson, Katherine.
    Come sing, Jimmy Jo.

    "Lodestar books."
    Summary: When his family becomes a successful country music
group and makes him a featured singer, eleven-year-old
James has to deal with big changes in all aspects of his
life, even his name.
    1. Children's stories, American. [1. Country music—
Fiction. 2. Musicians—Fiction. 3. Family life—Fiction]
I. Title.
PZ7.P273Co 1985 [Fic] 84-21123
ISBN 0-525-67167-6

Published in the United States by E. P. Dutton,
2 Park Avenue, New York, N.Y. 10016

Published simultaneously in Canada by
Fitzhenry & Whiteside Limited, Toronto

Editor: Virginia Buckley   Designer: Riki Levinson

Printed in the U.S.A.   W
10 9 8 7 6 5 4 3 2

for
Mary Handley Watt Sorum

Streams of mercy never ceasing
Call for songs of loudest praise.

with love and thanks

Come Sing, Jimmy Jo

Where do you come from?
Where do you go?
Where do you come from,
My cotton-eyed Joe?

I come for to see you.
I come for to sing.
I come for to bring you
My diamond ring.

—APPALACHIAN MOUNTAIN SONG

Grandma stuffed a pinch of homegrown tobacco in her pipe, scratched a kitchen match on the side of the rocker, and puffed to make the light catch. "Awright, James," she said between puffs, her teeth clenched on the pipe stem, "I wanna hear you really tear it up now."

James hefted the guitar, which was more than twice his eleven years and nearly as long as he was tall. It was heavy and the strap cut into his shoulder, but he didn't care. He stomped his bare brown foot—three, four times to set the rhythm—and then, by cracky, he tore into it.

> Oh, my dad's a travelin' man
> Gone a long, long way from home
> And my ma is crying every night alone—

Grandma squinted against the acrid smoke and rocked back and forth to the beat, hardly moving the rocking chair, just her body, her shoeless feet planted on the porch.

James ended the song with a great flourish of chords and a slap against the side of Chester—the private name for his guitar.

"Whoowee!" Grandma waved her pipe up and down. "Boy, you near 'bout light my pipe without no match."

James could feel his ears going pink. He hunched his shoulders.

"Stand up, boy. Take a bow. Don't scrunch inside yourself like a puppy ain't housebroke. You done good. Just smile and nick your head a bit—that's plenty humble enough for a star."

James stood as straight as he could and jerked his head, just like he'd seen them do on TV. You could only get a couple of channels here on the mountain, and they had lots of snow, but one of those channels carried WQVR in Tidewater, Virginia, so he knew how real country stars did things.

"That's right. Now. Sing me a comfort song."

He licked his mouth and shoved his glasses up on his nose. First he hit a few gentle chords, and then, very softly, he began:

> There's a mansion over there
> 'Cross the river's stormy shore
> Where my mother waits in glory just for me—

Grandma didn't have her apron on, so she bent toward her lap and wiped her eyes with the hem of her dress. "Boy, that one will git me ever' time." She snuffled loudly through the three verses and the four repeats of the chorus.

"I'm sorry," he said when the last chord died mournfully. "I guess it makes you miss your momma."

"Mercy, no," she said. "I never missed that woman one thirty-second minute. She was a falling-down drunk what beat the tar out of ever'one of us nine kids. We was glad to see her go, tell the truth. You shoulda been at that funeral—more like

6

a wedding, ever'body so happy they 'bout died theirselves. Mercy. Mercy." She took the pipe out of her mouth and leaned back against the chair with her eyes closed. "Just a purty song's why I cry. I love to cry. You know that, boy. A song like that's pure delight. And, Lord, boy, you sing it like a angel." She began to rock slowly, her eyes still shut. "Next funeral comes along, I want you to sing that one with the Family."

"No!" It was as if she'd thrown him naked into Carlyle Creek. "You know I don't sing for nobody but you."

"Yeah," she said, rocking and smiling. "More's the pity."

He began to sweat he was so relieved. The very idea of singing in front of people made him want to heave his breakfast. He didn't understand the fright himself, so it was a wonder his grandma did. All the Johnsons were singers and string pickers. His own mother, now. Why, Olive didn't have a nervous bone in her teeny little body. She'd just get up there before a whole passel of people and let it rip. She was beautiful, too—yellow hair that hung nearly to her waist, big brown eyes, and a voice that could blow the colored glass out of the back of a church. Grandpa had a skinny, high voice that'd give you the shivers. Uncle Earl was pretty near as loud as Olive —with a voice that *boom-boom*ed all over the scale, from the bottom to the top. Jerry Lee, James's daddy, wasn't much of a singer, more a picker—best banjo in three counties, everybody said—but he sang backup in a sweet, soft baritone that James loved to hear. Even Grandma used to sing with the Johnson Family. She taught James everything—except how to want to sing and pick a guitar in front of people. There was no teaching that. Besides, she said, he was still a runt. He didn't mind when Grandma said things like that. It wasn't like when his uncle Earl picked on him. Grandma had raised him while the rest were off picking and singing. She had a right.

He started into the house to put Chester in the case. "Wanna stir the beans?" she asked without opening her eyes.

He put the guitar away in his room. He called the room his. When Olive and Jerry Lee were home, they all three slept in it. Earl slept in the big room where the kitchen and everything else was. The other little room belonged to his grandparents. That was all there was to the house. Nobody had time to add any more rooms.

The string beans had been cooking in ham fat since yesterday. The smell had gone straight into the wallboards. He took the long metal spoon off the hook beside the big iron stove and stirred. His glasses got so steamed up, he had to stop and wipe them on his T-shirt.

"Done yet?" she called from the porch.

"Yeah," he said, hooking the metal frames back over his ears. The beans were pale khaki-colored, just the way she liked them. "We can eat anytime."

She ate four servings of beans. He marveled at the amount of food the old woman could stuff into her skinny body. One plate was all he could possibly manage, and he was supposed to be a growing boy.

"Well," she said, glancing at the funeral-parlor calendar hanging by the kitchen cabinet. "They ought to be back today —tomorrow the latest."

He felt a stir. He never minded being here with just Grandma, but there was always excitement about the return of the Family. They had stories to tell, and Jerry Lee would have always written some new songs to share. After a day or two, the Family would start to squabbling—usually Olive and Earl, who acted more like brother and sister than in-laws. James, at least, felt that proper in-laws would not squabble. And as they bickered, the house always seemed to shrink like last winter's long johns. Then Grandma and he would be secretly glad to see them go. Except for Jerry Lee. They always missed Jerry Lee, but not the others. The house was plenty big enough for the two of them, and they had never fought in their lives. Well, sometimes a cross word or two in the winter, on those rainy or snowy or icy mornings when James felt it was far too messy to walk the mile down to the school bus, and Grandma, who could hardly read or write herself, felt called to preach a sermon on the blessings of education. But it was summer now.

"I'll walk down to the box after dinner and see if they wrote," he said. The Family hardly ever wrote, but sometimes if they knew ahead they were going to be late getting home, Jerry Lee would send a card. Usually he called. None of them was much on writing.

James told Grandma to go in to lie down while he cleaned up, but before he'd finished washing up the plates and forks, he heard the old station wagon grinding up the dirt road. "They're here!" he yelled toward his grandma's room and banged out the door, wiping his soapy hands on his jeans as he ran.

Olive was jumping out of the wagon almost before Jerry Lee had it stopped, throwing out her arms to James. He went running into them as he had since he could run at all. Olive liked him to make a big thing out of her return. "Whew!" she said. "You've growed so. Next time you do that you'll knock me to the ground." Olive always pretended he'd grown a lot while she was away.

And then he was hugging Jerry Lee, who could still pick him up and swing him around even though he was eleven now, and Jerry Lee was only five-foot seven or eight with his boots on. James hugged Grandpa, too, and allowed Earl to punch him in the stomach. "Still a runt, huh?"

"You ain't been gone a month. Whatcha 'speck?"

9

Grandma was saying as she came down the porch steps still buttoning the front of her housedress. "Caught me napping," she said to Grandpa.

He patted her arm. He wasn't too tall, but unlike most men who grew up in the mountains, he walked without a stoop. That made him seem taller than he was. His hair was thinning a little, so he parted it low and combed it carefully to hide the bald spot.

"You awright, Grandma?" Grandpa smiled at his wife like a preacher shaking hands at the back of the church and patted her arm again. James wished he'd kiss her, but he never did. He just patted her arm or her face. Jerry Lee hugged her tight and kissed her smack on the mouth. Earl and Olive each gave her a peck on the cheek.

"There's plenty of beans," Grandma said, putting an arm around Jerry Lee's waist. They were just about the same height. "I know how you like your beans," she said.

"I been smelling 'em since Morgantown," he said happily.

"Me too," said Olive under her breath.

The men dived into the beans. Grandma brought out last night's leftover corn bread. Olive nibbled a bit of the cold bread. No wonder she stayed so skinny. She could pretend to like Grandma's cooking just a little bit, James thought. It wouldn't hurt her to eat a few beans. But he could never make the Family behave the way he dreamed they should.

"You have a good trip?" Grandma was asking.

"Fourteen churches and ten tent meetings," Grandpa reported. His mouth was full so he spit a little corn bread on the *s*'s and *t*'s.

"Tell 'em about the two county fairs and"—Olive checked James and Grandma to make sure they were both listening—"and the radio show."

"Radio show?" James asked. "When?"

"You couldn't have got it on our old clunker," Earl said. "It was all the way from Wheeling."

"Wheeling!" Both Grandma and James cried out the name.

"How 'bout that?" Olive was smiling across her whole face. To mountain pickers and singers, Wheeling was on the road to heaven. Once you'd sung in Wheeling, over WWVA, nobody could look down their noses at you ever again.

"Just one song," said Grandpa. "Wasn't even a gospel song."

"And Miss Olive made sure she did all the lead," Earl was grumbling.

"Wheeling," Grandma repeated. "I never in all my life sang in Wheeling." James jerked around to see her face. He didn't want her sad. She smiled at him and quickly put more beans on Jerry Lee's plate.

After the meal, they left the heat and smell of the house to sprawl about on the porch. It was a sleepy time for the men. Grandma would glance at the door every now and then, remembering her afternoon soap operas that she was giving up in honor of the Family's return. Olive was wide awake, slapping at the flies, nervously pumping the rocker back and forth. "Well, James," she said finally, "what you been up to?"

"Nothin'," he said. He often felt shy in front of Olive.

"Just 'cause it's summer, don't mean you have to be no count," she said.

"Oh, he's been helping me ever' day," Grandma said. "Wanna git my pipe off the table, boy?"

He jumped up off the step and raced inside to show how quickly and cheerfully he obeyed.

"You ought to get shut of that pipe, Momma," Olive said. "At your age, it can't do you no good."

"At my age, it don't have to do me no good." She took

the pipe and the match James had thought to bring and nodded her thanks. Then she pulled a little bag of tobacco from
her housedress pocket and filled the bowl. Olive turned away
in disgust. His mother would only be here a few days. Why
couldn't she be nice to the old woman? James couldn't understand it.

After Grandma had puffed her pipe into life, she said. "So,
Wheeling. Where do you go from there?"

Olive leaned forward, excited. "We don't know yet, but
it looks real good. Maybe we'll get ourselves a manager."

Grandpa woke up suddenly. "Olive," he said, "hadn't
been no agreement about that feller."

"I know. I said *maybe,* didn't I?"

"Your *maybe*s have a habit of stepping all over other people's *wait a minute*s," said Earl. It seemed they were going to
start fighting before even one night had passed.

"What you need a manager for?" Grandma asked. "You
seem to be doing real good—Wheeling and all."

"That's just it." Olive was eager for an ally. "We got a real
chance, Grandma. This feller's got connections all over."

"We been singing as a family for twenty-eight years."
Grandpa had put on his preacher voice. "Jerry Lee here was
just seven years old when we sang at that camp meeting in
Aurora. Remember that, Grandma?"

Grandma was laughing. "How could I forgit? That was the
time I yodeled so high that a fight broke out. Half the meeting
thought I was inspired by the Holy Ghost and the other half
thought I was possessed by the devil. Nobody had ever heard
a sound like that coming from a human throat, they said." She
made excited little puffs jump from her pipe bowl.

"I remember that," Jerry Lee said. "I was so scairt that I
thought when I got up there, frogs might just hop right out
my mouth."

"You were scairt?" Grandma twisted from her seat on the steps to look back at her son sitting on the porch bench. "Whyn't you say so? You never let on."

"I wanted to sing too much," Jerry Lee said. "I figured if I let on how scairt I was, you'd tell me I didn't have to do it."

"You're somethin'," Grandma said in that soft voice she used especially for Jerry Lee.

James wanted to ask Jerry Lee how, if he was so scared, he'd made himself just get up and sing, but the chance passed. Olive had business on her mind. "He ain't asking nothing but—"

"Nothing but ten percent right off the top," Earl interrupted her. "Even before expenses."

"Nothing down. Nothing for taking a chance on us." Olive swung her hair around. "Look y'all, outside this holler, nobody's even heard of the Johnson Family. Don't kid yourselves."

Both Grandpa and Earl turned red in the face and started yelling at that. What'd she know? She'd only been with the Family ten years or so. Olive yelled back even louder, and since she was a soprano, her voice carried. James hoped it wouldn't upset the chickens. They'd stop laying if they got upset.

"Hush, hush," Grandma was saying. "Y'all ain't been in the house long enough to have a full fight yet. Give it a day or two to ripen."

Jerry Lee started laughing at that. James wanted to laugh, too, but the fighting always did something cold to his stomach, and he couldn't throw it off the way Grandma and Jerry Lee seemed to.

"Hey!" Olive was outyelling the men. "You better shut your mouths and get this settled. He's gonna be here any minute."

"Who's gonna be here?" Now Grandma was the loudest.

"Eddie Switten," Olive screamed. "Our manager!"

"Says who?" Earl roared.

Jerry Lee had disappeared into the house. Now he came banging out with his banjo over his shoulder. He put on his metal finger and thumb picks so he could make a racket, and then he began to rattle those strings louder and faster than any of the rest of them could keep up yelling. They shut up in surprise and frustration. Jerry Lee finished his lick with a great flourish and a *bang-bang,* and then in the voice of a carnival barker, he told them all to be quiet and calm down. In his normal voice, he said, "Momma, what do you think? You think the Johnson Family should hire a manager, or should we just keep on the way we been doing?"

Grandma smiled at Jerry Lee. "I get a vote?"

"More'n vote, if I have any say. You're the only one in this family with sense enough to patch a leaky roof."

Everyone was looking at Grandma now, but no one except Jerry Lee was smiling. "How can it hurt to hear the man out?" Grandma said. "This is a new day, with radio and telly vee and all. Maybe the Johnson Family needs to hear some new ideas."

"That's just what—" Olive began.

"Whoa!" Jerry Lee commanded. "All she said was listen. Right, Momma?"

"That's all I said. We're pretty independent cusses, us Johnsons. We don't have to take nobody's advice, 'less it suits us to do so."

Now nobody was happy, except Grandma and Jerry Lee. There was a cold silence. You'd have thought it was an icehouse instead of a front porch in summer. Jerry Lee took off his finger picks and began to strum his banjo quietly and hum.

James swelled up with love for him. His daddy was almost as wise and good as Grandma. James got up from the steps and slid up to Jerry Lee. "Daddy," he said shyly, "you know 'There's a Mansion Over There'?"

"Sure, son." Jerry Lee fiddled about until he found the right key. Then, looking straight at Grandma, he began to sing. Sometimes Jerry Lee had the sweetest voice in all the world. James was watching Grandma. She nodded at him and winked, so James began to sing, too—a high harmony that perfectly suited Jerry Lee's gentle baritone. Jerry Lee smiled down at him, and they both turned and sang for Grandma, who knocked the ashes out of her pipe so she could give herself over to weeping with pure and free delight.

When it was over and Grandma was hugging them both to her, still crying, a tall stranger stepped out from the shadow of the trees near the road. He was clapping his hands.

"Well, I never—" said Olive. "There he is."

"Whooweee!" the man said as he got to the porch. "Now *that* was almost worth the walk."

"Where's your car?" Olive didn't seem very happy to see the fellow.

"You think I'm gonna bring a 1982 Pontiac sedan up that cow path? I ain't even finished paying for it yet." He stuck a big freckled hand toward Grandma. "You must be Miz Johnson," he said. "Eddie Switten here."

Grandma shook his hand. "Pleased to meet you," she said.

"And who's this fine little feller?"

"That's my grandson," said Grandma. "James, shake hands with the gentleman."

James lifted his face and right hand. Everything about Eddie Switten was huge—his height, his chest, his hands, his head—everything except his eyes and his teeth. The eyes were too small for all his red hair and freckled forehead and were set a little too close to his big nose, and his teeth were small and pointed. James would have liked him better if the man hadn't called him a fine little feller, but he didn't hold it against the stranger. Most grown-ups were stupid about things like that.

"He's eleven," Grandma said. "He'll catch up."

"Well, he don't have to catch up to nobody, far as singing goes." Eddie Switten turned to the rest of the Family. "Where y'all been keeping him?"

Nobody said anything at first. Then Grandma said, "He's not much for performing. Just sings for me—and the Family." James guessed she didn't want to explain that this was almost the first time he'd ever sung for the Family.

"Well, we're gonna have to do something about that," Switten said. "Presto. Pronto."

"I didn't know we'd decided—" Earl began, but gave up. It looked as though Eddie Switten was already doing the deciding.

For supper Grandma made fresh corn bread and sliced off some of last winter's ham to go with the beans. Eddie Switten acted as if he'd never had a full meal before in his life. "Mighty tasty, Miz Johnson." He talked not only with his mouth full, but while actually shoving more corn bread into it. Jerry Lee and Earl generally ate a lot, but James had never seen the likes of this big-city eater. James couldn't help watching, his eyes so wide he began to feel they might stretch too big to slide back under the lids.

"You through eating already?" Eddie Switten asked. At first James didn't know who the man was talking to.

"Yeah, you, sonny."

James nodded.

"Whyn't you sing us something else while we finish?" He was waving his corn bread at James.

17

James looked in panic from Grandma to Jerry Lee. One of them would save him.

"Come on, boy," Grandma was saying. "I'll sing along with you." Grandma never sang for anyone else anymore—just James—because she was ashamed when her voice cracked and wouldn't do what she told it to, but here she was willing to sing in front of this greedy stranger. How could James refuse?

He got Chester from his bedroom and fetched Grandma's Autoharp from the mantel. Grandma pushed her chair back from the table and settled the Autoharp on her lap. James pulled the fire stool up beside her. If he set his eyes on her, maybe he could get through.

"How 'bout 'Keep on the Sunny Side'?" she asked. She turned proudly to the visitor. "I heard the Carter Family sing that in person when I was just a young 'un."

"That was a history-making song," said Eddie. James liked him better. He was showing the proper respect. Sometimes Olive and Earl acted like Grandma didn't know anything. Neither of them had ever heard the original Carter Family in person. James tuned his strings and smiled at her to show he was ready.

"Hold it a minute," Jerry Lee said. "Let me get my banjo. I'll play backup. How 'bout it, Earl?"

"Backup to a 'leven year old," Earl was muttering, but he got his mandolin and brought Grandpa the big bass fiddle from the back of the station wagon. All the waiting was making James nervous. He wished he and Grandma could go ahead and get it over with instead of making some kind of production out of it. Still, he liked the idea—his daddy wanting the rest of them to play backup for him and Grandma.

Finally they were all tuned and ready. Only Olive stayed

put—apart from all of them. You couldn't be scared or mad or worried when you were singing a song like "Keep on the Sunny Side." That song just bounced the downs right up. It didn't matter that Grandma's voice cracked. That woman had about the best sense of timing a singer could ever want. It just made the very hairs on your head rejoice. And James rejoiced. He hardly noticed when Grandma dropped back and gave him the lead. "Tear it up, boy," she muttered.

James sang a verse alone and then he turned to Earl and Jerry Lee. "Now you boys tear it up," he said. And tear it up they did, with a duo lick that would send most bluegrass pickers crying for home. The whole ceiling seemed to jump.

The last chord was still humming when Grandma said, "Now let's sing him a comfort song."

Jerry Lee sang the first line, "There's a land that is fairer than day—"

James and Grandma harmonized, "And by faith we can see it afar—" When they got to the chorus, Earl and Grandpa were fully in it. "In the sweet—" "In the sweet," Earl echoed way down in the bass voice that sounded like it rose from the bottom of a well. "By and by—" "By and by," boomed Earl. "We shall meet on that beautiful shore—" James had forgotten to be afraid. His voice floated loose and free, high above the rest. This is what heaven must be, he thought, singing and picking in harmony.

When they finished, Eddie Switten put his piece of corn bread down long enough to clap. "Boy want to sing something on his own?" he asked the room in general.

Out of the corner of his eye, James saw Grandma shake her head at the man. Nothing more was said. James wasn't sure whether he felt relieved or a tiny bit disappointed.

How it all got settled, James didn't know. He went to bed

before Eddie Switten left that night. He half woke to hear his parents in whispered argument in the dark, but he didn't wake up enough to know what they were arguing about.

The next day Jerry Lee milked Rosie for him and helped him carry the slop to the pigs and hoe the corn and pick beans. They chopped greens as well. It didn't seem like work when they were doing it together. Earl mostly sat on the porch picking, first his mandolin and then his banjo. He was fooling with a new bridge. He moved it an invisible distance down, tightened the strings, picked a minute, then moved it an invisible distance up, and tuned again. Earl was always buying accessories for his instruments. What he really wanted was an electric guitar, but the very word *electric* sent Grandpa into orbit, so he didn't mention it except when he wanted to make Grandpa mad.

Grandpa was peaceful now, just sitting and rocking and seeing how far he could spit his chewing tobacco. Grandma didn't allow spitting on the porch, and he didn't want to have to get up every time he needed to spit. As far as James could tell, Olive spent the whole day curled up on the bed drinking coffee and reading *True Confessions.* Olive believed in reading. She was worse than Grandma preaching to James about how he had to get himself a decent education.

Grandma was filling the house with the smell of light bread baking—the best smell in the world as far as James was concerned. She only made light bread when the Family came home. "Corn bread and biscuits are better for you," she'd tell James. But James knew it was because corn bread and biscuits didn't take any kneading, and when you have arthritis, kneading is no fun. He usually tried to fool her into letting him do it. But you had to watch. The woman had pride.

They would be gone tomorrow. Eddie had arranged for

20

them to sing in a place called Woodspring, over the line in Virginia. "Hate to leave," Jerry Lee said, sighing, "even for just the one night. I'm plumb tired of running around so much."

James wanted to say he wished Jerry Lee wouldn't leave, but the Family always had to leave, and he couldn't wish they'd leave Jerry Lee behind. Who would keep the peace?

"It wouldn't be so bad if you and Grandma would come, too," Jerry Lee went on. "I get so lonesome for y'all on the road."

James glowed from the top of his bristly hair down to his bare toenails. "I get lonesome for you, too," he said quietly.

Jerry Lee smiled and handed him a bunch of collards to put in the basket. Then he bent low to chop more. The sweat was raining off his head onto the dry dirt where he was kneeling. His face was dark red. He didn't look at James as he said, "Whyn't you come along? Just to Woodspring? You might like to hear the Family perform in public. You ain't heard us in years."

"Will Grandma come?"

Jerry Lee stood up and handed him the last of the greens. "We'll ask her."

But Grandma didn't go. She said it had nothing to do with Olive grumbling about how crowded the wagon would be with six people plus all the instruments. She said it was summer, and if she didn't get her canning done, they'd have nothing to eat come winter. "I ain't no grasshopper, chip-chipping about, thinking somebody else is making provisions. 'Sides," she said slyly, "I'd miss all my stories. Andrea's liable to marry Brent tomorrow, and you know what that would mean." James thought he ought to stay to help her with the canning, but she said everything was already picked and he'd just be in the way, so he went.

When the station wagon broke down in the middle of Nowhere, Virginia, James wished for the hundredth time that he'd stayed home. Olive and Earl weren't paying him any mind. They were fighting over whether you could substitute a knotted polyester necktie for a fan belt—Earl said you'd be crazy to, Olive said it couldn't hurt to try. That, Olive declared, was the trouble with men—they never wanted any simple solutions, it was nuclear war or nothing. Grandpa couldn't figure out what nuclear war had to do with a broken fan belt, so he stretched out to sleep on the backseat. James was tiptoeing up and down the road, trying to get some feeling back in his toes. He hadn't worn shoes since May, and his poor toes were squeezed together like ninety-nine men on a boardinghouse bed. He should have asked Grandma to trim his toenails last night. It was too late now, and they were cutting into his flesh something awful. Olive was frantic to have him proper, even in the stupid car.

If he hadn't had the sense to stay home with Grandma, the least he could have done was to start walking down the road with Jerry Lee. Once out of sight of Olive, he could have pulled off his shoes and let his poor little toes spread out in the dust of the road.

"We got to do something," Olive was saying. "We don't get going soon, there's no way we can make it there by seven. I told Eddie we'd be there by seven at the very latest."

"Then you shoulda got decent directions. Wasn't for you we wouldn'ta got lost in"—Earl stuck up his fingers to count off the towns—"Rich Creek, Narrows, Pearlieburg, Pembroke, Parrot. . . ."

"You'd have to be a ant brain to get lost in a town the size of Parrot." Olive was hair-curling mad. "One street and you can't find it. Whyn't you leave the driving to Jerry Lee in the first place?"

"We didn't even want to be in Parrot!" Earl yelled back. "We're supposed to be in Woodspring."

"Well, it's over around here somewhere," she said. "Eddie said you couldn't miss it—right between Radford and Blacksburg. If we keep heading east, we're bound to hit it."

"Cow chips! We don't even know if we're on the right road. None of these towns been more than one street wide. You miss that one little biddy street, you might as well be in Paris, France."

"Well, if you pigheaded men would stop, just once, and ask somebody for directions . . ."

"*You* were supposed to have the dadburned directions, Miz Biggety. None of the rest of us was all that fired up about singing for the Drewry family reunion in Splinterhole, Virginia."

"Woodspring's got two traffic lights and four churches."

James couldn't stand it. He kicked a rock off the road. Now his toes hurt at the tips, too. If Grandma were here, she'd get them to shut up. Or Jerry Lee. Why hadn't he stayed and sent Earl for help? But James knew the answer to that one. Other than Grandma, Jerry Lee was the only member of the family who kept his brains in the right compartment. James would just have to shut his ears and wait. Jerry Lee would be back soon with help.

And he was—not soon enough to keep Earl and Olive from waking Grandpa, who was so mad he kicked a new dent in the side of the wagon—but soon enough to calm them all down, to change the fan belt, and having gotten proper directions at last, to get them to Woodspring by ten minutes before eight.

Eddie Switten was fit to be tied. He ran down the driveway at the sight of the station wagon, waving his arms and yelling. The reunion had been going on all day on the church grounds of the Holiness Tabernacle. A lot of people were picnicking right among the graves. They'd set up a single spotlight for the Family to sing in. There were no mikes, no place to change clothes. The Family was still flushed from fighting and anxiety, but it seemed to fire up the music to a pitch James had never heard on the porch at home. Finally, well past dark, the crowd let them stop and rest. James brought the Family a big tin pitcher of sugared ice tea and some Dixie cups. They all drank like overplowed mules.

"Want me to get more?" James asked as he poured the last drops into Jerry Lee's cup.

"No, but I got somethin' else I wish you'd do for me."

"Sure."

"Play backup guitar for the next song."

James felt as if he'd turned into one of the churchyard tombstones.

"We don't have no guitar 'sides Olive," Jerry Lee said, "And I got a taste in my mouth for singing 'Keep on the Sunny Side.' You know it ain't the same without a really good guitar backup."

"I ain't got my guitar," James said, but he knew before Jerry Lee went toward the wagon that it was Chester making that bump under the blanket there in the back.

"It's dark," Jerry Lee said. "Won't hardly nobody even see you in a weak little light like this one."

"Oh, for goodness' sakes," said Olive, "if the boy don't want to—"

"I said I'd do it," James said, even though he hadn't.

Jerry Lee was right. By the time they got up again, it was dark as the woods. The little spotlight hanging from the corner of the church building hardly lit up the Family, much less the crowd sitting on folding chairs and blankets and graves. James slung Chester over his shoulder. He put his left hand on the neck. The strings fit perfectly into the calluses on his fingers. His right hand hovered briefly over the hole in Chester's polished belly. Then the music began. James felt as though he were picking in a dream. There were no real people out front, just the feel and sound and smell of the Family gathered close around him—Olive's Gladiola Nights perfume and Jerry Lee's familiar sweat. It was almost like being on his own porch. Even when the rest dropped back and gave him the lead on the third verse, he hardly faltered. He just closed his eyes and conjured up Grandma's face smiling at him, with her pipe bobbing up and down while she nodded in rhythm.

It would have been different, maybe, if he'd known that the fat man leaning against the gravestone of Ella Hewes Roebuck, Beloved Wife and Mother, was Norman Wallace, the manager of the *Countrytime* TV show. Eddie Switten had persuaded him to drive all the way up from Tidewater, Virginia, to hear the Family, especially the youngest Johnson who, as Eddie had said, was the sweetest little thing to come along in country music since little Anita Carter yodeled at the Old Dominion Barn Dance in 1947.

3

James couldn't believe it. Jerry Lee had tricked him into singing at Woodspring. And now both Jerry Lee and Grandma were trying to persuade him to go on to Harrisonburg where *Countrytime* was sponsoring a special show. Everyone, including Eddie Switten, was on the porch, and he, James, was the center of attention—the one unrepentant sinner at a camp meeting.

He squinched his eyes and lips together so that he wouldn't cry. He was terrified of acting like a baby in front of Olive and Earl, who were saying he was too young to sing with the Family anyway—too inexperienced to trust on a stage.

"Suppose he panics?" Olive asked. "Ever'body'd blame me. I'm the boy's mother. They'd think I was shoving him into something he didn't want."

Why did Olive have to make sense for once? He didn't like agreeing with her against Jerry Lee, against Grandma.

"I don't think," Eddie Switten said, "I don't think"—he cleared his throat—"I b'lieve Wallace wants the whole Family —just like he heard you in Woodspring."

"The kid only did backup for one number," Earl said.

"He's your strong guitar," said Eddie flatly. "And he sings pretty good, too." He turned to Olive. "No offense, Olive, but you do more holding than picking."

Olive gave Eddie a funny look. "Are you saying we don't get to sing in Harrisonburg without the boy?"

Eddie coughed. "I'm not sure. All's I know is that Wallace really took to the kid, and if I was you, I wouldn't show up without him. Besides"—Eddie's little eyes shifted sideways— "y'all do good in Harrisonburg, Wallace just might want to take you back to Tidewater for the regular TV show."

It wasn't fair. Putting their big chance for television on him. Suppose he got up there and nothing came out? That had happened on the porch once, with no one listening except the Family. Suppose, heaven help him, he burst out crying and ran off the stage?

"I don't like it," said Earl. "He's never been a part of the Family. He don't even know how to sing our songs."

Yes, I do, thought James. It made him mad, Earl thinking he was stupid. Grandma had taught him everything his own ears could not.

"He knows them," said Grandma. "I promise you he can sing and pick any song you ever heard of." Which was a slight exaggeration, but it made James feel better. He didn't want anyone thinking that the reason he wouldn't sing was that he *couldn't* sing. Yet *wouldn't* seemed so selfish. All he wanted to do was sit down and cry. Nobody understood him—not even Grandma. Well, maybe she did a little bit, because just then she was saying, "Come on, James. Let's walk down to the box. See if there's any mail."

27

Grandma knew better than anyone that Willis Warford didn't get the mail in the box until the middle of the afternoon, but James guessed what she was up to. She wanted the two of them out of there.

They walked across the yard to the road. It was lined with cedars that Grandpa had planted more than forty-five years before when he had brought Grandma to the farm as a bride. She had been fifteen and he had been seventeen. It was smack in the middle of the Depression, but "We was young," Grandma loved to tell James, "we didn't know Despair well enough to shake his hand, much less make him a member of the family." At first she and Grandpa sang for the sheer pleasure of being young and alive, but then a kind of sorrow crept in. They had two babies die almost before they saw their first mornings, and when the war came, Grandpa walked down the mountain to Wesco and joined up.

James reached out and took Grandma's hand. It made him sorrowful to think of those long years when she had tended the farm all alone. She had sung then to comfort herself. They crossed the rail bridge that James had helped Jerry Lee repair after the spring rains. There was hardly a trickle of water running under it now in July.

"You know there ain't no mail."

Of course James knew. "I figured you wanted to say something, privatelike."

"I don't know how to say this, boy."

James could wait. For a few minutes they just walked quietly, matching steps. Four bare feet in the dust and ruts. Then Grandma stopped and raised his chin toward her face. "I know you're scairt. That ain't no shame. But, boy . . ." She cocked her head and sighed. "You got the gift." Her blue eyes were almost too bright and sharp. James looked away, down at his feet, to avoid the hurt of her gaze.

28

She sighed again. "Sometimes the gift seems more like a burden, but if you got it, you got it. It ain't fittin' to run from it. I love you, boy. I don't crave to have you scairt, but I don't want you sinning against your gift, neither." She dropped his hand and put both her hands on his shoulders to turn him toward her again. "You understand what I'm trying to say?"

He shook his head. He really didn't.

She sighed once more, took his right hand in her left, and resumed walking. "How can I explain it?" She felt in her pocket, but she had apparently left her pipe behind. She gave a little cluck of annoyance. "The Lord don't give private presents," she began. "If he give you somethin', it's only because he thinks you got the sense to share it or give it away. You try to keep the gift to yourself, it's liable to rot. Remember how the Lord give the manna to those Hebrew children? They had to use it or pretty soon it start to crawl with the maggots."

James tried not to think of himself crawling with maggots. "Maybe I could just wait a while—'til I'm taller. I wouldn't be so scairt if I was bigger."

"Yeah, you wait a year or two and that sweet angel voice of your'n liable to turn into a crow call. You ever hear a boy thirteen or so try to sing? Sound worse'n I do." She chuckled.

"You sound good to me."

"Don't try no sweet talk on me, boy," she said. "I'm giving you the Word of God."

Something blipped inside James's stomach. "God ain't said nothing to me," he said stubbornly, ignoring the blip. "If God wanted me to go to Harrisonburg, whyn't he tell me?"

She dropped his grasp, swung around, and put a big rough hand heavily on his head. "He give you the gift, James. That's all he got to say."

She was too hard and stiff—worse than a traveling evangelist. He'd never seen her this way before. She frightened him and made him mad at the same time. The tears were already gathering, threatening to spurt right out.

She began to crinkle in front of him. "Don't cry, boy. You'll break my old heart." She threw her arms around him. He did cry. They both cried. Finally, she wiped his face with her apron and then her own. "Even old Moses was scairt," she said.

"And Daddy," he whispered.

"And Jerry Lee, too," she said. "Well, boy, what do you say?"

"I'll go," he said. "I'll try this once, but if it don't work out . . ."

"Lord, boy, if it ain't right, you can always come home."

The next three days went by like a summer storm. Eddie Switten took charge like the thunder, and everyone just scampered around. Jerry Lee drove James down to Wesco to buy him new jeans and Western shirts with string ties and, joy, a real pair of Western boots with two-inch heels. When they got back, James found that his name had been changed.

Olive was the one who took him into the bedroom to explain it to him. "Eddie's been thinking, and he thinks *James* sounds kinda formal. See, sugar"—she'd never called him *sugar* in his life—"your average country music fan just can't warm up to a name like James. Look at Johnny Cash. He don't call himself John."

"He don't call himself Johnny Jo neither."

"Well, Johnny Cash ain't four-feet five. Eddie wants you to have a name that's kinda, you know, cuddly. Says it will bring out the mother in the fans. Most of the big-city fans are ladies."

Cuddly? *Cuddly?* "Nobody told me you was gonna change my name."

"Look, sugar, I'm not asking you to do anything I'm not willing to do myself."

"What do you mean?"

She giggled nervously. "Eddie thinks *Olive* just makes people think of Popeye's girlfriend."

James smiled despite himself.

"They're gonna call me Keri Su."

He liked *Olive* better. *Keri Su* sounded more like a Barbie doll than a mother, but he didn't say so.

"Jimmy Jo Johnson. It's just a brand label." Grandma tried to comfort him. "You're really James. That ain't gonna change."

But how could he be sure? Too much was changing already.

J ames stood in the shadows, listening to the sounds from onstage. Jerry Lee and Earl were battling with their banjos, each trying to pick faster than the other could follow. It was an old game his father and uncle played, and usually James loved it—the music as swift and clear as two mountain creeks in the spring thaw. But that was on the porch or in the kitchen, at Grandma's. Now he willed himself to listen, to forget the heaviness of Chester hanging like a dead calf in his arms. As he waited, his shoulders strained with the burden of it. He tried to shift the load, but the leather strap cut into his neck. He tried to clear his throat, but the guitar dragged down all the more, and his throat seemed clogged with sawdust.

At last he managed a cough, a strangling kind of cough that came so close to ending in a vomit that he bolted toward the backstage bathroom. Just as he turned, Eddie Switten grabbed his shoulder and swung him about, not roughly, but so

James could not mistake the meaning. "Near time," Eddie said through his little, pointed teeth. "Can't miss your entrance."

Then, before James could explain about having to throw up, the banjo battle blammed and crashed to its climax and was lost to applause, and Olive was saying, ". . . for the first time on any stage, the youngest member of the Johnson Family, who me and Jerry Lee are proud to call our boy. Please welcome, won't you, Jimmy Jo Johnson!"

The far blackness erupted in firecrackers and whistling rockets as Eddie shoved him stumbling into the light. James caught himself and half ran, half skipped to where his mother stood smiling in the blinding brightness, one arm out to him, the other holding a mike. She was blurred like a bad snapshot, not only by the light, but because Eddie Switten wouldn't let him wear his glasses on stage. "Makes the boy look like a Baptist deacon," he'd said.

"Tell the folks what you're gonna sing for 'em, Jimmy Jo," she said, moving the mike down in front of his mouth. He stared at it as though it were a copperhead lifting itself up out of the scum of the millpond. His lips had turned to rock.

"Well, awright, sugar," Olive said in her supersweet Keri Su voice, "I'll tell 'em." She turned from his frozen face toward the light. "This here song is one of my all-time favorites. Though I can't say Jerry Lee likes it all that much. Maybe you can figure out why. It's called"—her voice rose—" 'My *Momma* Is a Angel Up in Heaven, But *Daddy* He Is Heading Down to Hell.' "

Out of the laughter the banjos and bass sprang up toward the tune. Suddenly James's dead guitar came alive in his hands, and like a miracle in the Gospel, his tongue was loosed and he began to sing:

33

Oh, I'm but a little child
Just on earth a little while,
And you'd think I'd be so happy and so fine,
But the day my momma died,
Daddy went away to hide
His sorrow in a bottle of cheap wine.
Ohhh, in this wide world I'm all alone
    and grievin'
It's the saddest tale a little child can tell,
My momma is a anjul up in hayven,
But Daddy he is heading down to hell.

James waited a moment while the banjos and bass jangled and thumped, a fiddle yodeled away over the top and the Dobro whanged out a nasal variation of the melody. *Countrytime* had hired a backup band, and his guitar was not really needed, but he began to play anyway for the pure pleasure of it. Olive—or was it Keri Su?—smiled down at him, her head nodding in perfect rhythm. She and James began the second verse together, smiling at each other. Then turning a face of sorrow to the audience to show that they knew how sad the song really was, they continued. It went too fast. They were on the final chorus before he was nearly ready to stop. All the men were singing now and Olive's birdlike voice rose over it all in a high sweet obbligato.

"Oh, my momma is a anjul up in hayven. . . ." He smiled once more into his mother's bright brown eyes, and then turned toward the sea of upturned faces, twisting his expression and his warm soprano voice around the final line, "But my poor daddy's heading down to he-yell."

Beyond the footlights, the dim bodies in the high school auditorium were screaming and stomping and slapping their hands together. Some of them even jumped to their feet:

"Whooo-eee!" Olive's free arm was around his shoulder. She gave a little pressure with the inside of her elbow, so he would remember to bow. Obediently he ducked his head, just the way Grandma had taught him, but he wanted to look out at them and smile. He wanted to yell his gratitude. He'd done it! He'd sung in front of hundreds of people, on a real stage, and they'd liked him. Shouldn't he let them know how good they made him feel? Maybe he would have stayed out there grinning all night long, but the Keri Su voice of his mother was saying "Thank ya, thank ya," and she was nodding at him to skidaddle so she could announce the next number.

James obeyed, because he knew he must, but when he got to the edge of the curtain, he turned and blew them a kiss—as though he were two years old and they were all his grandma. The audience shrieked its delight, and backstage James could hear Keri Su—sounding a little like Olive—working hard to calm them down again. Before the show could go on, Eddie Switten had to push James back on for a final chorus of "My Momma Is a Angel Up in Heaven"

Eddie slapped James's shoulder as he came off the second time. "Boy," he said, "you go on back to that dressing room and tell Gus I said give you a giant Pepsi."

James didn't want a Pepsi. He wanted to go on stage and sing some more, but he went on back to the dressing room. It was really a math classroom, with problems still on the board from the spring before. The desks had been pushed to one side and a screen put up at one end so Olive could dress there. But it was like having a dressing room. It wasn't like having to change in a filling station or the back of the wagon. They had been on TV, too—*Countrytime,* broadcast by all twenty local stations in Virginia, West Virginia, North Carolina, and Tennessee that carried the regular show.

If only Grandma had been here, his joy would have been

complete. Still, she could see the show through the snow on the old black-and-white in the kitchen. That was something, anyway. He was glad Jerry Lee had put up the big antenna. Grandma had laughed to see it. "That thing's so big and heavy, liable to bring the whole house crashing over on its nose!" she'd said, but she loved the telly vee, as she called it. She watched the soaps as faithfully as she went to church. And tonight she had watched him, James, singing for hundreds of people.

There was no sign of Gus. James wouldn't have been brave enough to tell Gus to get him a drink anyhow, no matter what Eddie said. Gus was as old as his grandpa and worked as stage manager for *Countrytime* whether at home or on the road. No, it didn't matter how well he'd done tonight, James was not about to tell old Gus to fetch him a Pepsi. He found his glasses and one of Olive's *True Confessions*—"I Gave My Baby to a Total Stranger"—but he was too jiggly inside to concentrate.

"Well, I think that settles it," said Eddie when the show was over and the whole Family was back in the dressing room changing clothes. "The boy done real good, and he's a real crowd pleaser."

"He was mighty scared out there." Olive spoke so quietly from behind her screen that James wasn't quite sure he'd heard her.

"Hell," said Eddie. "Everybody 'at's any good gets scared out there." He took a pack of Camels out of his shirt pocket and stuck one in the corner of his mouth, feeling under the clothes piled up on the row of desks that were serving as dressing tables, looking for the book of matches that he'd laid somewhere.

"Eddie," said Grandpa. "Everybody knows I wasn't hot on getting us a agent in the first place. It's the young 'uns who

36

wanted you, but by daisy"—he held up his unbelted pants with his left hand while shaking the forefinger of his right at Eddie's back—"if you're gonna represent the Johnson Family, you're gonna have to watch that heathen tongue of your'n."

Eddie didn't even turn from his searching to glance at the old man. "Yeah, sorry. No offense, old timer."

Why were they discussing cuss words? They were supposed to be talking about the show—about how the Family had done—about *him,* James. He couldn't stand it. "Did I do okay?" he asked, looking at Jerry Lee.

Olive stuck her head around the screen, her mouth opened, but the words came from Eddie. "Okay? I'll say. You raised the roof, little feller. When you turned 'round and blew that kiss, they coulda eat you right up."

"You blew a kiss?" Olive asked, ducking back behind the screen. "When?"

"Just before he left the stage the first time. I wish I'd thought of it. Well, never matter, we're writing it into the act as of tonight."

"Wait a minute," said Earl. "I don't remember coming to any agreement about the kid being a regular member of the Family at all. You were just going to use him tonight. That's all I agreed to."

Olive's head popped out again, and everyone stopped dressing to look at Earl. He was stripped to his boxers, and his ears were very red. "I ain't got anything against James, you know that. But liking the kid don't mean I'm sure he's ready. He's only barely eleven."

"You was only nine," said Grandpa quietly.

"Yeah," said Earl, "and you never have treated me like a full member. Nobody ever told me that Grandma was going to 'retire' to make room for Olive."

"Keri Su," said James's mother through her tight, red lips.

"That's another thing. Nobody asked me about these fancy names, either."

"And nobody asked you to change yours, Earl," said Eddie. "Now look, man, the reason I was hired, least the way I understand it, was to help y'all get out of the tent meeting business and into the big time." He turned to Earl. "What you rather do, Earl, live in Tidewater, Virginia, and be a *Countrytime* star or go back to the sawdust trail?" He didn't wait for an answer. "Besides, folks, it don't necessarily mean Tidewater is the end of the rainbow, either. *Countrytime* looks like the big time now, but Eddie Switten's a man of jumbo dreams. I'm looking to Wheeling, Nashville even, and I don't mean a hundred years from now. I'm talking the *fore*-seeable future. You folks have potential. You need handling. And I'm the guy who can do it. But I can't do it without your *co*-operation. What do you say?" He swung around to include them all in his question. "Are you with me?"

"That's why we hired you," said Jerry Lee. Then he turned to his younger brother. "We ain't shoving you over, Earl. We're all in this together, but if we don't follow Eddie's advice, I can't see why we're putting out all the money."

"You were big for hiring him as I recall." James could tell by the edge in Olive's voice that she was mad at Earl again— so mad she didn't care how much she stretched the facts. Earl's mouth fell open, but Olive pretended not to notice. She could have made it solo—everyone said so—but she'd chosen to belong to the Family, and it just made her furious for Earl to talk like she was some kind of outsider that had pushed Grandma into retirement. Why the woman was over sixty and hadn't been able to do the high harmony for fifteen–twenty years.

James hoped his momma wouldn't feel the need to say to

Earl what was going on in her head. And she didn't have to. They'd had the fight often enough that they did it now in code.

Even Grandpa knew what was going on. "Okay," he said. "None of that."

Eddie Switten was the only one in the room who was puzzled, but he wasn't concerned with past Family squabbles. He just wanted to be in charge. "Good," he said. "I'm glad we understand each other. Now, the first thing I want you to do, Keri Su, is drive down to Tidewater and get you a house."

"Look, Switten," said Jerry Lee. "We haven't got the money to buy a house in Tidewater. You know that."

"Well, rent it then."

"And get stuck with a lease?" objected Earl.

"I'm gonna let you in on a little secret," said Eddie, smiling over the book of matches he pulled out from under Grandpa's yellow-and-black plaid shirt. They had to wait while he carefully struck a match and lit his cigarette. Nobody asked him not to smoke in the dressing room, they just wanted to hear what he had to say. He leaned his head back and blew a great cloud of smoke toward the ceiling.

"Yeah?" said Earl. They were all squinched with the waiting.

At last Eddie stuck the cigarette in the corner of his mouth, and with a great flourish, he pulled some folded papers from his inner jacket pocket. He waved these in the air and then, still without a word, put them back in his pocket and took another long drag from his cigarette.

Grandpa was the first to stop staring and begin to dress again. Eddie's theatrics made him impatient. Life was too short to be bothered with such shenanigans. He caught James staring at him. "Get dressed," he mumbled. "Time you was in bed, anyway."

Olive emerged from behind the screen fully dressed. She

39

went over to the desks and poked about for a hairbrush. "Why don't Gus clean up this mess?" she asked. "Can't find nothin'."

"Momma used to make it her business to keep things neat," Earl said.

Olive grabbed the brush and began brushing her hair hard, staring down into the little cracked mirror that was propped up on a desk top and leaning against the chalkboard. Her mouth was shut up tighter than a mason jar.

"Eddie," Jerry Lee said in his quiet, patient voice, "we're all tired. You got something to say, just say it, hear?"

James could tell Eddie would much rather have taken another hour getting to the point, but he went on and broke his news. "Six-month contract. At *WQVR–Countrytime*—the home show in Tidewater, Vee A. You won't do the whole show every week, but you'll be the only regulars. Now put that in your pipe and puff it."

For what seemed a long time, no one said anything. Olive just kept on brushing her hair, squinting and leaning toward the mirror. "Well," she said at last, "the first thing they're gonna have to do is get me a decent dressing room. I ain't gonna put up with no propped-up mirrors and bad light for six months."

James couldn't believe his ears. He knew good and well the Family had never had a real dressing room, not to mention the promise of six whole months singing in the same place. His mother must have lost her mind.

"I'm gonna have to have some more leads," Earl was saying. "You realize we were on more than an hour tonight, and I sang the lead exactly one time. James got more time than I did."

"Behave yourself, Earl," Grandpa snapped. "I'm ashamed of you. You act like you're twelve years old."

Earl's ears went crimson again.

James wanted to scream. Six months on *Countrytime* and they were fussing about mirrors and leads.

"We appreciate that, Eddie," Jerry Lee said in his sane, baritone voice. "Thank you. We're real pleased you could work it out."

Eddie was watching them, head cocked. He thinks we're stupid, James guessed, or weird. He knows anybody else would be jumping up and down. He wanted to say something to make Eddie realize that he understood what a contract meant. "Me too?" he asked. "Am I in the contract?"

"Sure," Eddie said with a quick glance at Earl. " 'Course you are. It's for the whole Family."

"We'll see, sugar," said Olive at the same moment. Her head was two inches from the mirror, and she was studying her nose. "We'll have to talk some more about it."

J erry Lee had folded up a quilt in the back of the wagon so James would have a place to sleep. This would also keep Earl from complaining about how crowded the backseat had got all of a sudden. James was too excited to sleep. Lying there, he could feel the humming of the tires in his belly, in his teeth even. He sang songs in his head to the rhythm of it, as though it were a guitar with only one chord, a chord that went with nearly everything. He saw himself singing everywhere—on the porch and in the kitchen at home, on the stage at *Countrytime.* He had seen pictures of the Grand Ole Opry's huge stage, so he put himself on that, too, but then backed off. He didn't want to dream so big it would pop in his face. He pictured Grandma in the *Countrytime* audience, smiling and puffing her pipe. No, that couldn't be. No smoking. He took the pipe out of her mouth. "So worked up, I plumb forgot," she said by way of apology.

His glasses were cutting into the side of his head. He raised his head enough to take them off and find a safe place for them between Chester and Earl's banjo. He loved his glasses. Grandma had driven him in the pickup all the way to Wesco to get them. It took two trips and nearly fifty dollars, but she wanted him to see the board at school. The glasses were just like the ones John Denver wore, but James didn't say so. He and Grandma didn't really approve of John Denver. He sang too much folk and pop to be genuine country.

Grandpa was snoring in the backseat. James incorporated the sound into his music making. Every now and then, Olive would say something to Jerry Lee in a staccato soprano, and Jerry Lee would baritone a reply. The wagon was too noisy for James to pick out the words, but he really didn't want to. He just drew the sounds in like solo licks from backup instruments.

Olive must have turned around from the front, because he heard her voice clearly asking Earl if he, James, were asleep.

"I dunno," said Earl. "Hey! You 'wake boy?" James could feel Earl punch his top foot. He pretended not to notice. "Yeah, he's gone."

"Earl, I swear," Olive said, forgetting to use her sugar-coated Keri Su voice, "sometimes you ain't got the sense God give a chigger. I didn't mean for you to try to wake him. Lord. He's just a baby. He needs his sleep."

"You asked me was he 'wake," muttered Earl. "How was I to know 'less I asked him?"

"You ready to drive awhile, Earl?" Jerry Lee asked.

"Don't make no difference," Earl said in the tone of voice that made James know it made a lot of difference. "Can't sleep nohow."

When Jerry Lee cut the engine, the music inside James stopped, too. He lay unmoving, his body still feeling the pulse. The doors slammed. The engine started up once more, and the car jerked back onto the highway. Earl was not the world's smoothest driver, but soon the car was in third gear and moving rapidly along.

Olive was saying something to Earl—about how fast he was going, James was sure. Earl snapped something back. There was no change of speed. James must have dropped off, for the next thing he knew, Jerry Lee was shaking him. "Wanna use the rest room?" James stumbled sleepily toward the service station. They were off the interstate now. "Want something to eat?" Jerry Lee asked when he came out. He shook his head. He was too sleepy to eat. He climbed back onto the quilt. The rest were all in the station at the food and drink machines. Through the open windows of the wagon, he could hear their talking and the clang of the dispensers, but he couldn't make out any words until he heard Olive's voice quite near the car.

"I still don't understand how you could agree to it. The boy's only eleven years old."

"Olive"—Jerry Lee's voice was much quieter than hers— "I been singing in public since I could stand up."

"You call what y'all did back then singing?"

"Well, yes, I do."

"Listen, sweetie, the biggest day in the Family's whole life was the day I walked through that cabin door."

"Shhh! The boy's in the car."

"What did I say?" she asked, her voice dropping to a whisper.

They moved away from the window back toward the station, still whispering. James didn't know what she'd said, either. It sounded like the same old fight to him—the one Earl and Olive carried on day in and day out. Maybe Jerry Lee didn't want James to know his mother was against his being

44

in the Family. But he knew that already. It didn't really matter all that much. Grandma said he had the gift and Jerry Lee believed in him. Momma . . . Olive . . . Keri Su—whatever her name was supposed to be—would come around. All he had to do was sing the way he had tonight. Eddie Switten had said he had "done real good," and Olive—Keri Su—wasn't going to cross Eddie Switten. James took off his belt, unbuttoned the top of his jeans, and wiggled into a more comfortable position.

He was barely aware of the others getting into the car and the last lap of the trip. He didn't even open his eyes when Jerry Lee picked him up and carried him to his bed. He wanted to wake up enough to tell Grandma about the show, but he was too far into sleep. He knew that it was she who had pulled up the sheet and kissed his cheek, but that was the last thing he remembered until they called him for supper at five o'clock.

They were all sitting around the table, except Grandma. She was taking loaves of bread out of the oven, causing the kitchen to smell like the love of Heaven.

"Well," said Earl. "The dead has rose up."

"Oh, shut up, Earl," said Olive. "The boy was wore out."

Grandma turned. She was using her big apron to pad the steaming loaf pan in her hands. "Well," she said, "you really blowed the roof right off that show last night."

"Did you see me?" James was wide awake now.

"Well, Channel Six was having a blizzard most of the evening, so I didn't see all that much, but brother, did I ever *hear.*"

James shoved his glasses back to the bridge of his nose. "Did you like me?"

"Sugarlump, I'd like you if you was calling hogs."

"No, Grandma, I mean, was I good?"

45

She turned the bread out of the pan onto the cutting board. "You was good," she said very softly. And then, quite loudly, "'Course, I don't have no taste."

He ran to her and hugged her close, the smell of the bread and her tobacco making him so glad to be near her he ached with it. "Woman," he said borrowing Jerry Lee's voice and one of his expressions, "woman, you could tease the taillight off a lightning bug."

She pushed him back and pretended to frown. "Go on," she said, "you getting mighty uppity." Her eyes were bright. James went quickly to his chair. At times like this, he loved her so much it pained him—like eating ice cream that's too cold.

Sometimes James thought that he must be the most stupid person in the world. Why hadn't he realized it? It wouldn't take the brains of a cream puff to know that if he became a member of the Family, he would have to leave home, leave Grandma. What had he thought? He really hadn't thought, but maybe somewhere in the back corner of his mind, he'd thought she'd come, too. When it finally dawned on him that neither she nor anyone else expected her to leave the place and come down to Tidewater with them, James was horrified. He confronted her on the porch where she was snapping beans into her apron.

"You can't stay here all by yourself with no one to watch out for you."

"Sure I can," she answered. "I was here all through the war by myself, and in those days I didn't even have no neighbors. Now they's the Jennings not more 'n a quarter mile away to the south and the Prudens not much more'n that the other direction."

"Please," he begged, "please come with us."

"Can I bring Rosie and the hogs and the chickens, too?"

"You can sell them," he said. But he knew, even as he said the words, that she couldn't. The place was for always. Tidewater was for six months. "You'll be so lonesome," he said sadly. "I better stay home with you."

"Oh, I don't know," she said. "Jennings' old hound just whelped. I might get me one of them teensy, woonsy, *ugly* little pups. Then I wouldn't hardly know you was gone."

He tried to laugh, but it came out sort of *hnk* through his nose.

"I'll see you ever' Friday night. Well, maybe not *see,* but I'll sure as death hear you. That's better than seeing the likes of you. A little telly-vee snow might even help. Who knows?"

He didn't even try to laugh.

"C'mon, boy." She grabbed his arm. "'Course we're gonna miss each other. But you got the gift. I can't hide you under my own private little bushel. It would be a sin in the sight of God."

"But what if—" He didn't know how to ask it. He wasn't really sure what he was trying to ask. "But what if I go down there and it all— What if I get different?"

"Different?"

"I mean, what if I was to really turn into Jimmy Jo Johnson?"

She pulled him down into her lap, right on top of the beans, and began to rock him as though he were four years old. "You feel yourself turning into some Jimcracky citymade Jo, you just come on home to your grandma. She'll wash you and bleach you and hang you out to dry. Awright?"

He nodded, his head tucked under her chin. "Then I'll never change," he promised.

Jerry Lee drove Keri Su—talk about change, Olive was turning into Keri Su faster than a locust sheds its husk—down to Tidewater to find the Family a house. The first show of their six-month contract was the Friday after Labor Day, and they wanted to be settled before the holiday. "'Sides," Keri Su said, "we got to get this cute little button"—she punched James's nose with her index finger—"into one of them nice big-city schools."

James fought back the panic. Why was everything going to be so different? He thought he could handle one or two things, but every inch of his life seemed pinched in a new direction.

The new clothes he didn't mind—and he positively loved the boots. Jerry Lee had made sure they were plenty big enough for his feet—it was almost as good as going barefoot —and they were genuine cowhide leather with pointy toes, designs of flowers at the rims. And best of all, they added two inches to his height. No, the clothes were the best part. Leaving Grandma was the worst. But she was the one who had told him he had to go, so he kept stuffing the fear and pain back into the dark inside his head. Didn't do to pull it out and look at it too close.

Jerry Lee and Keri Su came back from Tidewater within the week—too soon for James. He hadn't finished saying good-bye to the farm. He'd been planning to clean the creek while it was trickle-sized. There was always brush and leaves and trash brought down in the spring from higher up the mountain. Once he'd found a still unopened can of Coca-Cola. He had taken it home and split it with Grandma. The mountain water had kept it cold. It was the best-tasting drink either of them had ever had. They both thought so. But he'd only got a few yards of the creek cleaned, going up from the bridge, when his parents returned.

They kept finding more things to load into the wagon. Grandma insisted they take some of the canning. "Save you cooking," she told Keri Su, but James saw the expression on his mother's face. She was fixing to be a star in Tidewater. She wasn't planning on too much cooking anyway. Before long, the wagon was packed tighter than a pickle jar, with mattresses and chairs tied on the top. Jerry Lee kept checking the ropes while Earl stood by and told him their old heap'd never make it with a load like that. At last Jerry Lee pronounced them ready to go. James gave Grandma a little one-armed hug. He was scared if he really held on to her, he'd never be able to let go. She patted him on the head, playing that he was always taking off like this—that he'd be home in no time. Neither of them cried. They didn't let one little biddy tear dribble between the two of them. James was proud of how brave they were, but none of the rest seemed to take notice one way or the other. People who were always leaving places didn't seem to know how it was to be tore right down the middle of your soul.

"Lemme see your fingernails," Grandma said. James held out both hands, nails up, for her to inspect. Like a true picker, the nails on his left hand were cut just above the quick so they wouldn't click on the frets, while on his right, they were long enough to make a good purchase on the strings. "Left hand's awright," she said. "The right could be a woonsy bit longer and a mite smoother. Not to speak of cleaner. You got that file I give you?" He nodded. "It's a mercy you never bit them like Earl."

"C'mon." Earl jerked his head impatiently. "We gotta get a move on."

Grandma winked at James. He winked back and climbed into the little hole Jerry Lee had left for him in the rear of the wagon, fast—before the tears came.

The first thing James learned about Tidewater was water, water, and more water. Just coming across the bridge into Tidewater took longer than driving the pickup to the Jennings' place. There were boats on the water, too. The only boats James had seen before were the tiny rowboats or outboards people took fishing on Carlyle Creek and the South River.

Here there were all kinds—sailboats, small motorboats, boats with putt-putt motors on back, but others big as houses. That didn't count the navy ships, which were like huge gray floating cities. The cars zooming past made plenty of noise themselves, but there were airplanes and helicopters to add to the confusion. And a tunnel. Lord have mercy. It scared him nearly to death, going down under all that water. He ducked his head and squeezed his eyes shut, so as not to see the dirty white-tiled walls caving in on him.

"What's on top of us?" he asked.

"Water," said Earl.

"It's okay, boy," Jerry Lee called back. "Ain't gonna fall in."

How did he know? It was strange and smelly. Maybe you could die of poisoning from the fumes. Suppose they got stuck. Would they run out of air altogether, like in a mine? Something was rising up in his throat. This hole under the water was forever going to be between him and home. He couldn't ever see his grandma again unless he went through it—if he got through it at all.

Then suddenly they were going up, and he could see light. They were back on the endless bridge, under the hazy August sky—with the boats all around, and the cars and trucks whizzing past, and the gulls circling and crying above.

"You can breathe now, boy, we're through."

"Oh, Earl, don't tease him," Keri Su snapped. "I don't like it so much myself."

"I was in a mine once't," said Grandpa.

"I didn't know that," Jerry Lee said. "When was you in a mine?"

"Back in the Depression. I was desprit for a job, and my cousin Garland—You 'member Garland over to Slab Fork? Well, Garland tole me he could get me a job in the hole. He's lying through his teeth. Couldn't nobody get a job those days, but I went over there anyways. He took me down one day. I like to died of fright. I got out of there faster than a greased hog on butchering day. That's when I decided I'd be a scratch farmer the rest of my days."

But he hadn't been. He'd left Grandma to be the scratch farmer while he'd gone off to war. Then soon as her voice went, he had left her again to perform with the Family. But how could James blame him? Wasn't he also leaving Grandma to go pick and sing for strangers?

The Tidewater house was very grand. It had six rooms plus an inside toilet with a shower and bathtub, just like in a magazine. There were lights and electric plugs in every single room, more than one plug in most rooms. The kitchen even had an electric stove, and the refrigerator had a freezer section with a different door. Best of all, James had a room all to himself. It was a little room right off the kitchen. There wasn't any real furniture in it—just a mattress on the floor—but he had a separate closet, with shelves to put his clothes on and plenty of room for Chester.

"I'm sorry we ain't got you no bed yet," Jerry Lee said. But James didn't mind at all. He had been so sure he'd have to sleep with Grandpa—who snored like a freight train—or worse, with Earl. It was a sweet surprise to have his own little place, tucked away from all the others. Of course, he had to go all the way upstairs to use the bathroom, but that didn't matter, as long as he had his own place. It did make him a bit uncomfortable to see how close all the neighbors were. Some of the houses on their street were stuck on to the next house. James didn't think it was quite decent, but city people didn't seem to care.

They didn't take long to put their things away. It was still light, so Jerry Lee suggested they go for a ride and a hamburger. "I don't know if my bottom can go another mile," Keri Su grumbled. "I got saddle sores already."

"Aw, come on," said Jerry Lee. "I wanna show the boy where the schoolhouse is. It's bigger'n the Wesco courthouse," he told James.

And it was. It was only one story high, but it sprawled all over the place, like a huge yellow factory. In front was a white sign with straight black letters marching across it—GENERAL DOUGLAS MACARTHUR ELEMENTARY SCHOOL. The *General* was spelled clear out, just to show you they meant business.

"Well?" asked Jerry Lee, twisting around to the backseat where James was sitting with his head poked out the window.

"Whew," said James. He didn't know whether to be proud or scared.

They got lost looking for a hamburger stand. They found themselves on a highway—four lanes of traffic going with you and four against you, and both sides of the road lined with nothing but used-car lots. There were cars and lights and flags all over the place—everything lit up bright as noon. A Smilin' Jack's with an orange banner bearing a huge, grinning face dared them to stop.

"Get your head in the car, sugar!" Keri Su commanded. "You want it snapped off clean at the neck?"

James pulled his head in quickly. He tried not to think of his body ending in a bloody stump riding along in the wagon while his head bounced down the highway around the wheels of cars and trailer trucks coming up the road. Earl was sitting next to him, laughing as though he could read James's mind. Homesickness hit James's stomach like a lump of raw dough. Why wasn't Grandma here? Why wasn't he home with her?

Then, without warning, Jerry Lee's sweet voice rose up over the noise of the road:

> I am a poor wayfaring stranger
> While traveling through this world of woe;
> There is no sickness, toil, or danger
> In that bright world to which I go.

It was one of Grandma's favorite comfort songs, old as the mountains it came from. James swallowed hard, hung his chin over the front seat so his head would be close to his daddy's, and then, his voice barely quavering, joined in a high harmony:

53

I'm going there to meet my father,
I'm going there no more to roam;
I am just going over Jordan,
I am just going over home.

Jerry Lee reached back with his left hand and patted James's cheek. They did another verse before Grandpa joined them in his reedy tenor, and still another before Earl was booming the bass. James wasn't sure, but he thought even Keri Su was humming on the last verse. By then they were pulling into a McDonald's, and everyone was feeling better.

Eddie Switten had booked the Family to sing at a fair in York County on Labor Day. They piled into the wagon that morning, James in the back with the instruments again. He had it all figured out. This time he'd scrunch down, never peeping out the window, and he wouldn't know they were going through the tunnel until they were safely out the other side. It didn't quite work. He could still feel the car going down into the tunnel and the strange hum that told him they were there, but it helped not to look. He sang "Poor Wayfaring Stranger" inside his head and pretended not to hear Earl yelling, "Watch out! That piece in the ceiling up ahead there's 'bout to— Uh oh!"

"Shut up, Earl!" Olive's voice, definitely Olive's and nowhere kin to Keri Su's. Grandpa's nervous cough, the whining *hmmmmm* of the wheels, and then they were up and out, onto the bridge again. He'd like to see the boats, but somehow, if he wouldn't sit up for the tunnel, he had no right to sit up for the boats. Or maybe James was afraid of what Earl might say if his head suddenly popped up.

Everything was running late at the fairgrounds. The first several groups had sung longer than they were supposed to, and most of the crowd in the stands had wandered away in search of lunch by the time the Family got to the makeshift stage. James didn't blame them. He was hungry, too, although he wasn't sure whether it was hunger or fright that was churning butter in his stomach. In the end, they only sang three songs. Earl took the lead in two and Keri Su in one. James didn't even get a special introduction, much less a lead. He was nothing but backup guitar. He tried not to feel disappointed. After all, the idea of singing leads terrified him, he should be glad the way things worked out. If Earl hadn't lorded it over him, complaining to Jerry Lee about the way James had played, James would have minded less. But he refused to give Earl the satisfaction of back talk, just pressed his lips together, as he put Chester into its case.

Jerry Lee noticed. He came over to where James was. "That was good picking, son," he said. "Don't let Earl get to you. We've been needing our own backup guitar for a long time."

The next morning Jerry Lee drove him the eight blocks to the schoolhouse. The rest were sleeping in late. When his daddy stopped the engine and started to get out, James suddenly didn't want him to come in. "I'll be okay," he said.

"What? You mean you don't want me to go in with you?"

"It ain't you. It's me. If I'm gonna be a member of the Family, I got to stop being such a baby."

"Aw, son, don't pay Earl no mind. He's just a overgrowed bully sometimes. He don't mean nothin' by it."

"It's not Earl," James said, almost believing it. "It's me. I got to learn to stand on my own two feet. You ain't gonna be here at this school playing backup for me."

Jerry Lee grinned. "Okay, man, go to it." He slapped James on the bottom and got back in the car.

James stood up straight and headed for General Douglas MacArthur Elementary School. There was one long, wide step and then the door. Before he opened it, he turned. The wagon was still in the parking lot. James waved. Jerry Lee gave a little wave. James stood there until, finally, Jerry Lee started up the engine and drove slowly away.

Once inside the office, facing an enormous woman with a mountain of bright yellow hair piled up on her head, he wondered if he had done the right thing sending his daddy away. The first question she asked was, "Where are your parents?"

He didn't want to say in the car and in the bed, so he mumbled, "They work."

"They what?"

"Work," he said loudly, then ducked his head.

She pulled out a long form. "Take this home and have them fill it out."

"Now? I can't stay?"

"If you have proof of your immunizations with you, otherwise . . ."

He didn't even know what language the woman was talking, much less what she meant.

"I don't have nothin' but a notebook and pencil."

The woman's sigh was so loud it sounded like taking the cap off a car radiator on a hot day. "How'd you get here this morning?"

"My daddy drop me off."

"And didn't bother to come in? I swear, that's the problem with this world. Parents have no sense of responsibility. I suppose they didn't bother to find out that school opened *last* week, either."

He hated her for blaming Jerry Lee. Maybe they should

have found out when school opened, but Jerry Lee had wanted to come in. How could he tell this woman that he, James, was the one who sent his daddy away? So he lied again. "My daddy had to go to work," he said. "He couldn't come in because he had to go to work."

She reached for the phone. "Is your mother at home?"

James shook his head. "We don't have no phone yet, neither."

"Oh, that's just peachy," she said. She reached her long red-nailed fingers out to reclaim the form. "What grade are you in?"

"Six."

She looked him up and down. "You're awfully small for sixth grade. When is your birthday?"

"June twenty-first," he said.

"No, I mean what year?"

"I'm eleven," he said. He was always forgetting what year that made.

She sighed again. "Your last school? You know that?"

"Wesco, West Virginia."

"I should have known," she muttered, not saying what it was she should have known, although James was sure it was nothing good. "All right," she said. "If there's nobody home, I'll go ahead and put you in the sixth-grade class *temporarily,* pending the reception of your transcript from West Virginia and your proof of immunization." She stopped and frowned at him. "Do you know what I'm talking about?"

James just pressed his lips together and shoved his glasses up his sweaty nose.

"I'll write a note to your parents with this form, explaining what you need to properly enroll." She began writing. "That won't be a problem, will it?"

"Ma'am?"

"There is some adult in the household who can read, isn't there?"

James didn't know whether to be shocked or mad. "My momma reads all the time," he said fiercely.

"I thought she worked," the woman said without looking up.

"When she ain't working." Boy, he wished Grandma was here to put this priss face into line. Even Earl would do.

With the cushion of her index finger, the woman carefully pressed a button by the phone and spoke into a box. "Mr. Dolman, I have a new student for you. Could you send someone down to the office to get him?"

There was a crackle. Out of the box came a voice that sounded almost like a snarl to James. Why had he sent Jerry Lee away? Grandma always said Jerry Lee could charm the birds right out of the trees.

The boy that came to get him was about his own size, but very trim, with a face bordered by ears that lay perfectly flat against his neatly shaped light brown hair. He was wearing khaki pants and a blue shirt with a tiny curled-up crocodile on the front where the pocket should have been. The color of the shirt was exactly the color of his eyes. Even his feet were neat —gleaming white sneakers with three perfect, sky-blue stripes.

The woman was saying something. Too late, James realized that she had told him the neat boy's name.

"Ma'am?"

"William Short," she repeated sharply.

William Short, or Will, as he preferred to be called, was the smartest person in Mr. Dolman's sixth-grade class. For days James reckoned himself the dumbest. Somewhere in between them lay the rest of the class—boys and girls from about

James's and Will's size to men and women almost big enough to be their parents. They were all shades, too—white, black, and various tints of brown and tan that could mean anything from Filipino to Latin—an endless variety. It made James dizzy to think of it. At Wesco everybody had been country-white—except one family who called themselves black, but, to tell the truth, were lighter than the farm kids who worked in the sun.

Rising above everyone else in Mr. Dolman's class was one boy who was very tall and very black. He had a funny name —Eleazer Jones—but nobody laughed at it. No one called him simply Eleazer, either. He was always Eleazer Jones. He was at least thirteen, maybe older, a giant among pygmies. His black hill of hair put him three inches taller than Mr. Dolman. Eleazer Jones was skinny, the way a bird rifle is skinny—all that power ready to go. If people talked behind his back, it was very quietly and in the tone of voice that made James realize that at General Douglas MacArthur Elementary School, Eleazer Jones was a star. Will Short was the smartest person in the class. By all rights, he should have been a star as well, but as the fan magazines say, "You got to have star quality to make it big." Will Short lacked star quality.

So did James. Certainly, at school. Once Jerry Lee dug out the paper which proved to the office that James had had all his shots—that's all immunizations were, shots, and West Virginia required them just as much as Virginia did—James faded into the scenery. He sat in a corner at the back of the room—thank you, Grandma, for the glasses—and worked as hard as he could. He was behind, he could tell that from the first day, but if Jerry Lee helped him at night, it wouldn't be too bad.

Of course, he didn't like Mr. Dolman. You weren't supposed to like Mr. Dolman. Mr. Dolman acted as though he were the general in the school's name. Every day he put a motto on the board: No Personal Considerations Should

Stand in the Way of Performing a Duty (U. S. Grant, 1822–
1885). Under the daily motto went the names of those who
had to stay after school. The list was usually longer than the
motto. Eleazer Jones's name was on it nearly every day—Will
Short's, never.

7

The world comes in different colors. The farm was a deep green. The stage was electric orange. School was gray. When he was with Jerry Lee, the house was blue like a bright October sky; with Keri Su, it was a throbbing pink—too strong to leave your eyes on for very long. Grandpa made everything a pale green. And Earl, well, what did Earl make? Sometimes no color at all, sometimes a muddy khaki, sometimes flashes of that same disturbing, throbbing pink.

The Family made their first regular appearance on *Countrytime* on Friday night. Mr. Wallace made a big thing of *first regular appearance,* pretending that the time they'd been on the show in Harrisonburg didn't really count. Jerry Lee didn't have much time to help James with schoolwork. They were too busy rehearsing. The TV station was crowded and wouldn't give them rehearsal space except on Fridays, so they worked in the living room of the house and fussed about the sound being too different in the house for them to tell anything about how they were doing.

They—that is the grownups—had all decided on one thing. For several weeks James would do only one song. They would use *Countrytime*'s pickup musicians for backup, so they wouldn't miss his guitar. Even Eddie Switten thought James should appear sparingly in the beginning. Even Jerry Lee. There was another fight about what number James should do on the first show. Earl was all for "That Heavenly Train," which would limit James's solo to exactly one line—"Even little children got to get on board." Keri Su thought a duet in which she and James would be featured—she more prominently than he—something like "My Mother's Bible," would be "awful sweet." Jerry Lee suggested that James might like to choose what he was going to sing himself. Even Grandpa opposed that idea. "The boy ain't hardly sung in public. How's he gonna know what the fans like?"

Eddie Switten took over. He came to the house Wednesday evening, asked James to sing for him, and after four numbers, settled on "My Dad's a Travelin' Man." "That'll wring the ladies' hearts," he said. "Plus we don't want to limit him to gospel."

The rehearsal was set for Friday morning beginning at nine. It never crossed anyone else's mind that for James, Friday was a school day. In the car on the way to the station, they passed General Douglas MacArthur Elementary School. The crowds were milling around the playground, waiting for the bell.

"Oh, my goodness," Jerry Lee said. "We probably should have sent a note to the school."

"No!" said James. He could just imagine Mr. Dolman's face as he found out that one of his soldiers was taking off a day of duty to pick and sing.

"Oh, I'll send a excuse on Monday," Keri Su said. "They'll be proud as punch to have one of their little boys a regular on a TV show. Just you wait and see." She had obviously never met General Dolman.

It was a long day of mostly listening. James's fingers itched to play, but he had been told that if he wanted to sit and listen, he must not make a sound. So he sat there with Chester across his lap, stiff all over from keeping himself still. When they finally got to his number, he was so anxious to sing and pick that he never once thought about being scared. Besides, there was no one to be frightened of. There was no audience and the people behind the cameras and in the booth didn't seem to be paying attention. Had it been this way in July? James'd been too scared to notice. Probably rehearsed with his eyes shut or something stupid like that. No, the high school auditorium had been much bigger than WQVR's studio. Without his glasses, he'd been too nearsighted to see the technical crew. There was something to be said for nearsightedness.

That night there was an audience. But by the time they finally let him on stage to sing, he was so crazy to tear into it that he was hardly scared at all. Besides, the faces in the audience weren't distinct—more like piles of hair on round, yellowish melons. He smiled at the melons before he began and threw them kisses as he left. The melons squealed with delight. It made him feel fake as plastic flowers on a grave. Only when he was actually singing and picking did he feel right. He was with Grandma then, singing on the porch, looking down over the yard at the hog pen and Rosie's shed with the henhouse on the side, and looking up over the ripple of hills that rolled like waves to the higher Appalachians in the misty west. It was the music that tied him to home, to being James.

Mr. Wallace wanted them to be accessible to the fans after

the show. James stood as close as he could to Jerry Lee while the melon heads, now wearing fuzzy eyes and noses and mouths and set on bulky bodies, came swarming up the steps onto the stage. To James, they all seemed to be female, older than Keri Su and younger than Grandma, all with puffy hair—mostly blond puffs—and glasses that slanted and had shiny diamondlike bits at the temples. One of them poked her face right down into James's. "You so sweet, I could eat you right up," she said, grinning as though she just might. Another knelt down right on the bare floor of the stage and hugged him, nearly smothering his face in her huge bosom, her strong, sweet smell making him choke. They chucked him under the chin, they rubbed his hair, they called him their little sunshine, they kissed him wetly on the cheek—even, sometimes, right on the mouth. He was poked by brooches and eyeglass frames and the pointed corners of guitar-sized pocketbooks. There was no one to help him. The fans had torn Jerry Lee from his side, and James was too short to see any other Family member.

"Keri Su," a shrill voice called out, "he's such a precious little angel. Me and my friend were trying to guess how old he is. You got to settle it for us, now. Is he eight or nine?"

"Why, he's nine," he heard Keri Su say. "In the summer, so he's just barely nine. I reckon you're *both* right." His own mother.

"What a little sweetheart!" "So smart for his age!" "I bet he has lots of little friends."

"He sure does," said the proud mother voice. "Just lots."

The impassive face of Eleazer Jones flashed across James's brain, the small neat face of Will Short, the multicolored class. Not a friend in the lot.

"Wouldn't that be a thrill?" crowed an unseen voice. "Having little Jimmy Jo Johnson for a friend?"

James felt sick to his stomach. Lord, he prayed, please don't let anybody at the school know. What would somebody like Eleazer Jones do with a "precious little angel" whose own mother said he was two years younger than he really was just to make him seem cuter? He pushed his way out from between two polyester pantsuits and headed for the dressing room. "'Scuse me. 'Scuse me."

He could hear Keri Su apologizing for him. "Plumb tuckered out, I reckon."

"Well, of course, 'way past his little bedtime." It was hardly half past eight o'clock. Mercy.

He sat alone on a stool in the men's dressing room and stared into the mirror. He wanted to make sure that he, James, was still staring back, that part of him was not withering up like a plant in drought. He tried to conjure up a picture of Grandma, but got instead the large face of Mr. Dolman. "How's mommy's precious little angel?" Or the creature in the office. "You lied. Your own mother says you're nine years old."

He plunked a few chords on Chester—"a poor wayfaring stranger"—but he could hear the others coming down the hall, so he put Chester on the dressing table and curled up quickly in the overstuffed chair, pretending to be asleep.

Keri Su came through the door already sputtering about the way he had acted, but both Jerry Lee and Grandpa shushed her.

"He did okay for the first time," Eddie added. "He'll get used to it."

"Why did you tell that woman he was nine years old?" Jerry Lee asked.

"I don't know. I's just trying to make her happy. She wanted him to be eight or nine, so . . ." James could almost see her shrugging her shoulders with his eyes closed.

"I told you from the beginning the kid would never work out."

"Now, Earl," Grandpa was saying, "he done all right. You might try encouraging him a little. Don't you remember how it was when you was a young 'un?"

Earl mumbled something James couldn't hear.

It was midnight before they got back to the house. He felt like one of those possums that didn't make it across the road as he stumbled into the house toward his mattress and fell onto it without undressing.

In a few minutes Jerry Lee came in carrying Chester. He put the guitar case down near the mattress and then knelt down beside James and began to take off his boots. James roused himself enough to unbuckle his belt, but he was glad to have Jerry Lee help him pull off his dungarees and get under the sheet.

"You done real good, son," Jerry Lee said. "Them fans 'bout went wild, but you can't do much about it. They the ones keep *Countrytime* on the air." He patted James. "I guess you thought you's being hugged by a bunch of grizzlies."

James tried to grin. "I'm sorry I run," he said. "I'll do better next week."

"Sure you will. Try not to mind about your momma. She's so anxious that the fans like us that she just goes a little overboard trying to please 'em."

James nodded. It wasn't Jerry Lee's fault. Besides, next week he'd know what to expect.

He wondered if Keri Su would be mad at him, but it seemed almost the other way around, as though she was afraid he might be mad at her. She went out of her way to be nice to him all weekend. She even asked him Sunday afternoon if he had any ideas as to what he'd like to sing on the show on Friday. So he told her he wanted to do a duet with her, and she turned pink, she was so pleased.

Jerry Lee had been doing breakfast, but Keri Su was the one who got up early Monday morning and made him strawberry toastie-pops. He would have hated them if he'd allowed himself to, but he was obliged to feel grateful, so he just swallowed them without passing judgment. When he was ready to leave the house, she licked her finger and tried to priss a curl out of his short hair—something she hadn't done since he was a baby. Then she handed him his excuse for school, written on pink stationery. "There you go, sugar. Have a nice day."

James nodded and allowed himself to be kissed as he stuffed the excuse into his book bag. Later he stopped at the filling station, borrowed the restroom key despite the mean look from the attendant, and went into the dark, wet cubicle marked MEN. There he tore up the excuse into pink confetti and flushed it down the toilet. He sat down on the seat, and on a yanked-out piece of lined notebook paper, he wrote in pencil, imitating as best he could his mother's curly round handwriting: *James was sick.*

Then tiptoe to the cloudy mirror, he smoothed down his hair and put on his glasses. Keri Su didn't like him to wear them in front of her, and now more than ever, they seemed a way to hang on to that part of him that was still James.

He handed the key attached to its huge wooden label back to the attendant, ignoring the man's stare. "That's the last time, you hear? You kids got to learn to use the school toilets, you hear?" He kept yelling "You hear?" at James's back.

On the playground, he melted into the crowd as best he could. It's hard to melt when you don't have any friends. You have to think invisible. Since no one paid him any attention, he fancied that he'd managed a disappearing act. The bell rang. James let himself be shoved toward and into the building. The kids were like fans swarming onto the stage, except for their faces. There wasn't any eagerness, any of that strange hunger of fans pushing toward the light. Nobody was expecting light inside General Douglas MacArthur Elementary School. The classrooms didn't even have windows.

James didn't look at Mr. Dolman when he handed him the excuse. Then he thought he should. Mr. Dolman wanted people to look him right in the eyes. So James looked—only Mr. Dolman had his eyes down studying James's note, and the gesture was wasted. "You've got a lot of work to make up," the teacher said.

Relieved, James smiled, then quickly brought in the corners of his mouth, so as to appear serious. "Yessir." He went down the straight, narrow aisle to his desk in the back of the room. By the time he took his chair off the desk and set it on the floor, turned around, sat down, and read the motto for the day—There Is No Excellence Without Great Labor (William Wirt, 1772–1834)—his own name was under the words.

James didn't mind. He had nowhere special to go after school. There were other names on the board by three o'clock —Leroy Folker, a pimply boy who apparently never did his homework, and of course, Eleazer Jones and company. Eleazer Jones was given detention for the mysterious crime of having the wrong expression on his face. As soon as his name went up, five black boys, in rapid succession, committed offenses worthy of detention: throwing waste paper at the basket from a distance of six feet and missing, throwing waste paper at the basket from a distance of six feet and hitting, watching this sports event and grunting "Two points," trying to go to the rest room before the previously excused person had returned, and speaking the unspeakable word at the pencil sharpener loud enough for Mr. Dolman to hear it.

At five after three the room was almost as crowded as it had been at three. Mr. Dolman slapped a math ditto sheet in front of James. It might as well have been Chinese. What was he supposed to do? He glanced up at the front of the room to see Mr. Dolman glaring around at the detainees, daring them to make a sound or put a forbidden expression on their faces. The punishment would be double detention. Perhaps, thought James, if he sat very still without moving a muscle— He imagined himself as a tiny little frog that knows there's a big copperhead in the pond, his slanty eyes just waiting for the teeniest flicker of life, then—*chang*—gotcha! No sir, Mr. Copperhead, I ain't giving myself away. I ain't even breathing in and out. I ain't even wiggling the whites of my eyes. James's eyes felt dry and hard as Easter eggs, for even with his head lowered, he didn't dare to blink.

He began writing a song in his head.

> Oh, you're a copperhead
> and I'm a mighty tiny frog,
> But you don't frighten me,
> you don't frighten me.
> You're a big old diesel truck
> and I'm a tortoise on the road,
> But you don't frighten me,
> you don't frighten me.

The room erupted with the sounds of people scraping to their feet, of chairs being set on desks. James got up quickly, but not too quickly, and did exactly what everyone else was doing. He slipped the still untouched ditto sheet into his bag and moved out the door, right between the tall form of Eleazer Jones and one of his dark-skinned cohorts. It worked. Mr. Dolman didn't notice him. They moved in a body to the outside door—just a few more steps to freedom. For a second, James held his breath. Then they were out in the light, on the low step leading to the building. James turned and smiled up into Eleazer Jones's face. Eleazer Jones grinned back. "What's goin' down, white mite?" he asked.

"Nothin'," said James. He felt ten feet tall. Eleazer Jones was the deep purple of a king in the Bible.

8

At first James was puzzled. Why would Will Short want to tutor him during recess? Since the first day when he had fetched James from the office, Will hadn't seemed to pay him any mind. Now all of a sudden, he was marching up to Mr. Dolman's desk, offering to give up his recess time to help James with math, language arts, reading, and social studies—all the areas in which, according to Mr. Dolman's loud public announcement, James's "lamentable previous schooling" had failed to prepare him. Afterward, Will Short had offered to coach him. It took a few days for James to understand that Will Short would rather *miss* recess than *have* almost anything else. Like James, Will Short was small for his age and friendless. But unlike James, Will Short was highly visible. Nobody ever actually attacked him on the playground, but a lot of people seemed to enjoy snarling at him. So when an honorable alternative to recess presented itself, Will Short jumped at the chance.

James, on the other hand, liked recess. Being invisible, he could wander around watching other people without their seeming to notice. The weather was beautiful and even the smoky city air seemed fresh compared to the windowless classroom. He hated giving up his freedom, but he knew that he had to begin catching up with the class or he would lose his invisibility. Mr. Dolman was looking his way more and more. He didn't notice the average kids—just the very smart or very dumb or those who wore the wrong kinds of expressions on their faces. The height of James's ambition was to be totally and completely average.

Will Short was not a great teacher, but he was a great help. James wasn't the least bit afraid of him, so he could keep asking Will questions until, finally, the mysteries would crack open from sheer banging at them. *Least common denominator,* which sounded like a curse from an Egyptian tomb in the mouth of Mr. Dolman, became sunshine clear to James when he realized that it was the littlest number they could all dance to. Now, what was so hard about that? "Whyn't you tell me that in the first place?" he asked Will.

"Because you made that up. Fractions don't dance."

"Everything dances," James said. Will just looked at him oddly and went on to the next problem.

Maybe of all God's little creatures, Will Short was the only one who couldn't dance. Maybe he'd had it ironed right out of him. It made James feel protective toward Will, and he tried harder so that Will could feel good about being his coach. Will needed that.

As the weeks went by, James—with Will's help—began sneaking up on average, but now there was another factor threatening his invisibility. "Why is it, Johnson, that you are invariably 'sick' on Fridays? Very peculiar. Three Fridays in a row now. And every Monday this grubby little note, 'James was sick.' Sick of what, Johnson? Sick of what?"

James had learned not to answer such questions. It just made Mr. Dolman angrier to be answered. So James listened and schemed. If Mr. Dolman called home— Oh, please God, don't let him call.

The following Thursday night James complained of a great bellyache. It would be totally impossible for him to rehearse on Friday. Maybe he shouldn't even be on the show unless he got really well rested. When the Family left for the station at twenty of nine, he watched the wagon turn the corner and then threw on his clothes and raced to school. He got there while the bell was still ringing.

Since he was there and invisible, his name didn't go up under the motto. In a way, he was sorry. James enjoyed sharing detention with Eleazer Jones and his court, but he did have to rush home and hop under the covers before the Family got there. They always came home between rehearsal and show time.

When he turned into the street, the wagon was already there. Maybe they hadn't missed him yet. He crept around to the back of the house. The Family was rehearsing in the living room, Keri Su yelling as much as she was singing. James was too short to reach the bedroom window. He found a wooden crate in the garage and climbed up on it. The screen was tight, but he finally managed, with a lot of knuckle scraping, to get his fingers under it and force it up about eight inches. Then he had to tug and yank and shove at the window itself— without breaking his fingernails. Fortunately, the Family was making lots of noise in the front, which covered up his banging. He pulled himself to the sill and wriggled through the narrow opening. Then he closed both the screen and the window as quietly as he could and sneaked under the covers.

By now, of course, he had to go to the bathroom. He lay there for a while trying to listen to the music and forget about it, but there was a terrible smell coming from the kitchen and he couldn't concentrate. He got up, stripped to his underwear, and padded out into the kitchen. The peculiar smell was coming from a pot on the stove. It was enough to give him a real bellyache. He tried to breathe through his mouth as he sped through the kitchen. At the threshold he stopped to make a show of yawning and stretching.

"Awright, Earl," Keri Su ordered, "take that bass line one more time." Jerry Lee gave him a smile; no one else even glanced at him. He climbed the steps slowly, looking down on the Family. Their heads were bent over, concentrating.

When he came back down, Keri Su and Earl were arguing as to which one was taking the lead on the third verse of "Lonesome Whistle."

"Hey," Jerry Lee said, grinning up toward him, "let James try it."

"James is sick," Earl said. James couldn't tell if Earl was being smarty or not.

"You ain't too sick to sing tonight, are you, boy?" Jerry Lee persisted.

"He said he was sick," Keri Su said. "Can't you leave the boy alone? I swear. How are you, sugar?"

"I might be able to do a verse," James said, "then go lie down in the dressing room."

"No," Keri Su said. "You too sick to go to rehearsal, you too sick to perform."

"It don't necessarily follow," Jerry Lee began. "I remember once—"

"I'm his mother. I reckon I should know what's best."

Then suddenly, in the Keri Su voice, "I'm going to tell the fans that Jimmy Jo's a little under the weather. Fans like to share your sorrows and woes."

Oh, mercy.

"You can watch us on TV tonight, sugar," Keri Su said.

"Sure," James said.

"And you'll be all well by next week, and won't all your fans be happy to see you then?"

"I reckon."

"Now you just jump back in the bed, and soon's we through rehearsing, I'll get you a little soup, you hear?"

James nodded. There was nothing he could do except go on back to bed.

Later—he didn't know how much later, it felt like hours—the door opened. Jerry Lee came in, closing the door behind him. "You okay?"

James nodded.

"Everything awright at school?"

James wasn't quite sure how to answer, so he waited.

"Look, son, I know that's where you went today."

James sat up quickly. "Do— Does—"

"Naw, the others don't know. I was the one come back to check on you. That fake bellyache act. I done that myself often enough. Only it was to stay out of school—not to get into it." He grinned. "I gotta figure something bad wrong with a kid fakes a bellyache so he can *go* to school."

"Teacher was going to call home if I missed any more Fridays."

Jerry Lee sat down on the mattress. "You ain't been giving him your momma's notes?"

James shook his head.

"You ain't ashamed?"

75

"Oh, no, it ain't that." James sat up and grabbed his daddy's hand. "I'm proud to be part of the Family. You know that."

"You don't think the other kids will understand?"

"Likely not." With his thumb, he rubbed the callus on Jerry Lee's index finger.

"How 'bout the teacher?"

"Grandma used to say 'Everything dances.' I ain't so sure. I ain't seen no music in that man."

"I see."

"He'll fail me if I keep missing school."

"You want to stop singing?"

"I can't do that. No. I don't wanna do that. I got the gift."

Jerry Lee just sat there for a while thinking. "How come," he said, "this world wants to pull you in different directions all the time? I swear."

He wasn't asking James for an answer, but James tried anyway. "Maybe if you was to explain to Eddie, he could talk to Mr. Wallace. Maybe they could let me rehearse after school or something."

"Earl and your momma wouldn't like not having a break. It would make Friday a mighty long day."

"I reckon."

"But it's worth a try, now, ain't it?" He smiled and smacked James's knee. "Here comes your momma with her healing soup. I think it might be a good idea if it tasted like magic." He winked.

James winked back.

The fans sent cards, flowers, and demands for little Jimmy Jo's phone number so they could personally recommend sure cures for his mysterious ailment. WQVR didn't give out the phone number—Eddie Switten's orders—but a few of them got it through information anyway. Apparently Jerry Lee and Eddie worked things out, though, because late Wednesday afternoon Eddie came over to the house bearing a batch of get-well cards. "I left the calf's-foot jelly over to the station," he told James. "Sorry I forgot."

"That's okay," said James. "I'm well now."

"It ain't calf's-foot jelly you need for a bellyache," Keri Su said. "It's chicken-feet soup. Why, I fixed up a batch Friday, old family recipe, and by Saturday morning the boy was bouncing 'round like nothing ever been wrong."

"Yeah," said Earl. "We never got no lunch Friday 'cause we had to try five stores before we could find one would sell us chicken feet. Then we get home, we spend another couple hours fighting over who's gonna sing what on 'Lonesome Whistle.' It's a train song, for crying out loud. Some people who thinks chicken feet cures all ills ain't bright enough to recall that 'Lonesome Whistle' has always been bass lead all the way. With all the ruckus, we hardly had time to rest before we had to turn around and get back to the station."

"Yeah," said Eddie, smooth as butter, "I been thinking about that. That all-day Friday rehearsal just ain't working out good, somehow."

"How you mean?" Grandpa jumped in. "We been working like plow mules."

"That's just it. Too much in one day," said Eddie. "I been talking to Wallace." He stopped to light his inevitable Camel. "He says the station can switch you to Thursday evenings, say five to ten with a supper break." He took a puff to let this sink in.

"Well, I don't like it," said Earl.

"Earl," said Jerry Lee, "you hardly shut up from complaining about Friday being so long. Now what's your beef?"

"I just don't like it, that's all."

"That man," said Keri Su, turning to Eddie, "wouldn't like it if you give him Christmas in a Cadillac."

"Well," said Eddie, *puff-puff,* "it ain't really our decision nohow. Wallace done decided."

"How come ever'thing starts out like a discussion and ends up like a order?" Earl demanded.

"'Cause he's the boss and I'm the manager," said Eddie, but so easy, Earl could hardly yell back.

Saved. Saved. Saved. James wanted to jump up and dance for joy, but he only moved his head enough to catch Jerry Lee's eye. They gave each other a quarter wink.

The Thursday rehearsal went fine. At eleven o'clock Mr. Wallace came trotting out of the booth all the way into the studio to say so. He patted James's head with a fat pink hand that had white curly hairs on top. "Good to have you back, feller. We missed you last week."

James said "Thank ya" as politely and humbly as he knew how. He didn't take to Mr. Wallace much, but the man had saved him, there was no doubt in James's mind about that. So he was going to be extra respectful.

After he got home, he still had homework to do. He had to write a stupid report on the problems of agriculture in the Netherlands. How come those Dutch farmers thought they had problems anyway? All those neat, flat, well-fertilized fields. They ought to see some of them West Virginia farms where the bumper crop was rocks. Ever try to grow anything besides rocks on the side of a hill? That's what Grandma did, and did anyone write chapters in social-studies books about her problems? Just look at the pictures. Everyone of those Dutchmen had a cow fat as a barn. You got fat cows, you don't have no serious problems of agriculture. How about a picture of poor old skinny Rosie? Naw. The only cows could get their pictures in schoolbooks were cow pinup girls.

The more James thought about it, the madder he got. Maybe it was the hour—it was well past midnight—maybe he was a little drunk on getting to sing again, but next day when Mr. Dolman called for the reports to be passed in, James looked down at his paper, and this is what he saw:

> The main problem of agriculture in the Netherlands is that them farmers don't know when they are well off. Anybody got flat land and a fat cow should shut up whining about their troubles and go take a look at somebody really got problems of agriculture like Eskimos and mountain people. Then maybe they'd know what real problems are. . . .

The hairs stood up on the back of his neck. He couldn't hand that in. What in the world had possessed him? He looked around wildly for a place to stuff it.

"Johnson."

"Yessir," he mumbled.

"What's the matter? Didn't you do the assignment?"

"Yessir. No sir!"

Mr. Dolman had walked down the aisle. He picked up James's paper and stood there, right beside James's desk, reading it. James could practically feel the heat bouncing off the man's body. Then, pronouncing every single word as though it were snake venom he was scared he might swallow, Mr. Dolman read the whole composition aloud to the class, including the part about James's grandmother growing rocks. The way the teacher read it made James shrink in shame. He'd betrayed his grandma, making people snort and giggle at her

79

and at how hard she had to work. He hadn't meant that. He really hadn't. He wanted to burst into sobs and deny everything he'd said. Finally the teacher was silent. He crunched James's paper into a hard, little ball. "You may dispose of this, Johnson," he said, putting the ball down on James's desk, "while I add your name to the board."

James stumbled up to the wastebasket, never lifting his head. He felt so ashamed and ugly, worse than Judas in the Bible. Of course the class was giggling. How could he blame them? He must be the biggest fool—the dirtiest traitor—in the whole world. Then, just as he passed Eleazer Jones's desk, a hand half caught his arm. James turned. "Right on, stick man," the black king muttered, guaranteeing that his name would be added to the list as well.

J ames was supposed to sing "My Mother's Bible" with Keri Su for the show. She was pleased that he made a point of wanting to sing a duet with her. He'd sung the song lots with Grandma, and it was a comfortable one for him. He hadn't soured a note in rehearsal. So what was the matter? The hamburger and fries he'd eaten for supper began rolling around in his belly, and his mouth was so dry he couldn't work up enough spit to wet his lips. He turned to go back to the dressing room, moving straight into the big body of Eddie Switten.

". . . back again and feeling fine. Please welcome little Jimmy Jo Johnson!" Eddie shoved him toward Keri Su's voice.

"Now, Jimmy Jo, the folks is mighty glad to have you back this week, so how 'bout a word?" She stuck the mike into his nose.

What was he supposed to say—*James was sick?* He almost

snickered. "Thank ya," he got out. "Much obliged for all your cards and letters—"

Keri Su swooped the mike back to her own face. "—and other expressions of sympathy." She gave him back the mike.

He wasn't dead. Mercy. "Now my momma and I are going to sing 'My Mother's Bible.'" He turned right to the huge square eye of one of the cameras, daring it to scare him. "I want to dedicate this song to my grandma in Blue County, West Virginia."

The fans shrieked their approval. Keri Su turned pink beneath her powder and paint and forced a toothy smile. He was sorry to displease her, but he had to make it up to Grandma somehow. He had to take away the sting of Mr. Dolman's voice and the laughter in the schoolroom. He had realized that in order to hold on to being James, he had to keep Jimmy Jo separate, but he hadn't known until today that he had to keep secret the part of James that belonged to home and Grandma. He'd betrayed that secret. He'd somehow made his grandma seem a crazy old hillbilly when she was, like the words of the song he was singing, "precious and worn."

With his voice he did what his body could not—he put his arms around his grandma's old body and told her how beautiful she was to him. Maybe through the air waves she could see and hear, could tell that he was still James, that he hadn't forgotten her, that he would never slip up again in a way that would make people sneer at her. *I didn't mean for it to happen, Grandma. I love you. I want to come home.*

He poured everything into the song—all the pain of the day, all the homesickness of the weeks. When it was over, the tears were rolling down his cheeks. He bowed and ran off-stage, and not even Eddie Switten could make him go back on for another bow.

He ran to the brightly lit dressing room, shut the door, and switched off the light. Then he felt his way through the dark to the farthest corner of the room and sat down on the floor with his face to the wall.

He must have fallen asleep, for he was jarred awake by a blamming on the door and Gus yelling for him to get on stage. James jumped to his feet just as the door flew open. "Kid?" Gus's head was stuck in, and he was trying to see through the darkness. "Kid, you in here?" Then he flashed on the light. "There you are. Get on stage. They're asking for you."

James nodded. He grabbed a washcloth, ran it under the cold faucet, and wiped his eyes. He could see in the mirror that he'd smeared his makeup, so he had to take time to wash his face more carefully. Gus *humph*ed impatiently in the doorway. "Come on. Come on." Then Eddie and Mr. Wallace were there urging him to get a move on.

It was like the flood in the days of Noah. As soon as he got to the back of the lighted area of the stage, a great wave of words and shrieks and large, perspiring bodies engulfed him. He held on to himself not to lose control. He wanted to run, but there was no escape. He was pressed in on every side. Women kept grabbing him as though he were the choice item on the bargain table. Pens and scraps of paper were jammed under his nose. As quickly as he signed one piece, it was snatched from his hand, and another five or six were jabbed in his face. Several people asked him questions at the same time, but nobody waited for an answer. They just wanted to hear their own voices yelling out the questions.

There was no air. He began breathing too fast, trying to get air. *Dear God, don't let me die here or even fall out in a faint.*

They'll crush me to death. He was hot and dizzy. The sweat poured down his face and between his legs.

Then Jerry Lee was picking him up. "'Scuse me, ladies, he's still not up to scratch. 'Scuse me." Jerry Lee was shorter than lots of the fans, but they cleared a path for him. James closed his eyes and leaned on his daddy's chest, hearing through his body the sounds of Gus and Mr. Wallace clearing the studio, asking people to go on home.

"Whew," Jerry Lee said, putting him down on the easy chair. "Them fans was like crazy people tonight."

"Wasn't it great?" Keri Su said. Her brown eyes were sparkly with excitement.

"Well, I think it's hard on the boy," Jerry Lee answered. "They like to smother him alive."

Keri Su came over and knelt by the chair. "You gonna be a star, Jimmy Jo, you got to be more friendly to the fans. See, most of these people lead mighty dull lives. You and me, we're like sunshine to them. You understand, sugar?"

He nodded.

"Well, I think one of us should try to stand close and not let them run all over the boy."

"I can't see how we can do that, Jerry Lee," she said. "Lots of the fans want to talk to me personally."

"The boy ain't the only one has fans," Earl said.

"Yeah," said Jerry Lee, "I know. I think I'm the one should stay by him. The rest of you just spread out wide. It'll break up the crowd a little." He threw James's pants to him for him to change into. "I only signed one autograph and that was because they couldn't push through to the boy." He grinned. "They said having Jimmy Jo's daddy's autograph was almost as good as the real thing."

Earl made a rude noise in his throat. Keri Su jerked her

84

head up and glared at him. For a second, Jerry Lee's face went dark red. Grandpa was turning from one to the other. "Hush up, Earl," he said, even though Earl hadn't opened his mouth.

James didn't like the looks on their faces. Something that he didn't like one bit was going on over his head. He kicked off his boots and snatched off his stage jeans and yanked on his old dungarees. He kept his head down, pretending to concentrate on the zipper. His hands were shaking. He took off his Western shirt and pulled his T-shirt over his head. He sat down and put on his sneakers and tied the laces, and still no one had said a word.

Finally Grandpa *harumph*ed and mumbled, "How 'bout us getting ourselves out of here?"

In the car no one said anything. Usually on the way home Jerry Lee would sing, but he just drove the car, eyes straight ahead. Tired as he was, James sat up stiffly on the backseat, so as not to touch either Grandpa or Earl. He could feel them straining away from him as well. They had all cut him out of the Family for some reason they wouldn't make clear to him. He felt like a guitar string tuned too tight, ready to whang busted any second.

They'd forgotten to leave a light on the porch, so they had to stand there while Jerry Lee fumbled in the dark with the house key. "Dadburn city," Grandpa said. "Have to lock up ever'thing."

"Phone's ringing," Keri Su said. "Hurry."

"I'm doing the best I can, Olive," Jerry Lee said very quietly. The door fell open, and Keri Su nearly tripped over him getting through the dark house to the kitchen phone. As James went past her on the way to his room, she held out the receiver to him. "It's for you."

He took it without a word, just as though he got phone calls every night. "Hello," he said.

"Boy?" The voice at the other end sounded through the crackling.

"Grandma! That you?"

"Last time I checked."

"How come you calling? You okay? You ain't sick or nothing?"

"Nah. Nah. I just calling to thank you for the song." She was shouting over the bad connection.

"You heard me?" He yelled back. "Was I awright?"

"Awright? Boy, my apron's so wet, all I need is a bar of Octagon soap to launder it." He could hear her chuckle. "You all well now?"

"I'm fine. Did you really like me?"

"Would I call you up and scream over this dang contraption to say you was no good?"

"It was all for you," he said. "I miss you something terrible."

"Well, that's nice," she said. "Tell your daddy to bring you back up here 'fore this pup of mine gets bigger'n you."

"You got your dog?"

"Yep. Named him James after this runty kid I know'd once't." She was still hollering.

Grandpa and Jerry Lee had come to the kitchen by now. "Ask her does she want to talk to Grandpa or me," Jerry Lee said.

He hated to give up the phone. It was as though there were pure air coming through the line, reviving him. But Jerry Lee looked so sad, he had to. "Grandma," he said, "Daddy and Grandpa want to talk to you. Thank ya for telephoning me. It really made me feel great."

86

She knew how much he needed her; she forgave him even without knowing he had shamed her. He lay down on his mattress, put the pillow over his head, and cried himself to sleep like a baby.

By the fourth week of October, he didn't have to spend all of his recesses with Will Short. He had reached his goal of average, invisible schoolwork. The first day in the schoolyard he felt a little bit like a man who'd just been let out of jail. He breathed in the autumn air. Will Short was at his elbow.

"What are you going to do during recess today, James?" he asked.

"Nothin'," said James happily. "What are you gonna do?"

"Well, I don't know exactly," Will said cautiously. "We could talk about the book report for next week."

James didn't want to spend his first few minutes out of jail discussing imprisonment. "I don't think so," he said. "I think I'll just walk around and see what's going on out here."

Will nodded, his face the worried face of the little old man in the loose-dentures commercial. As James began walking, Will walked too, close as possible without actually touching. Not that James cared. In fact, he rather liked Will wanting protection from him.

"They're coming toward us," Will whispered.

James looked up. Sure enough, Eleazer Jones and his court were heading straight for them.

"Run!" ordered Will through his teeth. "Back to the building."

"They ain't gonna do nothin'," James said. "Hush up."

Eleazer Jones came up close. "Mite," he said, "you know that man over there?"

"What man?"

The King jerked his head toward the chain-link fence bordering the south side of the playground. James followed the motion. There was a man standing on the other side of the fence, tall and skinny, his shoulders slightly hunched like a mountain man's. A chill went through James. *Like somebody walked over my grave,* he thought. He shook his head. "I never seen him before in my life."

"He come here every day this week. He say he want to talk to you," the tall boy said.

James shook his head again.

"You want me tell him get lost?"

James nodded. It must be some fan who had found out where he went to school. "I'd be obliged," he said.

Eleazer Jones moved toward the fence, his admirers trailing like ducks behind their mother. Will Short was staring at James, his mouth open.

"C'mon," said James. "Let's go to the building."

Will Short scurried to keep up. "What was that all about?"

"I don't know," said James. "I never saw the man."

"No," said Will. "I mean you and that Eleazer Jones. He acts like he's supposed to take care of you."

James had been so worried about the man, he hadn't thought of Eleazer Jones's behavior seeming strange. "I think he likes me," said James.

"Likes you? Why? Why would he like you?"

"Maybe he feels sorry for me," James said.

"Maybe." James could tell Will was impressed.

When school was out, Will Short walked the first couple of blocks with James and then split off to go to his own house. James quickened his step. There was a rusted black pickup truck driving too slowly up the other side of the street. James turned down the first street and, as soon as he was out of sight, began to run. When he got to his house and was going in the door, the black truck turned the corner. James slammed the door.

"That you, sugar?" Keri Su called from the kitchen.

"Yeah," he answered, moving over to the front window. The truck was going slowly past the house. James thought, though he wasn't sure, that the driver's head twisted to look out at the house. Was it the man by the fence? It had to be.

"Problem?" Jerry Lee had come up behind him and had his arm around James's shoulder.

James shook his head. He didn't want to say anything. It seemed silly. If the man were to follow him again, he'd say something, but not just now. Not while Jerry Lee was keeping his worries to himself, keeping James on the outside.

10

Although James kept watch, the man with the black pickup wasn't around the next day—or the next or the next. Gradually, James relaxed. Just some nosy fan who had been easily discouraged. Besides, James had something really good to think about for a change. Because of all the football games, *Countrytime* wasn't going to have a show Thanksgiving weekend, and the Family was going home to West Virginia as soon as school let out on Wednesday. James considered being sick on Wednesday so they could leave a day early, but decided he'd better not risk it. He was nearly invisible to Mr. Dolman these days.

James practically danced to the house Wednesday afternoon. It was as though since September he'd been seventy years old and suddenly, by some magic, had turned eleven again. No, five—back before he'd ever been to school, when all the world he really knew was that rocky hillside.

I'm just a poor—*toodletido*—wayfaring stranger—*tooka doo-*

dle doodley do, he sang inside his head, jazzing it up with an imaginary fiddle obbligato and throwing in banjo, guitar, and mandolin as well. Travelin' through—*whang, whang, tooka doodle di doo*—this world of woe— This time the fiddle ornamentation was fancier than a Christmas tree. Oh, he wished it would all come out of his hands and mouth the way it sounded in his head—*toodledido toodledi tiddle di tiddle di*—

He danced right up the steps, into the house. "I'm here!" he yelled. "Let's go."

For a minute there was no answer, then Jerry Lee's voice from the kitchen. "Back here, boy. I'm not quite ready."

James bounced into the kitchen. Jerry Lee was standing at the counter slathering mayonnaise on bread. "Making us lunch so we won't have to stop so long."

"Good," James said. "Where's ever'body?"

Jerry Lee spread the mayonnaise very carefully to each corner of the bread. "We got this call from a club over to the Beach. Olive—Keri Su—thought it was too good a chance to pass up."

"I don't know what you mean."

Jerry Lee slapped the ham on the bread and slammed down the lid of the sandwich. "Yeah, well, it means that them three are going to stay here and play this club over the weekend."

"What about us?"

"Well, I don't know about you, old buddy, but if I don't get out of this burg and back to the mountains pretty soon, I may just wither away." He put the sandwich in a plastic bread wrapper with the others he had made and carefully folded up the loose end. After he had put the sandwiches and a couple of bananas and a bag of cookies in a paper sack, he turned back to James. "I told them I thought you'd rather go home with me."

"Sure," said James. He was sure, wasn't he? "Sure, of course." It was all he had thought about all week. "I'm ready anytime. Just let me get my stuff."

He sat close to Jerry Lee, not just because they'd have to go through the tunnel, but because he wanted to say with his body how glad he was to be going home with him. "How are they gettin' out to the Beach?" On the bridge it occurred to him that he and Jerry Lee were driving away in the only car.

"I rented 'em a Buick. Baby blue. It's her favorite color." He glanced over at James and smiled a crooked way that made James hurt for him. "Your momma was like a little girl with a new doll." He squinted at the road. "This old heap ain't got much going for it."

"It works fine."

Jerry Lee grinned and put his right arm around James and drew him even closer. "I reckon," he said. "Maybe so."

James wanted to say, *Don't be lonesome. I'm here with you.* But he couldn't. He tried to stay awake, though, in case Jerry Lee wanted to talk—he didn't . . . or sing—he didn't. They listened to the radio—all kinds of pop and rock, even caught the news and weather.

"The weatherman says it's going to be clear and sunny for the weekend," James said, in case Jerry Lee had missed it. "That's good, ain't it?"

"What?" Jerry Lee was on another planet.

"Clear and sunny. Ain't that good?"

"Yeah. Fine."

"I changed the dog's name" was first thing Grandma said after she'd hugged them and asked where everyone else was and pretended that it was just fine that only the two of them had come home for Thanksgiving.

"How come?" James asked, glad to change the subject.

"He can't sing on key, and it was giving him one of those inferior complexes to be the namesake of a famous country telly vee star when he couldn't sing a lick."

"Oh, Grandma."

"Yep. Order to keep him from sulking around with his tail between his legs, I had to change his name to what he does best—Squirt. He's a heap site happier now, ain't you, Squirt?"

Even Jerry Lee smiled. He hugged Grandma again. "How 'bout some hot biscuits and gravy for two starving hillbillies who ain't put their teeth into a real biscuit for nigh onto three months?"

"Oh, go off, you," she said, pleased as could be. She'd never say that Olive couldn't cook worth doodlydi-squat, but she didn't mind too much if someone else hinted at it.

James picked up the puppy and scratched his neck. He wanted to be loyal to Olive. He really did. She was his mother, and though she wasn't like other people's mothers, she loved him in her way, even when she was so set on being Keri Su and making him into Jimmy Jo. Like Jerry Lee said, she meant well. Besides, what did he know about other people's mothers anyway? The only other mother he knew to speak of was Grandma, and she was a special case. Olive's mother had died when Olive was just a little girl. How was Olive supposed to know about mothers? Hadn't she made that chicken-feet soup when she thought he was sick? She told him it was what her mother had made her once. That's probably all she could remember about mothers—chicken-feet soup. And though no one said it right out clear, he was pretty sure that the reason she had run away from home was because her daddy beat her. A person like James, who had had Grandma and Jerry Lee loving him all his life, shouldn't be so hard on her, but still he

93

forgot to be understanding when he looked at the hurting in Jerry Lee's face.

The next day while James and Grandma fixed the dinner, Jerry Lee chopped and split firewood until it reached the top of the shed and there was no place else to put it. Now and again Grandma would go to the window and peer out at him.

"I think he's upset 'cause the others didn't come home," James said. He felt a need to explain Jerry Lee to her.

"I 'speck that's it," she said, but she didn't sound convinced.

James was kneading the bread dough that he'd sneaked away from Grandma while she was staring out the window. He punched it down several times before he said, "I'm thinking I shouldn'ta gone down there with the Family."

"Oh?" She didn't look up from the onions she was chopping for the dressing.

"They fight about me a lot, Grandma."

"Who fights about you?"

"Well, Earl and Momma, mainly. Earl thinks I'm trying to shove him over, but I ain't, really I ain't."

"And your momma don't like Earl shoving back on you?"

"Not exactly." Now that she was asking him, he wasn't sure why Keri Su was so often mad. Her words said that it was Earl she was fighting with, but it wasn't as though she was trying to favor him over Earl. Actually, if he thought about it, she wasn't so thrilled when James took the lead, either. She liked it when he sang duets with her. In fact, the time he played sick, she'd seemed happier with him than when he was doing just what she said she wanted him to do. She went to a lot of trouble to make him that soup. She didn't usually go out of her way for him. "I can't figure Momma out," he said at last. "I don't know what she wants outta me."

"Maybe she don't know, either," Grandma said. Then,

very softly, "She was always the star before, James. Now she's gotta share that with you." *Chop, chop, chop* on the cutting board and *crack* outside as Jerry Lee split still another log. "I know she loves you, but it ain't easy when you're still not more than a girl yourself to make room for another person, even when you love the other person."

James flipped and punched the springy dough. It was ready to put to rise, but he didn't want to let it go. It was warm under his hands, and the rhythm of slap, punch, turn, and dig with the heels of his hands was a comfort—but not comfort enough. Something was catching in his throat. "Well, what am I supposed to do?" he asked her. "I just make Momma and Earl unhappy if I sing, but you and Daddy tell me I gotta do it because I got the gift. What am I supposed to do?"

She shook her head. "Nothin's ever pure, James. Joy and pain always show up in the same wrapper."

"Earl says she shoved you out."

Grandma looked up sharply. "I don't shove so easy," she said. "If I move over, it's 'cause I choose to."

"Didn't you want to sing no more?" The thought of never singing again was rising like a great spiked ball inside his gut.

Her face softened. "Nobody loved to sing more'n me," she said. "I woulda give anything to sing straight through to Glory without a pause. But my voice give out. You heard me. You know."

He didn't insult her by trying to say otherwise. He knew her voice was gone.

"That was just about the time that Olive come along. Poor waif. But she could tear up a song, even then. Afterward you was with me. It all worked out." She mixed the onions with the stale bread and melted butter and began stuffing the turkey Jerry Lee had brought her from Tidewater. James divided the

95

dough, patted and folded half of it to rise in the loaf pan, and began making the other half into rolls.

Finally she said, "Is it just too miserable? Do you crave to stop?"

"No." He wouldn't look at her. "I don't crave to stop, but I wish you was with us."

"Well, that don't hurt my feelings none," she said, wiping her hands and putting the bird into the huge black oven. "Let's you and me give that feller out there a good weekend, awright?"

He put a dish towel over the rolls and set them on the back of the stove. "Whyn't I get the guitar and the Autoharp, so's we can make us some music while ever'thing's cooking?"

"By cracky, Squirt, I think the boy is getting some sense at last."

They made a lot of music over the weekend. When they were too stuffed to breathe, they picked. Jerry Lee even tried the fiddle. Real fiddling is powerful hard, and Jerry Lee hardly dared play in front of them, much less in front of an audience, but he still practiced, hoping to be good enough someday. Grandma and James told him over and over how much he was improving, and that seemed to cheer him a bit.

They sang a lot of sad songs, too. It's funny about sad songs. They don't really make you feel sadder when you're down. They even seem to take the sting out of the worst of it.

"I've wrote me a new song," Jerry Lee said, pulling off the thumb and finger picks he used for rousing tunes. "Wanna hear it?" Of course they did. The music was gentle, with easy chords, so James and Grandma caught on to it and played backup after the first few lines. It was a song about an old man who lives alone in a tumbledown house in the hills. One day he finds a bird with a broken wing and takes it home and nurses it to health. Slowly, the bird gets well and begins to sing for the man, and the old cabin is filled with beauty. But when spring comes, the bird flies away. For the first time, the old man is lonely, because before the bird came and filled his house with song, he hadn't known that it was empty.

"That's about the prettiest song I ever heard in all my born days," said Grandma, wiping her eyes with her apron. "I swear, you gotta do that one on the telly vee."

"What do you think, James?"

"Oh, Daddy, it's beautiful," James said. And it was, so sad and pure that it rearranged his insides.

"I want you to sing it," Jerry Lee said.

"No," James said. "You should sing it. It's your song."

"I wrote it for you."

James looked from his father to his grandmother. "You think I can do it?" He didn't want "Broken Bird" to come across as some kiddy song. It would be awful for people to think of it as cute or darling.

"We'll teach you how to do it right, won't we, Jerry Lee?" And they did, stopping only to eat and sleep. They sang the song until it ran through his veins like rich, red blood. And he knew beyond a twinkle of doubt that "Broken Bird" belonged to him, and he could give it as a gift.

They hated to leave. All three of them cried a little, and the puppy whimpered to keep them company in their misery, still the road back was a happier one than the road there had been. He and Jerry Lee sang and joked, and James slept for long stretches of highway—no longer anxious for his daddy, just comfortable being near him.

They were late getting back Sunday night—later than they'd meant to be, as the holiday traffic on the bridge and in the tunnel was like a logjam on the South River. But the house was empty.

"Still at the club, I reckon," said Jerry Lee.

"Clubs is always late," agreed James, as if he knew.

He didn't see the others until he came home from school on Monday. Keri Su was in her pink quilted robe with the frilly collar, drinking coffee at the kitchen table.

He went straight back to where she sat. She was reaching out her arm, so he went close and let her kiss him on the cheek. She smelled heavily of perfume mixed with coffee.

"How's your trip, sugar?"

"Fine." He wasn't sure if he ought to say something about missing her, because in the end, he hadn't. But he had at first, so he said, a little stiffly, "I was sorry you and Earl and Grandpa couldn't go, too."

"I was sorry too, sugar, but we got this good gig over to the Beach."

He nodded. "Grandma says to tell you 'Hey.' "

"I guess she's spry as ever."

"Seemed to be fine," he said. What a stupid conversation. "Ever'body else gone?"

"Earl and Grandpa are sleeping. Jerry Lee's out somewheres."

He went to the refrigerator and stared into it. "Did Jerry Lee tell you he wrote me a new song for the show?"

"That's nice." She said it lightly, as though she didn't care. And she probably didn't just then.

It was after she had heard "Broken Bird" that Keri Su began to care.

"That ain't no little boy's song," she said.

"I wrote it for him," said Jerry Lee.

98

"Well, when he grows up, he can sing it," she said, turning to Eddie Switten for help. "Don't you think that song needs more'n a kid's voice?"

Eddie was perched on the end of the sofa with his arms and legs crossed. "The boy done it great," he said. "I think it'll go over just fantastic."

"I'd like to try it," she said. "I'd just like y'all to hear me do it before you decide."

Eddie and Jerry Lee looked at each other. James could feel that Jerry Lee was angry, and he was sure of it when his daddy spoke very quietly. "How about Earl? Don't he want to try it, too?"

Earl shrugged. "Not my style." Then to James's surprise, he added, "C'mon, Keri Su, let the boy have the song."

She opened her mouth to say something, then shut it again.

"I want Wallace to hear the boy sing it," Eddie was saying. "If he says it don't suit, I ain't arguing."

But Wallace liked it. When James got to the mike Friday night, he said, "This here's a new song that my daddy wrote for me, and I'm singing it for him." And he did, putting into the song all the pain of the ride to West Virginia and the joy of their time there together. When he finished, he turned to Jerry Lee and held out his hand so they could take the bow together. His father's eyes were bright with tears.

It was funny how he didn't seem to mind the fans that night. In fact, it was as though he was standing in a glowing circle. He smiled at each one and signed their autograph books and scraps of paper. They weren't greedy and grabbing, but sad and lonely, their faces almost hungry. *Don't be sad. Don't be hungry.* He wanted to reach out to them all and heal their hurts. How rich he was. How full of good things. Jerry Lee had written a wonderful song, and James had opened his

99

mouth, and the song had come to life. He had been possessed by it, as though it were a magic spell. The enchantment had poured out from his body through the air—all the way to West Virginia. Maybe Grandma would call. He hoped she would, although he didn't need her to say that he had been good.

She did call, but all she did was cry, the puppy yowling with dismay in the background, until they both had to laugh. He went to bed without talking to anyone. He didn't want to talk anymore. He just wanted to lie there in the darkness, holding inside his body the fierce sorrow of the music. His fingers, his head, his chest, even his toes rang with it, and he could not hold it in. He had been swallowed by the hugeness, the greatness of it—like Jonah in the belly of the whale. The vastness filled him with wonder, but he was not afraid. This must be how it feels, he thought, this must be how it feels to have the gift.

11

The club didn't want Grandpa. An old grayhead picking a bass fiddle, with a reedy mountain voice, was too old-fashioned for the kinds of customers the club attracted, the manager said. He hired an electric bass and a steel guitar to back up Keri Su and Earl, and signed them to perform for six weeks of Sunday nights. Nobody said out loud that Christmas, which was on a Sunday, was only three weeks away.

On Saturday Earl took all his savings and bought a car. It was only a '79 Plymouth, but it was baby blue, and Keri Su loved it. The two of them left for the club the middle of Sunday afternoon—a cold, rainy Sunday. Grandpa was out of sorts for being bumped, so he complained of tired blood and went off to bed as soon as the car pulled away.

Jerry Lee and James were glum, too, but each tried to pretend he wasn't for the sake of the other. They watched a football game on a network channel for a while, and then switched to WQVR and watched a bowling tournament,

RETA E. L. LIBRARY
CHADRON STATE COLLEGE
CHADRON, NE 69337

though neither of them cared anything for football or bowling. By four o'clock, they were just staring out the window at
the rain.

Jerry Lee suggested they go to a movie, but when they
looked at the paper, there was nothing either of them wanted
to see. About five, they drove through the gray drizzle to
Anna's Chicken House and got a bucket, plus fries and cole
slaw and something Anna—who must have been a Yankee on
the basis of the evidence—called biscuits.

"Land o'Goshen," Jerry Lee said as he spread the food out
on the kitchen table. "If this Rock of Gibraltar is a biscuit, I'm
Mother Maybelle Carter."

"Wish Grandma was here," James said.

Jerry Lee nodded. "Tell you what," he said. "Let's you and
me make biscuits."

"You know how?"

"I should. I seen her do them hundreds of times. So have
you. It don't look that hard." Jerry Lee got out flour, salt, and
milk.

"You need soda," James remembered, "and lard."

They found baking soda, but no lard, so they substituted
margarine. The chicken and fries were stone-cold by the time
the biscuits were brown, but Jerry Lee and James were very
proud of themselves when they called Grandpa to supper.

He was the one who took the first bite. His nose wrinkled
up toward his forehead.

"Ain't they good?" James and Jerry Lee both leaned forward anxiously.

Grandpa put the biscuit down. "Let me just put it gentle.
These biscuits make Olive's taste like the Bread of Heaven."

Jerry Lee took a big bite and promptly spit it out. "Boy,
you'd think we was trying to poison ourselves. Taste it,
James. I don't know what the world we did."

James took a tiny bite and then pinched it out with his fingers. He felt as though he had a mouthful of bicarbonate of soda. "Phlaaaa."

Jerry Lee stood up. "I think we'd better get us the original recipe." He laughed. "These likely to be the most expensive biscuits you ever set your teeth into before we get through." He went to the phone and dialed. They all waited.

"What's the matter?" James asked.

"I dunno. She ain't answering."

"Likely milking," Grandpa said.

"Mighty late for that," Jerry Lee said, turning from the phone, his face pinched up in worry.

"We just talked to her Friday night," James said. "She was awright then."

"Yeah," said Jerry Lee. "I'll try again later." He got the despised Anna biscuits out of the sack. But none of them were hungry anymore.

Jerry Lee tried to call all evening, every half hour or so.

"Maybe something wrong with the line," Grandpa suggested about nine.

"Yeah, that's probably it," Jerry Lee said.

"She was okay night before last," James said as though to assure himself. Actually, all she'd done was cry on the phone, but the crying had sounded natural, hadn't it? Surely, he of all people would have noticed if something was wrong. He knew her better than anyone in the world, didn't he?

At eleven thirty she still wasn't answering. The three of them had been trying to watch TV, but James would have been hard put if anyone had quizzed him on the programs. At midnight when there was no answer, Jerry Lee went past them from the kitchen and climbed the stairs. Five minutes later he reappeared carrying his little nylon suitcase. "I'm driving up," he announced. "Like as not, the phone's just out, but I gotta see." James and Grandpa jumped to their feet, both wanting to go.

"You got school," Grandpa said. "You know how mad she'd be, you skipping school to come check on her."

"Grandpa's right," Jerry Lee said, but sadly, as though he really wanted James along. "You stay here and tell Olive and Earl where we're at." He waited, without sitting, while Grandpa packed his case. "I reckon I should try once more," he said. James held his breath, listening for his voice from the kitchen, but Jerry Lee came back without speaking. "I give her fifteen rings," he said. Then he looked at James. "Hey, don't worry, it's likely nothing. She'll kill us for coming all that way."

"Yeah," said James, "likely so."

He went to sleep on the couch, with the television blaring. Somehow he wanted the company of it. It scared him to have Jerry Lee worried enough to drive home, but he was glad Grandpa had gone, too. He wanted Grandpa to be worried about her. A man, no matter how old he is, shouldn't take his wife for granted like some old faithful hound.

Keri Su and Earl came banging in around two thirty. James sat up on the couch, waiting for them to see him. Keri Su noticed the TV first and stood over the set watching for a minute. A man was smooching all over a pretty blonde woman on the screen. When it went to the commercial, she switched it off. Earl had already walked straight past the couch into the kitchen without seeing James.

"Momma."

Keri Su jumped. "What you doing up?" she asked.

"Grandma—" he said, but it was all he could get out.

"What in the world?" she demanded.

He blurted it out—how they'd tried all evening to get Grandma on the phone to get the biscuit recipe—

"Biscuit recipe?"

—how she hadn't answered and hadn't answered until Jerry Lee and Grandpa got so worried they decided to drive up there to see if she was all right.

"I swear—that woman." Keri Su was steaming. "They must be outta their heads. Why didn't they just call Jennings to check? I swear. You know it'll turn out to be nothing. Then all that time and gas and— I swear."

James wanted more than anything for it to be nothing, and of course they should have tried calling the Jennings, so why was he so mad at Keri Su for saying it?

She looked at him and broke off her fuming. "Well, I'm dead. I'm gonna have a cup of coffee and get right on to bed. That's where you shoulda been hours ago." She took his arm and pulled him to his feet. "Oh, don't carry on so, sugar. She'll be all right. She's the toughest old bird in three states. Sometimes Jerry Lee act like he don't have good sense, that's all, taking on like this."

The next morning he got up realizing that he should have told Jerry Lee to call him as soon as he got there, but then his daddy would hardly have had time to get there yet. James's body was heavy with dread. It was like walking around dragging fifty-pound weights with every step, but he made himself go on to school, feeling somehow that if he behaved in an ordinary manner, there would be a perfectly normal explanation for Grandma's not answering the phone—as though if he sat around waiting, his worry would cause disaster.

He went through the motions of school, stumbling to his feet to recite the pledge, turning to pages in books as ordered, working on ditto sheets that were put down in front of him. He couldn't risk detention, today of all days. He had to get home as soon as he could. If Jerry Lee hadn't called yet, he would call the farm. He couldn't stand any more waiting. His body was loaded with waiting, it was rising in his throat, by three o'clock he would be choking on it. But suppose, even then, no one answered? Suppose they all three just disappeared off the face of the earth, like a dog that strays away and is never heard of again?

"Johnson!" He jerked to attention. "Would you kindly favor us with your presence?"

"Yessir." His heart was beating like a honky-tonk rhythm section. Oh, God, please, please don't let him put my name up. But of course Mr. Dolman did, with elaborate curlycued handwriting, under the motto: Do Noble Things, Not Dream Them All Day Long (Charles Kinsley, 1819–1875).

He sat through detention, not daydreaming, hardly daring to breathe. He couldn't stand it if he got double detention. He could feel Eleazer Jones glancing his way from time to time, but he couldn't acknowledge the King's sympathetic looks. At exactly three forty-four Mr. Dolman got up and marched the length of the aisle to James's desk. He put down a note. "The office sent it up. I told them you had a prior obligation." James opened the note with shaking hands. He knew Mr. Dolman would be reading over his shoulder, but he had to see: *Your father wants you to meet him in Anna's Chicken House after school.*

Why would Jerry Lee want to meet him in the fried-chicken place? It didn't make sense. What could be so awfully wrong? And how in heaven had he gotten back from Grandma's so fast? And why? Oh God, it must be worse than anything he could possibly imagine.

"Can I go?" he managed to choke out.

"May I go?" corrected Mr. Dolman, but he stepped aside. Good thing, or James might have run him down.

The chicken place was nearly empty at that time of day. One glance around told him that Jerry Lee was nowhere in sight. Nevertheless, he hurried through the length of the restaurant and checked the back corner booth and the men's room, just to make sure. Jerry Lee must have left already. James started for the door. As he did, a tall man got up from a side booth. "Jimmy Jo," he said. It was the man from the black pickup. James started to bolt, but the man caught his arm. "I ain't gonna hurt you," he said softly. "I just want to talk to you a minute."

"I ain't got time," James said. Fan or no fan, he didn't have time. "My daddy needs me."

"I'm your daddy," the man said, showing tobacco-stained teeth. "Your real daddy."

James looked the man straight in the eyes. "I ain't never seen you before in my life. Let go my arm before I holler."

The man let go. "Ask your momma," he continued softly. His eyes were very hard and bright. "Ask her wasn't she seven months gone when she got married."

"You lie!" James cried. He grabbed the door and slipped through, never looking back. He ran as fast as he could all the way home, but he needn't have. The man made no attempt to follow.

"You're late," Keri Su called out when he flung himself through the front door.

"I had to stay after." He was still panting for breath. She was sitting in her pink robe at the kitchen table. She was always sitting in her robe drinking coffee. He started to walk right past her to his room.

"Jerry Lee called."

Lord have mercy. He'd forgotten. He must be out of his head. How could he have forgotten? "What'd he say?"

She took a sip and put the cup carefully onto the saucer. For those few seconds James thought he might kill her, but he held it all in. "Your grandma's in the hospital," she said finally.

Oh, God, he knew it. He knew it. Please don't let it be bad.

"It ain't too serious." Keri Su kept on in her most matter-of-fact tone. "She went down to Wesco Saturday for a checkup, and the doctor put her in for tests or something. Jerry Lee and Grandpa are going to stay and take care of the stock until she can come home." She raised her cup and studied him over the rim as though he had turned another color. "You all right, Jimmy Jo?"

"I'm worried," he said more loudly than he meant to. "I'm worried to death."

"Well," she went on calmly, "Jerry Lee said not to worry. She's doing just fine."

"They don't put people who's doing 'just fine' into a hospital!" All the anger and fear of the last eighteen hours burst out. She heard the anger above the words.

"Watch it!" she said sharply. "Me and Earl are just as upset as you are. She's his mother, you know, and my mother-in-law."

He wanted to yell out, to ask *Is she my grandmother?* but he couldn't. All the strength had gone out of him. If the stranger was telling the truth, James didn't want to know.

The kitchen phone rang the next morning at eight o'clock. James got there in one leap from the table where he was eating his solitary bowl of Cap'n Crunch. Grandma. In the few seconds it took to lift the phone off the hook, he saw his wonderful, funny, wise old grandma in her black Sunday dress, dead and laid out in Thorogood's Funeral Parlor.

"Yeah?" he said all out of breath.

"James?" It was Will Short.

"What d'you want?"

"Hey, don't get mad. I'm just calling to ask if you heard the news."

What news? How could Will Short know about what was news in his life?

"No school today. Isn't that great?"

"No school?"

"Snow day! They said so on the radio. I heard it."

James looked out the window. "They ain't hardly enough snow to wet the soles of your shoes."

"Well, down here they don't know how to manage with snow. They're not used to driving in it."

"Awright," said James. "See you."

"Wait. You want to come over and work on your book report or something?"

"No."

"I could come over there."

"No!"

"I'm just trying to help you," Will said primly. "You can't do a picture book this time, you know." Will Short's feelings were not as neatly pressed as his pants.

"I'm sorry. I don't feel so good." It wasn't really a lie. He felt rotten with all the crush of the past two days. "I think I'll just go back to bed."

Will Short mumbled something and hung up. James was so relieved, he hardly noticed the disappointment in Will's voice. No Mr. Dolman. No stranger lurking about. James could stay home, close to the telephone. He went back into his room and lay down on top of the covers, staring at the ceiling.

He should never have left her. The work was too much. Strong as she pretended to be, she was too old to do everything alone. He saw her plowing behind Jennings' mule—which she rented for a few days every spring—her gray hair loose from the knot, blowing about her face. He was going to buy her one of those little ride-on tractors that mowed and plowed and did just about anything. As soon as he got some money. It was the first thing he was going to buy her. All she had to do was get well for him. *C'mon, Grandma,* he begged, *get well.* Was it her heart? Her lungs? She did smoke too much.

Some mysterious cancer eating away at her insides? He'd been too scared last night to question Keri Su—too angry.

The stranger stretched out a hand and smiled that hard, tobacco-stained smile at him. I'm your real daddy. Oh, God, say it ain't so. Say he's some crazy. He conjured up a vision of Jerry Lee to drive the stranger from his head. But the man was taller and kept shoving little Jerry Lee aside.

He slid under the covers with all his clothes on and pulled the quilt high over his head to shut out the sight. Oh, Jerry Lee, come back. I can't get through this all by myself.

There were voices in the kitchen. Keri Su and Earl were up. He put the covers down. They were whispering and gig-gling—so as not to wake him. But no, they didn't know he was here. They thought, didn't they, that he had gone to school an hour ago? He flung the covers off his body and lay still as a dead man on a slab.

"Quit it," she was saying. "I mean it, Earl." Then she giggled some more.

James jumped off the mattress and banged about his room, making as much noise as he could. The whispering and gig-gling stopped abruptly. The kitchen radio blared on. James went to his door and put his ear against it. There were no sounds other than the radio. He opened the door and walked out. They were sitting at the table across from each other. Keri Su's back was to the door.

She turned, her eyes wide in mock surprise. Earl kept his on his coffee cup. "What are you doing here, sugar?" she asked, glancing at the clock. "Ain't you supposed to be at school?"

James cleared his throat. "Snow day," he said. "Ain't that a joke?" He tried not to look at either one of them as he went to the refrigerator and got out the milk.

"Don't you need more than that for breakfast?" Keri Su was all solicitous.

"I ate early. When I thought I had to go to school."

"Oh." He saw her eyes cut across the table at Earl. "Then you went back to bed."

"Yeah," he said, studying a speck floating on top of his milk. "I went back to sleep." He could almost feel the heaviness in the room fall away.

"Well," said Keri Su, cheerfully. "How about a toastie-pop or something?" She started up from her chair to prove her willingness to serve him.

"No," he said. "Thank ya." He sat down at the head of the table with his milk and proceeded to fish out the speck.

"So," she said, even more brightly, "you got the whole day free, huh? Well." She tossed her hair. Earl glanced up quickly and then back down at his coffee. The three of them sat there, careful not to look at one another, at least not when they thought the others were looking. James's stomach was hard as week-old light bread. He needed to say something so they wouldn't think he'd heard them. He didn't want them to think he'd heard anything funny. Besides, what had he heard? Whispering and giggling. He hadn't really heard anything, now, had he?

"Did Jerry Lee call again?" He asked knowing full well that if the phone had rung last night, he would have been the first to get to it. "I slept so sound."

"No," said Keri Su. "Not after he called at noontime." She looked at Earl for just a flash before turning toward him. "He said not to worry. Now, I know that's easy to say, sugar, but it's really just tests, that's all."

"Tests for what?" His voice sounded squeaky even to him.

"Well, I'm not rightly sure. Heart or something."

"She had a heart attack." His own heart clamped down against his chest.

"No." Earl cleared his throat. "Not attack. More like a irregularity."

"What's a ee-regularity?"

"Oh, sugar, it just means that it don't beat exactly regular." Keri Su was helping Earl out. "Happens in old people all the time, don't it, Earl?"

"All the time," Earl agreed.

"They wouldn't have even put her in the hospital, Jerry Lee said, 'cept she had so far to go to the doctor's." Keri Su reached toward him to prink his hair. James leaned back out of her way.

"I should have stayed with her," he said. "I never should have left her."

"Well, how was you to know?" He didn't like Earl being nice. It wasn't like Earl to sound so understanding. "None of us knowed. She's always making out like she's Wonder Woman of West Virginia."

Keri Su giggled, a quick nervous sound that stopped dead when James looked at her. He got up and dumped the still full glass of milk into the sink. "Can we drive up there?" he asked, his back to the table.

"She's fine, sugar. She ain't near death. She ain't even really sick."

"I want to see her."

"Well, sure, sugar, that's natural. But you're like to scare her into a heart attack if you go rushing up there like you think she's in mortal danger or something. Right, Earl?"

"Jerry Lee said not to come," Earl said. "I asked him, should I come, and he said, no, it might just upset her."

"It wouldn't upset her to see me."

"Now, sugar, you know she'd be upset if she thought you was missing school."

"How 'bout Friday after school?"

"You know we got the show," Earl said.

"Even if your mother is in the hospital?"

Earl slammed his coffee cup to the table. "She's just in for tests! She'll be out two, three days. I swear, boy, you're getting all het up for nothin'."

"Come on, Earl, he's just a kid worried about his grandma."

"And I ain't worried? Is that it? You think I don't care what happens to her?" He was yelling at Keri Su in his usual way. "It don't matter that she always favored *him*. That don't matter to a kid. You still love her. You still care."

"Shh," said Keri Su. "Of course you do. Nobody thinks you don't love her, Earl." She reached over with her paper napkin and wiped up the coffee Earl had sloshed on the table. "We just upset. That's all. We just got to calm ourselves down." She got up from the table. "First thing, I best call Wallace and get us some more backup for Friday night in case Grandpa and Jerry Lee don't make it back. Then"—she patted James on the shoulder—"long as you're home, we better start rehearsing. Lots to do," she said, scooping up the dishes as though it were she, not Jerry Lee, who was accustomed to doing housework, to keeping everything going. She dumped the dishes in the sink and turned on the water. "Lots to do."

It was weird rehearsing with just Keri Su and Earl. In the first place they wanted to do a different kind of music—what Grandma would call Nashville honky-tonk—the kind a lot of the big country stars were doing these days. All the songs had spangles on them, making a hard, flashy sound. James played backup, but he knew what Keri Su and Earl were hearing in their heads was a steel guitar and lots of amplified, electronic instruments. A simple six-string guitar played with the kind of licks Grandma and Jerry Lee had taught him didn't match their style.

He could tell they were trying super hard not to lose patience with him, but that just made matters worse. He was used to Earl yelling and complaining. Today Earl was coaxing him and petting him like he was some kind of expensive but slightly stupid possum hound.

"Well, I tell you what," Keri Su said. It was about nine in the evening, and it had been a long and wearing day. James was sweating from frustration as much as exhaustion. "I tell you what. Why don't you forget backup this week? We'll get Wallace to fill in with a couple of boys from over to the club for the songs that Earl and me are doing. Then when you do your lead number, you can play for that."

They hadn't talked about any lead number for him. He had just about decided that they were going to squeeze him off the show altogether. "Awright," he said dully. He didn't much care anymore. Last Friday night, when he'd been drunk with the joy of music, seemed like a scene from another lifetime.

She leaned close to him and smiled warmly. "What would you like to do this week? Somethin' special?" James turned away, then quickly looked back and tried to smile.

"Oh, I dunno," he said. "I ain't got much heart for it, I reckon. Grandma sick and all."

"Bless you, sugar," she said. Why was she acting so motherly all of a sudden, just when he had to get himself unwound from her so he wouldn't get broken to pieces?

"I dunno what to sing."

"Well, sing something special for your grandma, then."

"She won't hear me."

"Sure she will," said Earl. "They got nineteen-inch TVs in ever' room of that hospital." Then he seemed to remember that they'd promised James she'd soon be out of the hospital, so he added, " 'Course, she'll more likely be watching from home by then. With your grandpa and your daddy." Earl smiled, showing all of his bright, straight teeth. It gave James the willies.

"I can't think tonight," he said. "Lemme sleep on it."

"Sure, sugar. You do that."

"Can I call Jerry Lee tonight?"

"Whyn't you just do that right this minute?" she said. "Make you feel better."

His fingers shook so, he had to hang up and redial three times before he could get through the whole number without a mistake. It began to ring. Once. Twice. Suppose nobody answered? He didn't believe he could stand it if no one answered. But before it had finished ringing five times, Jerry Lee was on the other end.

"Daddy?" was about all he could get out before he started crying. He felt as though he had been doing nothing but boo-hooing or trying not to boo-hoo since Sunday evening. He was sick of it. He hated himself for being such a baby, but he couldn't seem to help it.

"Hey, little buddy. It's all right. Doctor thinks she's gonna be fine. She just has to take it easy for a while. Hey . . . Hey . . . Ever'thing's fine. I promise. I wouldn't lie to you."

The more Jerry Lee tried to comfort, the harder James sobbed.

"Hey, boy, I'm not kidding you. She's having the time of her life. She hasn't missed a single one of her soaps. Doctor

wanted her to go down for a X ray at three thirty, and she told
him he'd have to wait 'til *General Hospital* got through. How
'bout that?"

James gave a barky laugh. "Sounds like herself, all right."

"She is. I promise you. Only reason she didn't call on
Saturday was she was afraid we'd worry."

"Hmmmph. Didn't she think we'd worry if we called her
and there wasn't any answer?"

"I told her that, but she said how was she to know after
she'd just talked to us on Friday that we'd be calling Sunday
for a biscuit recipe? She really got on me for that, boy. Us not
knowing how much soda to put in the biscuits. And you do
have to use lard—if you want 'em to taste like hers, you do.
'Lard the size of a egg,' she says. I said, 'Momma, eggs come
in different sizes, pullet to goose'—and she just laughs. 'A
regular size egg,' she says. 'James'll know,' she says."

"I wanna come up, but Keri Su says they can't bring me."

"No. Y'all got the shows. 'Sides I may be back myself by
Sunday."

"You gotta stay. Who'll take care of her?"

"Well," Jerry Lee said. "Daddy wants to be the one."

"Grandpa? He can't even cook as good as us."

"She can tell him what to do. It means a lot to him." James
could hear the pride in Jerry Lee's voice. Jerry Lee liked
having his daddy want to take care of his momma. James liked
it, too. "I miss you, Daddy," he said shyly. "I can't hardly wait
'til you get here."

"I miss you too, old buddy. You work hard on your schoolwork and sing pretty. I'll be there before you know it."

He hung up just as Keri Su came into the kitchen. "Oh,"
he said, "did you want to talk to Jerry Lee?"

"Well, sure. But it don't matter. Ever'thing okay?"

"Yeah. Jerry Lee says Grandma ain't missed one of her soaps yet."

Keri Su laughed. "I just bet."

"Jerry Lee says he may be back by this Sunday."

"Oh?" Keri Su cocked her head. "Good." James tried to read her face, but it was closed up.

"Grandpa's gonna stay and take care of her."

"You're joking." She yelled toward the living room. "Hear that, Earl? The old man's gonna stay and look after your momma."

"Well, I never." Earl came into the kitchen. His face, too, was closed. "Jerry Lee?"

With her fingernail, Keri Su was scratching up a bit of sticky from the oilcloth on the kitchen table. "He's coming right back. Maybe this weekend."

"I see. Well."

"You got homework, sugar?"

Homework. He'd completely forgotten. He had to have a book report done by tomorrow. And he didn't even have a book. He'd meant to get one Friday, but with all the excitement about the new song, he'd forgotten. Then Monday— But he didn't want to think about Monday.

"I forgot," he said and rushed into the living room. In the tiny case were mostly magazines—*Country Music* and *True Confessions,* a King James Bible—but you couldn't read the Bible all in one night, and three or four of Keri Su's paperbacks. He chose the thinnest one. The picture on the cover looked a little like Dolly Parton in fancy dress, but when he read the first page, it sounded as though it were all about history, so Mr. Dolman was sure to be impressed. Besides, it wasn't any little skinny kid's book with pictures on every page. It was three hundred eighty-four small print pages with no pictures at all.

It took him most of the night. He got through it—skimming from time to time, to be sure—but he read practically the whole thing. At 6:30 A.M. he wrote his report, careful to follow exactly the pattern on Mr. Dolman's ditto sheet and to count the words to make sure it was long enough. After all his work, he didn't want to give Mr. Dolman any excuse to fuss.

13

James could hardly keep his eyes open in school. He may have even fallen asleep, because later he remembered a dream about a cuff link that revealed his true identity, but he pushed the dream aside.

Keri Su liked to tell about the fan who dressed up like a delivery boy so he could bring her the one dozen long-stemmed roses himself. Earl always muttered that this had happened to Loretta Lynn, not Keri Su, but the point was the same. Fans did peculiar things to get attention. No matter what the man in Anna's Chicken House might say, he could not be James's father. The man was tall, nearly six feet, while James was a scrawny runt just like Jerry Lee. James had hazel eyes and the man had real dark, almost black ones. When James got that figured out, he felt as if the burden of his heart had rolled away. He was so glad he hadn't said anything to anyone about the guy. Jerry Lee would have been worried to death, and he had enough on his mind right now without having to fret over James.

"Johnson!"

James jumped, his knees blamming the desk. Mr. Dolman was standing over him waving some papers under James's nose. "Is this another one of your jokes?"

"No sir. That's my book report." He was confused. If there were any two things in the whole world Mr. Dolman was crazy for, they were history and patriotism. *Follow The Wild Wind* had more of both than a dead possum has maggots. "You said last time not to do any more skinny books with lots of pictures, so . . ."

Mr. Dolman rolled his eyes at the ceiling. "What have I ever done to deserve this?" he cried.

There was tittering, nervous tittering, as the class never knew if Mr. Dolman meant them to laugh or not. Still, to James's ears, it sounded as though everyone were confirming Mr. Dolman's scorn. The jerks. How many of them had read a three hundred eighty-four page book, full of big words and not a single picture, all in one night?

"I seem to have to keep doing this with you, Johnson."

James waited, staring at the middle finger on his picking hand. The dirt just seemed to congregate under that nail. He tried digging it out with his left thumbnail, but it was too short to do much good.

"I'm going to share this report with the rest of the class as an example of how *not* to write a book report."

He'd followed the ditto form. Mr. Dolman couldn't say he hadn't followed the form. And he'd made it plenty long. He'd counted all the words. James's middle fingernail went to his teeth, but he realized in time and snatched it away. The teacher turned and, half-sitting on James's desk, began to read:

Title: Follow The Wild Wind

Author: Cybil Von Steinway

Illustrator: Nobody. This book did not have any pictures.

Number of pages: 384

Chief characters: (List at least four with brief descriptions of each.)

1. Marguerita Del Gloria—Spanish princess who was kidnapped at the age of three and raised like she was the daughter of a famous pirate.

2. Philippe de Rouche—famous French pirate who kidnapped Marguerita Del Gloria at the age of three and raised her like she was his own daughter.

3. Erin O'Brien—old Irish woman who was the nurse of Marguerita Del Gloria.

4. Lord Byron Hamilton—famous English nobleman who was disguised like a famous Spanish pirate named The Dark One.

Summary of plot: The famous French pirate named Philippe de Rouche kidnapped the Spanish princess, Marguerita Del Gloria, when she was three years old and raised her like she was his own daughter. He also kidnapped a old Irish woman, named Erin O'Brien, to be the nurse for his daughter, who wasn't really his daughter.

Philippe de Rouche was a pirate, but he was a French pirate, so he wanted to sink all the Spanish ships and all the English ships, so the seas will belong to the king of France alone. He is very patriotic. He hates, more than the Devil himself, this mysterious dark-haired pirate of the northern seas, known only as The Dark One. He does not know that The Dark One is really the famous English nobleman, Lord Byron Hamilton, who is really not a Spanish pirate. He is really a English spy. But nobody knows this because Lord Byron Hamilton is supposed to be dead.

While Lord Byron Hamilton was a Spanish pirate, he captured Philippe de Rouche's ship. The name of Philippe de Rouche's ship is called Fleur de Fury. Philippe de Rouche is not on the ship right then, but Marguerita Del Gloria is. So is her nurse. The big problem for Lord Byron Hamilton is that he falls powerfully, devastatingly, eternally in love at first passionate glance with Marguerita Del Gloria. But he pretends to hate her and has her locked in a cabin on his pirate ship. The name of the ship is called The Wild Wind. One of his men named Simon Labeste develops a mad, hungry, animal passion for the breathtakingly beautiful young creature, so The Dark One, who is really Lord Byron Hamilton, has to kill him. With a broken heart which he must keep secret from all the world, he puts Marguerita Del Gloria and Erin O'Brien off The Wild Wind in the dark of the night on the shores of France. He does not reveal his true identity, but he does vouchsafe to his secret beloved a cuff link bearing the coat of arms of the House of Hamilton. That's his farm in England.

A big war starts in France, and Philippe de Rouche is very patriotic, so he gets thrown in jail because he likes the king and some other people want to chop the king's head off. When Marguerita Del Gloria hears that her father—who isn't really her father, but she thinks he is—is in jail, she rushes off to Paris, France, in the company of her faithful nurse, Erin O'Brien. Both of them get put in the same jail with Philippe de Rouche. They are all desperate. Erin O'Brien tries to keep up their spirits with amusing Irish tales, but it don't work. They must face Madame Guillotine, who is the guy who chops off everyone's head.

One fatal night, a wretched guard tries to have his way with Marguerita Del Gloria. Philippe de Rouche, gallantly, with no thought for his own safety, dispatches the wretched guard with his own hands, but gets killed himself. With his dying breaths, he tells Marguerita Del Gloria the secret of her past. The word comes to Lord Byron Hamilton concerning the dreadful fate of his beloved, and he hastens to Paris. It's kind of hard to explain how he busted into the jail, but anyhow he does. He snatched her up in his arms like a trembling flower of the woodland and carried her on horseback to The Wild Wind, revealing all, but she already knew because Erin O'Brien wasn't really a old Irish woman, she was really Lord Byron Hamilton's mother who had been kidnapped by the real Dark One when Lord Byron Hamilton was a baby. She could tell about everything by that cuff link, and she produced—to the amazement of all—the matching link, proving her true identity. And they all go off to America to make a new life in the new world of Promise.

So it was a real happy ending. Except for Philippe de Rouche, the famous French pirate, who got dead and the king who got his head chopped off. I guess they weren't too happy.

What I liked best about this book: I liked how everybody was real patriotic, and it was all about history.

What I did not like about this book: This was a real good book, except it would be better if it was shorter.

Mr. Dolman looked out at the class. They weren't giggling. They were absolutely still. He stood up from James's desk and turned all the way around, staring at everyone in the class with his eyebrow raised. *Well?* he seemed to ask the silence.

"Myself—I give it uh A." Every head turned toward Eleazer Jones. His long body was slouched down under the desk that was too small for him, his brown eyes half closed. "Ain't nobody else in this class ever read no three hundred eighty-four page book in their life," he said. The only eyes not on the King were James's. He was watching Mr. Dolman. The man wasn't moving a twitch, but James had the feeling that behind that stare was a regular Madame Guillotine, chopping off Eleazer Jones's proud black head right at the collar. Then, abruptly, in six giant steps, the teacher was at the motto board writing down *Eleazer Jones* and underneath that, *James Johnson.*

There were various crimes committed by the King's guard of honor, but mysteriously, Mr. Dolman never saw them. Or if he did, he pretended to ignore them. For when the bell rang, only James and Eleazer Jones had been sentenced to detention.

James lay his head down on his desk. If he couldn't go to sleep, he might die—right there in Mr. Dolman's sixth-grade classroom. His heart felt enormous and pressed painfully against his chest. See! He had to be a real Johnson, he even had heart trouble, just like Grandma. That was the kind of thing you inherited. Anybody knew that.

"Johnson."

His head flew up and snapped back as if he were riding a roller coaster.

"Is something the matter, Johnson?"

"No sir." He could hear Eleazer Jones elaborately clearing his throat. Mr. Dolman didn't look in the King's direction.

At three forty-four Mr. Dolman stood up. "Johnson," he said, "I've asked Mrs. Sheldon to choose a suitable book for you to report on. Please stop by the library on your way out of school and pick it up." He glanced at them both. "In the future, Mr. Eleazer Jones, please remember that it is I who gives grades in this class. Dismissed."

James was so tired he could hardly stand up, but he forced himself to his feet and out the door. Eleazer Jones was waiting just out of sight. "You awright?" he asked.

"Just tired," James said.

The tall boy fell in step beside him. "Walk you to the liberry," he said. They walked side by side without talking until they were nearly at the library door. Then James heard the King say in a shy, most unkingly manner, "I caught you on TV Fri' night."

"Huh?" James was awake now.

"Don't fun me. I know it was you."

"You didn't tell nobody?"

He grinned. "You think I brag to ever'body I watch honky music? I got me a rep, man."

"I don't want nobody to know."

"You oughta be proud, you some kinda celebrity."

"You think people would like me better if they knew? Really?"

The King cocked his head. "Naw. They be jealous."

"So don't tell. Please."

The tall boy nodded. "That man hanging round the fence. Do he know?"

"Yeah."

"You go on in, get your book. I wait for you and walk you a ways."

"That's okay, really."

"Listen, man. Some crazy dudes all time trying to kidnap celebrities. Like your book report say."

A chill went through James.

"Go 'head on. Get your book. Nobody's gonna hassle you with Eleazer Jones around."

14

They fought again about what James was going to sing on the show. Keri Su had told him he could choose, but then when he chose "Poor Wayfaring Stranger," she hit the ceiling. Well, maybe not the ceiling. She did it all in her sweet-sugar Keri Su voice, but she made it Olive-clear that she didn't want any old-time country or gospel on Friday's show. "How 'bout 'My Momma Is a Angel Up in Heaven'?"

James hung his head so she couldn't see that he was working his mouth and clenching his teeth. She'd told him he could do anything he wanted.

She pinched his chin with her thumb and index finger and lifted his face up. "Come on, sugar. Don't be a baby. This is gonna be one of them real fun shows."

"I think I'll get me some Pepsi," he muttered, moving his chin out of her grasp.

"He don't have to sing nothing if he don't want to." Earl

was standing in the kitchen doorway, leaning against the door-jamb.

So that was it. They were just going to squeeze him out. He opened the refrigerator door. For a minute he couldn't remember why. Then he saw the large half-full bottle and some cans of Pepsi. He chose a can and, in his head, dared her to object. He yanked the tab back and took a sip. "Okay," he said. "I'll sing whatever you think fits."

They settled on "My Momma Is a Angel Up in Heaven," doing it with lots of electronic backup and faster than James was used to, but he'd manage. He tried to think of it as a kind of present for Grandma. He could stand Earl and Keri Su pushing him around if it meant Grandma could have Jerry Lee there with her when she needed him.

The rehearsal Thursday night went all right. He was only doing the one song, so he spent a lot of time in the dressing room reading his *suitable* book and writing his *suitable* book report. At first he had been insulted by what Mrs. Sheldon thought was suitable for an eleven-year-old boy in the sixth grade who could read a three hundred eighty-four page book —well, almost all the pages—in one night. The book she had given him was far skinnier, with pictures and large print. And it was all about a girl. In the first grade. The longer he read, however, the more he loved the crazy little kid. Boy, would Ramona have ever run Mr. Dolman wild.

Friday he watched the early part of the show from the control booth. He didn't want Earl and Keri Su to fall on their faces, exactly, but it hurt a little that they sounded so smooth, so much of a pair. You'd have thought they never passed a cross word between them, that they'd been born in harmony. He'd heard them sing together plenty of times before, but never so sure, so at ease. Not his style, but good. Real good.

He wandered back past the rear exit toward the dressing room. Gus was there talking to someone who was outside wanting, it seemed, to be let in. "I don't care if you're Whistler's mother," Gus was saying, "you don't come backstage." Another crazy. James hurried to the dressing room and shut the door. He started across to the easy chair, then went back and pushed the little metal button that caused the door to lock. When he did sit down, it was on the edge of the chair, and his heart was going as though he'd just run a mile. He longed for Jerry Lee, for Eleazer Jones. He reread two chapters of Ramona to calm himself down. *Blam blam blam.* He jumped right out of the chair.

"Jimmy Jo?" It was Gus.

"Yessir," he said and quickly unlocked the door.

"There's a call for you."

Grandma. Oh, God, please let her be all right. He followed Gus to the phone in the stage manager's office. It looked more like a janitor's closet, but everyone called it an office to keep on Gus's good side.

"Jerry Lee?" James called into the receiver.

"This is your real daddy, son."

James slammed down the phone. Gus was looking at him peculiarly. "Some crazy fan," James explained.

"That the one who says he's your real father?"

How did Gus know?

"Don't give it a thought, kid." Gus went right on as if James had answered. "Remember Dottie Pierce? Was a regular here before y'all come?"

James nodded. He'd seen her on the show lots of times.

"I counted," said Gus. "I swear. If I had believed the calls, letters, telegrams, and bums that showed up, that woman would have had thirty-seven secret marriages."

"Really?"

"I swear. The world is full of crazies wanting to take a bite out of somebody else's success." He reached into a tiny ice box and pulled out two orange Nehis, yanking the caps off on a wall opener. He handed a bottle to James. "Picking on a kid, though. That's got to be the bottom."

James took a big swig of the Nehi, not because he was wanting a drink just then, but because he wanted to thank Gus. "I never believed the guy one minute."

"Good for you. First few times Dottie Pierce almost did. She'd say to me, 'Gus, maybe I was drunk and didn't know what I was doing or something.' " Gus shook his head. "I had to remind her that the strongest thing she ever put to her mouth was sugar-free Dr. Pepper. She was so shook up."

James laughed. "I never even told nobody," he said. "I knew it was just silly."

"Where this guy bother you before?"

"He come around school some."

"I think you better tell somebody if he's hanging around."

Of course Gus was right. "Yeah," James said. "I will. Soon's my grandma's better. I don't want to worry 'em about anything stupid like this right now."

There was a banging on the office door. "Gus! Gus!" It was Wallace. "You know where the kid is?"

His entrance. James shoved the Nehi back into Gus's hand. He ran his hands over his head and dashed out, stopping only to fetch Chester from the dressing room. He was almost late, but he made up for it. He had never sung on the stage with such a light heart.

"Oh, my momma is a angel up in heaven. . . ." It wasn't a sad song that night. It was full of fun. James could see the three of them watching on the big color screen in Grandma's hospital room. He sang right at the camera to make sure they'd know he was singing for them. He was so full of love that it just oozed out his pores, making everyone in the audience think he was in love with them.

With no Jerry Lee to stand over him to watch out, James was mobbed after the show. Twice he was knocked off his feet by people shoving up, trying to stick autograph books under his nose—but he didn't fall down, just against some other fan.

At last the crowd began to thin, and he could hear Wallace and Gus clearing people out. He began to stumble toward the dressing room. A few voices called after him, but the tiredness was beginning to seep into his bones, so he pretended not to hear. When he pushed open the dressing-room door, Earl and Keri Su were sitting there in their street clothes. It took him a minute to realize what that meant—how long they must have been waiting.

"Well," said Keri Su as he walked in. "Finally."

"I'm sorry," he said. "I'll be ready to go in a minute."

"Get me some coffee, will you, Earl?"

Earl got up without a word and went out.

James unbuttoned the top several buttons of his Western shirt and then began to pull it over his head. "I sweated a lot tonight. I 'speck this needs washing." She didn't answer. He turned his back on her, pulled off his boots and then his jeans, trying to act as though it didn't bother him that she was sitting there watching him change. "You and Earl sounded good as Dolly Parton and Kenny Rogers," he said.

"Humph."

He waited a second for her to go on, but she didn't. He put on his old dungarees and T-shirt and a sweater that had a little of the smell of the farm still in it. Pulling it over his head made him feel close to Grandma for just a second. He sat down and put on his sneakers, still waiting. The room was full of all the words she wasn't speaking. "How 'bout my number?" he asked. "Was it awright?"

"I don't know where you think you come off, trying to upstage your own mother," she said.

"What?"

"Oh, come on, boy. Don't give me that sweet baby act. I'm not a fan."

He knew he was sitting there with his mouth open, staring at her, but he couldn't help it. It was as though she had turned into Mr. Dolman right before his eyes.

Wallace came through the door followed by Earl carrying two coffees in Styrofoam cups. He handed one to Keri Su and looked around at James. James jumped up off the chair and knelt to finish tying his shoestrings. Wallace hollered out the door, "Gus, bring me a chair, hear?"

Gus came with the chair, then left, closing the door carefully behind him. Wallace sat down and motioned Earl to take the chair James had emptied. "Well," said Wallace, "I think we learned one thing here tonight."

James sat on the floor, hugging his knees to his body and scratching his chin on the rough denim. Keri Su took a long sip from her cup. James could hear Earl clearing his throat. Finally Wallace leaned back on the legs of his chair. "I think we learned tonight the kind of music *Countrytime* fans go for." He looked from face to face like a preacher at a revival meeting. Both Earl and Keri Su were staring into their cups, not looking back. "Now, that slick, new Nashville sound is awright for a club," Wallace continued, "but it don't go over so well here on *Countrytime,* now do it?"

No one answered, but that didn't matter. He went right

on. "Now I'm not sorry I let y'all talk me into this kinda show. Not at all. If we hadn't give it a real try, we'd never be quite sure what it was the fans wanted. But now we know, don't we? I'm just sorry Eddie Switten wasn't here tonight. I think it would have been good for him, as your manager, to hear and see it all just like we did."

James was not clear as to what all of them had seen and heard, but he wasn't about to ask any questions.

"Jerry Lee coming back soon?" Wallace asked. Keri Su nodded. "Good. I want him to have more say in the numbers. What you're singing. He's got a good feel for what our fans like." Wallace brought the chair legs banging down and leaned over toward James. "And I want this young feller featured. Folks can't hardly get enough of him." He slapped his thick thighs with both hands. "Okay. That's it. See you next week." He got up and went out.

James's gut felt like a bunch of fishing lines had tangled up inside. Wallace wasn't being fair. Even if he didn't like their style, he had to know Keri Su and Earl were good. And it was Keri Su decided she wanted James to do "My Momma Is a Angel" that went over so great. Wallace ought to give them a chance—let the fans get used to the sound. Still, the idea of being featured—

"Hurry up, boy," Keri Su said. Neither of them spoke to him again that night.

He got up on Saturday with the feeling that he had to tiptoe around them. The bright, overcharged atmosphere of the week had given way to a brown haze. They didn't come downstairs until nearly eleven, and then they both just sat hunched over the table drinking leftover coffee.

"You want me to fix you some breakfast?" James asked. No answer. "New pot of coffee?" No answer. He made the coffee anyway. They were sure to want it sooner or later, and he needed something to do. When it smelled perked, he poured some into their cups without even asking if they wanted more. Then he made some toast, buttered and spread jelly on it, and gave each of them a piece on their saucers. They didn't thank him, but they ate the toast, so it was some satisfaction to him. He racked his brain for something else he could do to show them he was sorry about last night. Nothing came to mind, so he just leaned against the kitchen counter and tried to pretend he was not watching them.

"You know what?" Earl was speaking to Keri Su.

"What?" she asked without looking at him.

"We ought to make that demo."

"What good would that do?" she asked. "You can't just make a tape. You got to push it."

"Well—"

"Ain't no way to push a demo 'less you take it to Nashville."

"Well—"

"You can't mean that. What would ever'one say?"

"Jerry Lee won't say nothing. No need for Grandma and Grandpa to know."

"You're out of your mind, Earl Johnson."

"No." He was looking straight at Keri Su now. "We drive down to Nashville first thing Monday. Make the demo there, where they'll do it right, then push it ourselves 'til we have to get back for rehearsal Thursday night."

"That ain't enough time to push a aspirin."

"If nothing happens, we go back the next week, or the week after Christmas when we ain't got no show." Earl leaned across the table toward her, as though he forgot James was there. "Like Wallace says, *Countrytime* ain't ready for our sound. Nashville is."

"But what about . . . ?" Keri Su jerked her head in the direction of James.

"Look," said Earl, "the boy don't want to hold us back. We didn't hold him back. We give him his big chance."

"This ain't the time to talk about demos," she said. "What'll Jerry Lee say, us looking like we're trying to cut out?"

"Olive, you know good and well Jerry Lee wants what's best for you. He's done nothing but encourage you since the day he met you."

"Yeah," she said, running her index finger around the rim of her cup. "Well, I feel better talking to him before we make any big decisions."

"Lord have mercy. I'm a grown man, Olive. I know what's good just as well as he does."

"I ain't married to you, Earl." She got up. "I gotta take my bath," she said. "Can you get the dishes, Jimmy Jo?"

He nodded, but he stayed frozen against the counter until Earl, too, left the kitchen.

Jerry Lee got home Sunday about five. Keri Su and Earl had already left for the club. James was watching a TV movie while he ate his supper of peanut butter and apple jelly sandwich. Keri Su didn't like him to drink Pepsi for meals, but she wasn't there, so he'd poured himself a huge glass with almost no ice. It would last through to the next commercial. The movie was a Western, which meant he didn't hear the wagon pull up for the shooting and screaming on the screen.

He did hear the doorknob rattle, and for a minute, he stopped breathing until he heard the key and Jerry Lee's voice calling "Hello" as he opened the door. James jumped up, sloshing Pepsi all over everything, and by the time he'd put the glass down and wiped his hand on his dungarees, Jerry Lee was hugging him. "Boy, seems like a hundred years. How you doing, old buddy?"

"Better," said James, "now you're here."

They talked until it was well past time for James to be in bed. James was hungry to know everything. Grandma was home, mad as a caged tomcat because the doctor had told her to quit smoking. Grandpa was clucking over her. "I don't think he's coming back," Jerry Lee said.

Something cold clanked inside James's brain. "How come?"

"Well, I don't know. I think it took something out of him for the club to say he was too old-fashioned. He heard it 'too old.' "

"He's good."

"Yeah, he's good for the kind of music the Family's been doing all these years, but . . ."

"Well, it's nice for Grandma."

Jerry Lee patted James's knee. "Yeah. She's grinning like a high school girl finally got herself a steady." He got up. "So? Ever'thing go all right this week?"

James nodded. He couldn't bring himself to tell Jerry Lee about the crazy stranger, and he wasn't going to be the one to tell Jerry Lee about the demo. He was asleep when Keri Su and Earl came in, so he never heard that discussion. All he knew was that by the time he got home from school on Monday, the two of them were on the way to Nashville. From the best James could make out, Jerry Lee had not only told them to go ahead, he'd put up most of the money to make the demo —since Earl had sunk all his savings in his car and Keri Su had spent all her earnings on new clothes. As she said, she had to look good both for TV and the club.

They made biscuits Monday night to comfort themselves. This time they got them right, red-eye gravy and all. "And tomorrow," Jerry Lee said, "I'm fixing us a pot of beans. You want string or pinto?"

"Pinto," James said, and he tried to act as though it were really exciting to look forward to beans and fatback.

There was a call from Eddie Switten that night. He'd lined up a Saturday show in Hampton. They were to replace the Kitler Brothers, who were a warm-up act for Jay Bliss. According to Eddie, it was a golden opportunity. He was talking so excitedly that James, sitting at the kitchen table, could hear the peaking and rumbling of his voice.

"Well, I don't know, Eddie," Jerry Lee was saying. "Keri Su and Earl ain't here right now. . . . Well, they're out of town. . . . Well, to tell the truth, they went down to Nashville. . . ."

"Nashville!" That was loud enough for James to hear.

"They got this idea they want to make a demo. . . . No, just the two of them. You know they been singing in that club over to the Beach."

From the racket at the other end, it was clear not only that Eddie didn't know about the club dates, but that he was furious with Keri Su and Earl for rushing off to Nashville without his permission. Jerry Lee held the receiver away from his ear while Eddie ranted. Finally, he broke in, "Awright, Eddie. Tell 'em we'll be there on Saturday. I'll work it out." He hung up before Eddie had time to yell at him any more.

"He sounds real mad."

"Yeah," Jerry Lee said. "Mostly 'cause he's afraid he'll miss his cut. He's flying down there tomorrow after them." Jerry Lee shrugged and gave a half laugh. "He don't let the big ones wriggle off the hook."

Why didn't Jerry Lee get mad and do something about it like Eddie? James watched the little man steaming around like a canning kettle. Why didn't he just blow his top? As for

James, he went around for four days cussing things: the stuck zipper on his best jeans, his lost glove, his math homework—even, on Thursday, the pencil sharpener at school that chewed three inches off his new Ticonderoga yellow No. 2. He got detention for that one. Eleazer Jones's name was already on the board, so James was perversely pleased. He hadn't had three words with the King since the day they'd walked home together. But, as usually happened, when Eleazer Jones's name went up, so, also, did five others.

At three forty-five the seven of them walked out of the building together. As soon as they hit the outside step, one of the King's court—a tiny, very black boy named Eugene—started dancing around in front of James, sticking his finger in James's face.

"You the one!" Eugene said. "I saw you. You the one!"

James looked at Eleazer Jones for a clue to Eugene's meaning.

"I saw you," Eugene repeated. "You the one on tee vee. You that li'l honky hillbilly with the git-tar, ain't you?"

James tried to walk past, but Eugene kept bouncing up and down right in his way. "Don't shake me, man. I saw you. Fri' night." Eugene plunked an imaginary guitar and began to sing, "Oh, my momma is uh anjul up in hayven. . . ."

The other boys' eyes were wide with delight. "You fooling, man. He really be on tee vee?" "You lying." "Go 'head on!"

James shook his head like poor Rosie trying to shake horseflies.

"Take off your glasses. I know it was you."

"Look like him." It was the deep, powerful voice of the King. "Look like him. That's all. Now ease up."

Eugene stopped dancing and moved aside. All the boys stood still and let James go past. James tried to thank Eleazer

Jones with his eyes. The King flicked acknowledgement under his half-closed lids.

At quarter to five Earl and Keri Su had still not returned. Jerry Lee and James drove glumly to the studio. "What you going to tell Wallace?" James asked when they were just a minute away.

Jerry Lee had his head cocked, watching the red light. "I reckon you and me will have to carry it," he said.

"Oh," James said, trying to keep from sounding happy. Forty-five minutes of singing with Jerry Lee. It would be just like Thanksgiving. Grandma would love it. But when they turned the corner into the studio parking lot, the blue Buick was sitting there.

There was no time to talk. Jerry Lee told everybody what to do when, and Keri Su and Earl could hardly fuss since Wallace had told them plain as day he wanted Jerry Lee in charge. Everything went smoothly until he said to James, "I want you to sing 'Broken Bird.' The fans been requesting a re-peat."

"Uh, Jerry Lee," Keri Su said quietly. "Could I talk to you a minute?"

"Go 'head."

"In the dressing room."

"You got something to say, Keri Su, say it."

She shook her head, and they went on with the rehearsal. Wallace had gotten an electric bass to replace Grandpa's old standing bass fiddle, so the sound was different from their usual, but certainly less honky-tonk than the week before. Wallace seemed pleased, at any rate, patting Jerry Lee on the back and laughing loud as a Baptist preacher at a church picnic.

"Wallace thought the show was shaping up good," James said to the side of Jerry Lee's head in the car going home.

"Um."

"That bass don't sound like Grandpa, do it? Wonder why Wallace got electric. He's always saying he likes the old sounds best."

No answer.

"Guess you was glad to see that Buick when we drove up."

A kind of snort while Jerry Lee shifted down at a light.

"Did I do awright?" He'd sung in three numbers, the most ever.

"Huh?" Jerry Lee watched the light change and started forward before saying, "Sure. You did fine. It's gonna be a good show." That was all.

At home James allowed Keri Su to kiss him good-night on the top of the head before he went to bed. He was glad when they all took their coffee into the living room. He could hear the rumble of their voices, but he fell asleep with the feeling that the rumbles had been tired, not angry sounds.

15

James was in the middle of singing "Poor Wayfaring Stranger" with Jerry Lee on Friday night when he looked out at the audience and realized that he was no longer seeing melons with hair. He still couldn't make out individual faces—he was too nearsighted for that—but he saw a sort of softness, he saw that they were people. Bunch of grandmas, he thought, a bunch of lonely grandmas wanting comfort.

When, at the end of the hour, Keri Su introduced him for the last time, he took the mike and smiled up at her and then smiled down at the audience. "I'm pleased so many of you like the song I sang for the very first time two weeks ago. It's got to be my very favorite song, and I'm proud to repeat it tonight"—and Jerry Lee hit the first lonesome chords of "Broken Bird." James sang it for Grandma and Grandpa watching together, but more and more he sang it for those faces out in front—all those lonely grandmas—his voice high and pure and full of a sweet sadness. It's a real mountain song, he thought, like the old, old ones that Grandma sometimes sings that no one knows where they came from because folks have been singing them for longer than anybody can remember.

They mobbed him after the show, but it was all right. Jerry Lee was close beside him, making sure he had air and room to write his name. It was easier now to write *Jimmy Jo*. He didn't put *Johnson*. *Johnson* belonged to James, and besides, folks got impatient when you spent too long writing your autograph. *Jimmy Jo* was all they wanted.

If Keri Su and Earl had something to report on their trip to Nashville, James hadn't heard it. They staggered off to bed as soon as they got home and didn't come down for breakfast until noon. As soon as they appeared, Jerry Lee started talking about the show Eddie Switten had lined up for them in Hampton that night. The Family was going to do only three numbers, and Jerry Lee wanted one of them to be gospel. "Nobody else is likely to do gospel, far as I can see," he said, "and a country show ain't right without gospel."

No one argued. When he suggested "Will the Circle Be Unbroken?" James was sure Earl would object. He'd heard Earl say once that the song had been written by an over-the-hill dinosaur. But Earl was acting like an assistant undertaker, all solemn and helpful.

"I'd say 'Broken Bird,' " Jerry Lee said to James, "but you just did that last night so beautiful, I kinda want to let it hang in the air awhile just like that." James couldn't fuss when his daddy put it that way, much as he craved to sing it again. "How 'bout you, Olive—Keri Su? You got something special you'd like to do?"

She shrugged. "Whatever."

"How 'bout 'Flowers of Crimson, Ring of Gold'?" It was a song he had written for her five years or so before.

"I ain't sung it in a coon age," she said.

"Then let's do it," he said. "Lead off with it. Then we'll have James sing 'Traveling Man' for a change of pace, and we'll end with all of us singing 'Will the Circle Be Unbroken?' " He looked around, but still no one objected, so he went on. "You'll have to do the lead in that one, James, since Grandpa's not here."

They were only one group in a string of warm-up acts, not even near the featured singer, a hotshot named Jay Bliss that James had heard on the radio but didn't much care for. Bliss was one of those slick ones—shiny like plastic and just as lifeless.

"Now when we go out there," Jerry Lee was saying, "the band is going to be feeling its way. After a phrase or two, they'll catch on, but we got to work hard at the beginning and pull them along 'til they get all the chords and beat. They're good, so don't let it worry you none. Just make sure you give them what they need to follow you easy, okay?"

James nodded, his mouth dry. What if he froze up?

"Now, this is a coliseum. That means big. You saw the outside, well, that means lots of people inside. But don't let that worry you overly. It's harder to sing to six people than it is to six thousand. I ain't fooling."

James kept wagging his head as though it weren't fastened on tight enough.

"Now, look, boy, I'm counting on you. I wouldn't't've brought you if I thought you couldn't do it."

"Yessir."

At least they all went out together. He stood close as he could to Jerry Lee while Keri Su introduced the Family. Then she turned to him and nodded. He felt stiffer than a dead snake. What did she want? It wasn't his turn to sing. It was hers. Then Jerry Lee was poking him and saying through his teeth. "Lead off. Lead off."

He fumbled on the frets until he found the chord, and then he started to play. He could almost feel the relief rolling off Keri Su's body as she eased into the lyrics, and then it was all right again. He was where he belonged—on a stage, picking and singing for a huge barn full of people who loved him. He knew they loved him. By the time he finished "Traveling Man," they were whooping and hollering, and at the end of "Will the Circle Be Unbroken?" they were on their feet stomping and clapping and singing along. It was as though six thousand people had become a family singing group.

The Family left right after. They wouldn't be needed again, and it would be easier to get out of the parking lot and back to Tidewater if they beat the crowd. James couldn't be sure from the backseat, but he thought he heard Jerry Lee humming up front. Sure enough, after they had pulled onto the freeway, Jerry Lee broke out into singing:

> Will the circle be unbroken
> By and by, Lord, by and by?

James leaned his chin up to his daddy's neck and added the high harmony. He loved the way Jerry Lee smelled—sweat and after-shave and hair oil and flannel shirt and heavy wool lumber jacket. James scratched his chin along the rough shoulder of the jacket. He felt deeply content, and he wasn't going to let the sight of Keri Su sitting up stiff on the front seat or Earl lounging against the corner of the rear door with his eyes shut—he wasn't going to let the two of them ruffle him. If Jerry Lee was happy enough to sing, so was he. He moved his cheek closer to Jerry Lee's and sang just for the two of them, hardly noticing when the car plunged down into the white-tiled tunnel.

James slept late on Sunday morning. When he finally got up and staggered out his door, Jerry Lee was sitting at the kitchen table reading the Sunday paper, which meant he'd already been up and out to the 7-Eleven. Jerry Lee never was much for lying in bed. "Morning," he said cheerfully as James staggered through in his underwear. He wished he'd put socks on. The linoleum was so cold his feet hurt.

On his way back from the bathroom, Jerry Lee stopped him. "Hey," he said, "listen to this."

"Can I put something on my feet? I'm freezing."

"Oh, sure." But he began reading anyhow, raising his voice so James could hear it from his room. " 'Last night, the singer said to be the hottest thing on the country-music circuit today, Jay Bliss, gave his fans in the Hampton Coliseum the cold shoulder. Maybe no one could live up to the billing this young man's been getting lately, but Bliss didn't even bother to try. . . .' "

James stood in the middle of his mattress pulling on his dungarees. Then he sat down on the edge to put on his sneakers and socks while Jerry Lee continued to read.

" 'But' "—Jerry Lee raised his voice even louder—" 'but the evening was not a total loss for those who came early enough for the warm-up performances. Substituting for the Kitler Brothers were the Johnson Family, current regulars on *WQVR–Countrytime.* Ten-year-old Jimmy Jo Johnson brought the huge crowd to their feet with an inspired rendition of the old A.P. Carter classic "Will the Circle Be Unbroken?" proving that the best presents come in little packages. For my money, Jay Bliss should take lessons in music, manners, and

146

charm from this pint-sized performer.'" Jerry Lee put the paper to his lap. "Well, old buddy, what do you think of that?"

James was standing in the doorway, his sneakers still untied. "I'm eleven," he said.

Jerry Lee grinned. "You sure are." And dropping the paper to the floor, he held out his arm. James came and sat on his lap. "Plus you ain't gonna stay pint-sized too much longer, either. Won't be long 'til I'm setting on your lap."

"What?"

Jerry Lee held up James's right hand in both of his own. "Look at these paws on you, boy. You got to grow up to them."

"No!" James jerked his hand back. "I'm gonna be scrawny like you. Ever'body says so."

Jerry Lee hugged him. "You don't wanna be scrawny like me, boy."

"Yes, I do. I always wanted to."

Jerry Lee laughed out loud. "That's the dumbest thing I ever heard. Don't you know it's the tall ones get all the girls?"

"I don't want no girls."

"Just wait."

"I wanna be just like you."

For a minute Jerry Lee rocked James in his arms, the way Grandma used to. Then, abruptly, he set him on his feet. "Okay. What do you want to eat? And don't think anything is too hard. Biscuits with red-eye gravy? Pancakes? Fried ham and eggs?"

When James chose pancakes, Jerry Lee snatched a box of Aunt Jemima out of the cabinet. "Presto!" he cried. Then he whipped out the oil, and an egg and milk from the refrigerator, and mixed it all with the grand gestures of a TV magician. "You know what I think we should do this Friday?" he asked as he was frying the batter.

"What?"

"I think we should do us a all-gospel show. It'll be nearly Christmas. Folks'll like it."

"I don't know about that." Earl came in, and after he had poured some coffee from the pot on the stove, he sat down. "Let's face it," he went on. "Gospel's about two things—death and sin. At Christmas people likes to think about something a little more cheerful."

"How 'bout 'Keep on the Sunny Side'?" James asked.

Earl gave a snort behind his coffee cup. "I mean something's been wrote in the last hundred years."

"Tell you what," Jerry Lee said, putting a plate of pancakes down in front of James. "At the end we'll do a medley of Christmas carols and get the studio audience to sing along."

Earl make another rude noise.

"What's the matter?" Jerry Lee demanded. "When that crowd joined in last night, it nearly took the roof off." He got the syrup from the cabinet and plunked it down on the table.

"Let me put it this way, big brother. It's not where I'm at right now."

"Where are you at, Earl?"

Earl grunted. "I dunno. I'm working on it."

They all stopped and listened to the sound of Keri Su on the stairs. She went directly to the stove and got coffee. They all watched as she sat down, propped her elbows on the oil-cloth, and began to sip, eyes nearly closed.

James watched her as he ate. She was terribly skinny. Where was she at right now? He had never known where Keri Su was at. Maybe Grandma was right. Maybe Keri Su herself didn't know. Twenty-five isn't very old. She'd been hardly older than he was now when she'd had him. There wasn't anybody like Grandma to take care of her when she was little. And then the flush of pure joy at the thought of going home next Saturday, of spending more than a week with Grandma, just washed Keri Su right out of his concern. Only a week to go.

James wasn't the only one who couldn't wait for the days to pass. Monday Mr. Dolman's classroom snapped, crackled, and popped with anticipation. Even Mr. Dolman seemed infected. No names appeared under the motto the entire day, and when the bell rang and a small whoop sounded, there was no bark of reprimand.

Eleazer Jones wrinkled his nose at James and mouthed something which James interpreted to mean that the King had seen the show again Friday night and had approved, but the tall boy was surrounded by his court and James had Will Short at his heels, so they didn't try to speak to each other.

Much to James's annoyance, Will didn't turn off at his own street but kept walking toward James's house. James wasn't listening, but every now and then he realized that Will was babbling on about Christmas and how his father might come from Buffalo to see him this year and was James going to be there and maybe they could go to the movies or something.

"No."

"No, what?"

"I thought you asked if I was gonna to be here. I ain't. I'm going to my grandma's."

Will Short's small, neat mouth widened slightly into a smirk. "The one that grows rocks?"

"Shuttup," said James.

"You were the one that said it," Will protested. "I didn't make it up."

But James wasn't paying Will any attention. There was a brown Plymouth parked in front of the house. Without a word, he left Will standing on the sidewalk and ran to his house. Company meant trouble as far as James could see.

16

There he is now," James heard Keri Su say to the visitor as he came through the door. "C'mon in here, sugar"—as though there were some way to come in the front door without coming on into the living room. Keri Su was perched on the far end of the couch. At the near end sat a young woman wearing a beige knit top and poofed-up slacks. A young man in jeans and sweatshirt was sitting on the straight chair. He was holding a camera.

"This is my son, Jimmy Jo," Keri Su said and gestured with her arm for him to come sit down beside her. "Now these folks are from the newspaper, and they just want to ask us a few questions." A flash flared, making him see white spots. "You can take off your jacket first." He sat down between the two women and took off his jacket, then he put it and his book bag on the floor by his feet. "Your glasses, too, sugar," his mother whispered. He obeyed, taking them off and holding them carefully on his lap.

"So," the woman said, leaning forward and smiling. She had a small tape recorder in her hand. "So. You're the young man who could give Jay Bliss singing lessons."

James looked around wildly. Where was Jerry Lee? All he got was another flash in the face.

"Don't mind Bob," the woman said. "He'll just take some pictures while we talk. We find they're more natural that way."

"Sure," Keri Su said. "We don't mind, do we, sugar?"

He sat up straight and still, blinking to rid himself of the spots.

"Now, how old are you?"

"He's just turned ten," Keri Su said quickly. He would have corrected her, except that his mouth wasn't working.

"And when did you first start singing?"

He tried to lick his lips, but his tongue was so dry it just scraped across.

"I swear, I think Jimmy Jo come out singing," Keri Su was saying. "None of us can remember a time when he wasn't singing. I guess when your momma's a singer, you just born with it. Right, sugar?" Why did she have to lie? She'd hardly heard him sing in her life before last summer.

"Well," the woman was saying, "the Johnsons are quite a singing family, too, aren't they?"

He thought he felt Keri Su stiffen beside him, even though her voice was smooth as a milk shake. "Yes, the Johnson Family's been singing together for many years."

"So your mom and dad just brought you up singing?"

My grandma, he thought, but the words didn't come out.

"That's right," Keri Su said. "We just naturally shared ever'thing with him. He's our one and only, you know."

"When did you start playing the guitar, Jimmy Jo?"

"Soon as he could pick it up." Keri Su laughed as if she'd made some kind of funny joke.

The woman smiled slightly and then bent herself right into James's face. "Tell me, Jimmy Jo, what is your favorite song?"

He was working up a little spit in his mouth so he could answer, but it took too long, Keri Su couldn't wait. "Jimmy Jo loves this duet we do together. Maybe you heard it on *Countrytime* three weeks ago?" The woman shook her head. You could tell she wasn't a *Countrytime* fan. " 'My Mother's Bible.' It's a real old-time country song. We're trying to pull this boy into the twentieth century, but he's stubborn as a plow mule." She giggled again.

"Then you like— What was that old gospel number you did in Hampton?"

" 'Will the Circle Be Unbroken?' " Keri Su said.

"Yes. That one. Is that one of your favorites?"

He started to nod in case Keri Su lied again, but she agreed. "Yeah. That's one of Jimmy Jo's all-time favorites." She gave James a little hug before leaning around him to say, "I don't know if you happened to hear my special number on that show?"

The woman shook her head. "I must confess. I wasn't there. I don't cover music. I'm a feature writer."

"Oh."

"My editor picked up on the review in the paper yesterday. We don't have a lot of"—she turned and smiled directly at James—"a lot of ten-year-old celebrities in Tidewater. He thought our readers would be interested in a story."

The photographer was bouncing about all this time, taking pictures from every angle. "Maybe Mrs. Johnson could move off the couch a minute and let me get a few shots of the boy by himself."

James shook his head. The last thing he wanted was his picture in the paper, but no one paid any attention. The photographer was firmly pushing Keri Su to one side, then telling her to go get James's guitar. Keri Su was making little *humpf* sounds, but she got Chester from his room. The photographer gently pried James's glasses from his grasp and handed them to Keri Su. Then the man took the guitar and arranged it on James's lap. He even put James's fingers where he thought they should be. I ought to play it just like this, James thought. That would give him a gosh-awful sound.

The reporter was fiddling with her tiny tape recorder. When she got it all set again, she turned full force on to James. "What would you say is the most satisfying part of being a star?" she asked.

He stared back so hard that she looked away. "The fans," Keri Su was saying. "Jimmy Jo is real touched by how the fans love him. Why, back awhile ago he was sick, they sent him cards and flowers and old family recipes. It was just beautiful, wasn't it, sugar?"

"So, is that right? You like the fans?" He pressed his lips together and nodded. You had to say you liked the fans. "Doesn't it ever get tiring—all that smiling? Signing autographs? Do you have to sign a lot of autographs?"

"You'll never know," Keri Su said, sitting back down on the couch beside him. "I ask him ever' Friday, 'You got writer's cramp, sugar?' I ask him. " She giggled and shook her head. "He's a real little sport. He wouldn't disappoint them fans for nothing."

"Is that right, Jimmy Jo?"

"Of course that's right. Jimmy Jo is like all of us genuine country singers. We know we can't be nothing without our fans. They the ones make ever'thing possible, and we love 'em for it."

154

The woman looked down at her watch and then clicked off her machine. "You have enough shots, Bob?"

"I'm okay," he said.

The reporter got up and stuck her hand out at James. He stood up and shook it. "You don't have a lot to say off the stage, do you?"

"He puts it all into his singing," Keri Su said.

The woman smiled, one side of her mouth higher than the other. "Well, thank you, too, Mrs. Johnson."

"Keri Su. Call me Keri Su. Ever'one does."

The door shut behind the visitors. Keri Su watched them go down the walk and get into the brown Plymouth before she turned around toward James. "What's the matter with you, Jimmy Jo? I never saw you act so dumb before in all my life."

James picked up his book bag and jacket in one hand and Chester in the other and headed for the kitchen. "I'm eleven." That was all he said.

Wednesday was the final school day before Christmas vacation. The last thing James wanted that day was detention, but Mr. Dolman kept looking at him. All day long, whenever James would glance toward the front, there was Mr. Dolman giving him the eye. James willed himself invisible. He slouched way down in his seat, keeping his head directly behind the head of Cindy Smultz, who sat in the desk in front of him. Cindy was big and wore her pumpkin-colored hair poofed out. His strategy should have worked, but everytime his eye got past the mound of orangy hair, he saw Mr. Dolman's face and had to dodge back.

Even Will Short noticed. "What's Dolman staring at you for?" he asked James at recess.

"He ain't staring at me."

"Yes, he is. You haven't turned in any more papers without letting me read them first, have you?"

"No, I ain't. And he ain't staring at me, either."

"You watch. After lunch. I know it's you."

But James didn't watch. He didn't even lift his head. He wasn't going to do anything to get his name on the motto board. Patience Is a Necessary Ingredient of Genius (Benjamin Disraeli, 1805–1881). The spot stayed clean, as it had since Monday. After one hundred and ninety-five years, the bell rang, followed by that blessed word *dismissed.* Still working to seem invisible, James slid out from behind his desk, silently put his chair on top, and walked right behind the well-filled-out Cindy toward the door. He had made it as far as the threshold when— "Johnson, James. One minute, please."

He didn't turn around. His body sagged to a halt as the rest of the class pushed and skipped past him into freedom. When he was alone in the room with Mr. Dolman, he realized that he would have to turn and face the teacher or be charged with "not looking in the eye." He forced his body about, toward the large desk. The teacher was leaning against it, holding out a newspaper.

"I suppose you've seen this already."

James shook his head. "We only get the paper on Sundays."

"Well, this should interest you, then." He shoved the folded-back paper at James. The first thing James saw was a picture four columns wide of a strange little pop-eyed boy with hair standing straight up on his head, sitting on a sofa. It looked as though someone had thrown a huge guitar at the boy's stomach, knocking the breath out of him. "Anyone you know?" Mr. Dolman asked.

He would have denied it if there had been any hope of getting away with a lie. As it was, James just hung his head.

"Looks as though you're a celebrity, James."

James shook his head. "Not really, sir," he mumbled.

"Well, somebody thinks so." He waved his hand at a chair set legs-up on a front desk, indicating that James should take the chair down and sit on it, but James pretended not to understand. "I guess," Mr. Dolman went on, shaking the paper slightly, "I guess this explains certain"—he bared his teeth in what must have been a smile—"certain peculiar absences."

James shuffled his feet. What was the man getting at?

Mr. Dolman bent over him. "You should have trusted me, James. I am not an unreasonable man. I would have been glad to give you extra help"—he showed his teeth again—"made allowances."

James looked down at his sneakers. The canvas had worn very thin at his right big toe. Maybe Jerry Lee would get him a new pair in Wesco over the holidays.

"I take it you were trying to keep this your little secret?"

James gave a short nod.

"Well, you can count on me. I must say, I have to admire a young man who doesn't want special favors or special attention. Good for you, James." He made a noise something like a laugh. It needed practice. "I think I can guarantee that no one else in this classroom reads the newspaper beyond the comics." He held the folded paper out. "Would you like this copy to send to your"—another smile—"grandmother in West Virginia?"

James took it. "Thank ya," he mumbled.

"Merry Christmas, James."

"Same to you . . . sir." He backed his way out the door

and raced home, pausing only long enough to jam the strange-looking kid with the big guitar into the trash can at the filling station.

But Mr. Dolman was wrong. There was another person in the class who read the newspaper. The phone was ringing when James walked in the house.

"It's for you, Jimmy Jo," Keri Su said and then went back into the living room to the magazine she had been reading.

"Who is it?"

"It's me—Will. Did you see the paper today?"

"We don't get the paper."

"James. There's this picture of you on the front page of the B section. With a guitar."

"Just someone looks like me."

"James, don't lie to me. I'm your best friend. I know it's you." He giggled. "Soon as I read 'Jimmy Jo Johnson hardly spoke, preferring that his mother answer for him.' Soon as I read that I was sure it was you. You're always pulling that dumb act."

"I gotta go."

"No, wait! I can't believe it. I know somebody famous."

"I just sing and pick. I ain't famous."

"Your picture's in the paper. It says you're on TV every week. How come I never saw you on TV? I watch all the time."

"I dunno, Will. I gotta go."

"James, wait. I mean, Jimmy Jo. Are you only ten, like it says?"

"My name is James and I'm eleven years old. Smart as you are, don't you know you can't believe ever'thing you read in the newspaper?"

There was a laugh at the other end—a fake, snorty kind of laugh. "You could have knocked me over. Honest. I called up my mom at work and told her, 'I'm best friends to this famous guy, and I didn't even know it.' She can't believe it. She was really impressed. She said I could call my father in Buffalo tonight and tell him, 'Guess what? Your kid is best friends to a celebrity!' He won't believe it either. . . ."

"Will—"

"What?"

"Don't tell nobody, hear?"

"What do you mean? It's the biggest thing ever happened to me. I been tutoring a TV celebrity. I already cut your picture out to put on the bulletin board by the principal's office. Gee, I wish I had a picture of you and me together."

"Will, have a nice Christmas. I gotta get off the phone."

"Yeah, you too. I'll be watching on Friday, Jimmy Jo. I won't miss it."

He'd hardly hung up when the phone rang again.

"Jimmy Jo? That was a fine picture in the paper today, but they got your age wrong, didn't they, son?"

James slammed down the receiver.

Keri Su called from the living room "Who was that?"

"This kid from school."

"And you hung up on him like that? That ain't nice, sugar."

"Oh. No. That second one was a crank call." He went into the living room. Keri Su was sitting on the couch.

"What did they want?"

"Nothing. Really. Just stupid." Should he tell her? Gus had said he ought to tell them. "Gus said when people get on TV they tend to get crank calls and stuff."

She nodded over her magazine. Her hair was knotted up on top of her head to show off her white neck. Keri Su had beautiful skin—like a baby doll's, so smooth and pale. "Gus ought to know," she said.

159

"Do you ever get calls? Like Gus said, Dottie Pierce got thirty-seven men claiming to be her secret husbands."

She looked up. He tried to read something in her brown eyes, but couldn't. "Fancy that."

"Nobody ever call up and said they was your first husband or nothing?"

"How could they?" Her voice was Olive-sharp. "I never been married before."

"It ain't the truth," he explained. "They just trying to get a bite out of the star—like the guy that brought the roses, you know."

"I see. Pretty dumb, if you ask me."

"Yeah."

Keri Su wasn't the one to talk to. Over Christmas he'd have lots of time. He'd tell Jerry Lee about the man then. Jerry Lee would know what to do.

They had known since Thanksgiving that Earl and Keri Su wouldn't be going home with them for Christmas, but somehow, James had hoped they might change their minds.

"We got us a contract, sugar," Keri Su said, playing with his hair. He wanted to put his arms around her right there in the middle of the sidewalk and beg her to come. It wasn't that he wanted her to come so much as it was that he was afraid of her not coming. But he couldn't tell her that, so he just stood there with his arms straight and close to his sides and nodded solemnly, pretending to be grown-up and understanding.

"Well," Jerry Lee said, "we'll look for y'all Monday night then."

"Yeah," answered Earl. "Tell Momma we'll see her soon."

Keri Su rushed back into the house and brought out two

packages wrapped in pink Santa Claus paper with bright red ribbons on top. "I got me some presents for my two special little guys," she said. "Now. Do not open until X-mas, you hear?"

"I ain't got you nothing," James said. "I ain't done any shopping."

"We'll do us some shopping on the way home, boy." Jerry Lee kissed Keri Su on the cheek and then put his arms around her. "We'll be waiting on you," he said. He and James got into the wagon.

Keri Su leaned in the window to give James a peck. "You be good now, sugar."

"Don't worry 'bout me none," he mumbled.

She gave a little frown and then touched him lightly on the nose with the tip of her finger before backing away from the car.

Jerry Lee wanted to do their shopping in Wesco where they knew the stores. By pushing the accelerator and watching out for the highway police, they managed to get to Wesco forty minutes before the stores were due to close. Shopping was not a problem for Jerry Lee. He already knew, apparently, exactly what he was going to buy and where. But James felt crowded and frustrated. He ended up getting bath powder for Keri Su, shaving lotion for the men, and nothing at all for Grandma, the very one he most wanted to please.

"That's all right," Jerry Lee said. "The robe can be from both of us."

He didn't want to give Grandma the robe Jerry Lee had bought. He'd never seen her wear a robe in his entire life. What would she think, them giving her a bathrobe? You don't need a bathrobe unless you're lazy—or sick. But he couldn't say this to Jerry Lee, who was going on about what a pretty color it was—midnight blue with light blue trim—and soft as goose down. Jerry Lee wouldn't tell him what was in the large box marked FRAGILE. It was Jerry Lee's present to the whole family, James included.

As they bounced up the last stretch of dirt road, James felt the old rising and tingling in his stomach that told him he would soon be home. He reached over and put his hand on Jerry Lee's arm.

Jerry Lee turned his head. "Feels good to get here, don't it?"

James nodded. They came round the bend, and there it was —the old cabin squatting low in the darkness, its windows glowing warm. When the headlights skimmed the porch, they could see two figures. James was out of the wagon almost before it stopped. He ran to the porch and grabbed Grandma. He could feel the bones through her thin cloth coat.

"Hey, boy," she said. "Handle with care. Ain't they told you how sickly the old lady is?"

"I never believe that," he said, leading her into the house, his arm around her waist. Grandpa went with Jerry Lee to bring in the things from the car. James could hear Squirt barking and yelping with excitement. He helped Grandma off with her coat and hung it on the clothes hook near the door, then hung his own jacket on top.

"You boys want something to eat?" she asked.

"Naw," he said. "We eat in the car."

"Glass of milk? Rosie been pouring it out." She wanted to get him something.

"That sounds fine," he said.

He watched her walk slowly to the refrigerator and take out a huge jug of milk. It shook in her hands. He must have started toward her, because she jerked her head impatiently to show that she could handle it herself.

The men came in, the dog bouncing around their knees,

all but tripping them. "Down, Squirt," Grandpa ordered. "Down. Will you call off this dog of your'n, Ava?"

Grandma carefully lowered the milk jug to the table and went to the door and opened it. "Out you go." The dog dropped his tail between his legs and skulked out. James took the moment to pour himself some milk. The jug was heavy. It was all he could do to keep from spilling milk on the table.

"You want milk, Jerry Lee?" he asked, avoiding Grandma's eyes.

"What? No. No, thank ya."

James put the jug away. How did you make a person like Grandma take it easy without making her mad?

They sat watching the flames through the small mica window of the stove, hardly talking. Since it was winter, the porch rocker was indoors, and Grandma sat rocking in it. Occasionally she would feel in her pockets as though groping for her pipe. She kept forgetting that she no longer smoked. James tried to think of something to say that wouldn't bring up either sickness or the missing family members, but his brain was full of chicken feathers.

How quiet it was in the country at night. No sounds of trucks shifting gears at the corner traffic light. No sirens in the distance. Only the whimper of the hound puppy lying against the door.

"Oh, thunder. Let him in, James," Grandma said. "The poor wretch has served his time, ain't he?"

James hopped up and let the dog in. Squirt went immediately to Grandma and put his front paws up on her lap and tried to lick her face. She scratched him under the throat and made little clucking noises.

"You see the show Friday?" James asked, surprised at how loud his voice seemed.

She put the dog off to the floor and reached out to James. He was suddenly embarrassed to get on her lap. Wasn't he the strong one now? He dragged the fire stool over as close to her as he could, so she could put her arm around him.

"I know'd you had the gift, boy," she said softly, as though she meant for only him to hear. "Ever' week though, seems like you get better and better. I'm so proud."

"I get scairt, you know."

She nodded.

"Sometimes I think I'm just going to freeze to ice out there, and nothin's gonna come out."

She was smiling with her blue, blue eyes and nodding.

"But ever' week," he continued, "ever' week I think you're out there listening. I got to sing for you." She tightened her arm around him.

"That electric bass—" Grandpa began.

"—ain't the same," Jerry Lee said. "Me and the boy both remarked on it. Just not the same sound."

"No," James agreed, "that's what we said. To get the real Family sound, you got to have Grandpa on the standing bass." He could almost feel his grandfather's pleasure across the dimly lit room. "Singing, too. I had to take the lead for 'Will the Circle Be Unbroken?' in Hampton the other night, and it just wasn't the same a-tall."

"Well, that is one of my special numbers."

"Ain't nobody can do it like you," Grandma said. "Remember how you used to love to hear your daddy sing that one when you was a young 'un, Jerry Lee?"

"It was always one of my very favorites," Jerry Lee said. "And I always said nobody could sing it like my daddy."

"Well." Grandpa got to his feet. "This is mighty nice, but

I think y'all must be tired, and I gotta get this little gal in for her beauty sleep."

Grandma snorted, but she let him help her to her feet.

It didn't seem like Christmas. Other years James and Grandma had spent the days before baking and cooking, preparing for the Family to come home. But this year there were no smells of Christmas cooking. There wasn't even a tree, so he and Jerry Lee got up before it was fully light and went out into the woods and cut a little white pine. They hung the old decorations on it and put their few presents at the base.

"Now, ain't that a pretty surprise?" Grandma said when she came out of her room. They gave her the robe and she made a big fuss over it. "Makes me look like the queen of England," she said, putting it on right on top of her housedress and old sweater. James gave Grandpa and Jerry Lee the shaving lotion. They both opened their bottles and smacked some on their faces, just as if they were making a commercial. Then James and Jerry Lee each opened a pair of mittens that Grandma had knit them. "Can't smoke," she muttered. "Got to do something with my hands."

Jerry Lee's big present was last. Grandpa opened the box and lifted out a suitcase-sized radio with bands and dials and antenna. "You can get anything on it," Jerry Lee explained excitedly. "Africa, if you want."

"Anybody here understand African?" Grandma asked. She was pleased as pie. She fiddled with the dials. "Hope it won't take off while I'm a-holding to it," she said.

"The man guaranteed you could get WWVA in Wheeling and WSM in Nashville," Jerry Lee said. "You always wanted a radio that could get all the good country stations." He clicked it on and began working the dial and the antenna.

The house was filled with the sound of "Joy to the World."

"Ain't that pretty?" Grandma asked. "Will it get Tidewater, too?"

"Oh, I'm sure," said Jerry Lee. "Bakersfield, Austin, anywhere in the world. And it ain't supposed to give you any static."

Grandma listened to the new radio and did sit-down jobs, like peeling potatoes, while James and the men made dinner. Grandpa jerked his head toward the radio. "Only thing 'sides her soaps that'll keep her outta mischief," he muttered. Jerry Lee beamed all over.

James and Jerry Lee didn't remember until Christmas night to open the presents Keri Su had given them. Since she hadn't sent anything to the others, it seemed best to unwrap their gifts in their bedroom. She had given them each a shirt—bright red cotton-knit shirts with a little curled-up crocodile—Will Short shirts.

"Mighty bright," Jerry Lee said. "Mighty cheerful."

"Yeah." What did he want with a Will Short shirt? It looked sissy. The color was sissy. Even the crocodile looked sissy. She probably thought he'd like having something just like Jerry Lee's, and he would, if it were a Western shirt or a lumber jacket. But a Will Short shirt— What was she thinking of?

"These are real stylish in the city." Jerry Lee was trying to explain to him. "I think lots of city folks wear them."

"Yeah."

The next day Jerry Lee suggested that they put the shirts on to surprise Keri Su when she came—let her see how much they appreciated them.

"They just got these little biddy short sleeves."

"After she gets a good look, you can put on your sweater. Come on, it'll mean a lot to her."

They were in the bedroom putting on their shirts when they heard the song. Earlier Jerry Lee had found WSM Nashville for Grandma, and she'd been listening all day, giving a running commentary on the music—whether it was real country, Bakersfield honky-tonk, bastard pop, or purity mess. Almost from the first chords, they thought they knew—although the backup was all a brassy, synthesized sound, and the rhythm was souped up with a heavy *donk-donk* beat. But when the voice came in, they both rushed from the bedroom.

There was no mistake. It was Keri Su singing "Broken Bird." And then the voice of Earl— The polished, metal sound of Earl and Keri Su singing together.

That's my song. It was all James could think. That's my song. Jerry Lee wrote it for me. Why are Keri Su and Earl singing it on the radio? It's my song.

"Folks," the deejay was saying, "that's a brand-new single, written and performed by a brand-new brother–sister team. You can say you heard it first here on WSM, and you can count on Brother Ed, that song is headed wa-a-ay up to the top of the charts. . . ."

Jerry Lee turned around, went into the bedroom, and closed the door behind him. Grandma shut off the radio.

"That's my song," James said, almost in a whisper.

"I thought it was Jerry Lee's song," Grandma said.

Grandpa walked out of his room. "Something wrong?" Grandma shook her head. James didn't know whether she meant she didn't want Grandpa to know or she didn't want to discuss it in front of James. But James had to get out anyway. He called the dog, grabbed his jacket, and went out the door —down across the yard, past the chickens and hogs and Rosie's shed.

He was shivering. Maybe it would snow and the road would close so Keri Su and Earl wouldn't be able to get home. They didn't belong here with the Family. They didn't deserve to be here with the Family. They didn't even want to be a part of the Family anymore. He kicked a dried cow chip loose. What were they trying to do? His heart was pounding as though he'd been running a long way. Didn't they have sense enough to know what they were doing? Didn't they care? First they'd got rid of Grandpa, and now they were acting as though he and Jerry Lee didn't exist. She was his mother. Didn't that matter to her?

He went on, into the woods. It was late afternoon, nearly dark under the trees. He liked that. There shouldn't be any sunshine. The wind should be howling. He sat down on a stump and tore apart a dried leaf. Then he cracked a branch across his knee. That was better. Not only did it make noise, it hurt his knee. He stood up and threw the jagged piece as hard as he could. It hit a tree trunk and crashed into the leaves. The dog started after it, but stopped, confused, as though he couldn't figure out where the stick had gone.

"Stupid!" James said aloud. He headed back. Angry as he was, he wasn't ready to spend a winter night in the woods. Besides, he should be there when the others arrived. He wanted, just once, to hear Jerry Lee tear into them.

He banged his way into the house. Grandma and Grandpa looked up. "Born in a barn?" Grandpa asked.

He turned and slammed the door. Then he jerked off his jacket and threw it at the hook.

"James." Grandma's voice was unnaturally controlled. "Pick up your jacket and calm down. There may be a perfectly good reason. . . ."

He couldn't believe it. Why should she take up for Earl and Keri Su? He went into the bedroom. Jerry Lee was lying on his back, his arms under his head, staring at the ceiling. He didn't look at James. James made as much racket as he could, but since all he was doing was changing shirts, it wasn't very satisfying. He stomped back into the big room where the old folks were still sitting, staring in his direction.

"I can't help it," he said. "They stole me and Jerry Lee's song. I got a right to be mad. Maybe I wanted to record that song. It was mine, and I sang it real good. I really did."

"Why don't you close the bedroom door," his grand-mother said. "I think your daddy's trying to rest." Something in her voice made him obey. "Now, you listen to me," she continued quietly so Jerry Lee wouldn't hear. "I know you're mad. I ain't blaming you. But I want you to get yourself tucked in and under control before they get here. It's up to Jerry Lee to speak to them about it, you hear?"

"He give the song to me. He wrote it for me. You heard him. He said so Thanksgiving."

"You listen to me. Whether you own that song or not, I do not care. I care what happens to your daddy in all this. I don't know just what's going on, but I lived long enough to know a delicate business when I see one. Your daddy's got enough trouble without you bulling in, you hear me?"

She could have socked him in the teeth and it would have hurt a lot less, but he wasn't about to let on. "I hear you," he said. "I'll start supper."

Jerry Lee didn't come in to eat. James was glad. What would he have to say to Jerry Lee? She loves you the most. It's like Earl says, you're the one she favors.

They heard the sound of the Buick, and then Earl was honking the horn—*shave and a haircut two bits*—to announce their arrival. Earl could sure pick the derndest times to be cute. For a minute none of them moved, but at last, Grandpa got up to open the door.

"You behave yourself," Grandma told James. "I mean it."

Jerry Lee came into the big room as Earl and Keri Su did and pecked Keri Su on the cheek. He was quiet, but he was often quiet. Keri Su was calling everybody *sugar* and ordering Earl to bring in the chocolate candy they'd brought from Tidewater. She hugged James and mussed his hair. "Miss me?" she asked. He just smoothed his hair in place.

James put food on the table for the two of them. Keri Su ate a bite or two of ham and drank three cups of coffee. Earl cleaned up everything in sight. He was talking in his loudest, jolliest voice, telling about the day-after-Christmas traffic that had plagued them along the way. Jerry Lee sat in the shadows near the stove, not saying anything. James kept waiting for the others to bring up something about the song, but no one did.

After they'd eaten, Earl noticed the new radio. "That's a beaut."

"They say it'll get Africa," Grandma said dryly.

"I'll bet," Earl answered. Not even then did anybody mention that it could get Nashville as well.

Before long, conversation died as though the battery had given up. They rocked or sat and watched the flames. But it wasn't a comfortable quiet.

"Want me to turn on TV?" Earl asked. "Or the radio?"

"Go ahead if you want," Grandma said, standing up slowly. "I think I'll go on to bed. How 'bout you, James? It's been a long day."

She was trying to get him out of there. She didn't trust him to keep his mouth shut. "I'm okay," he said. "I'll take out the dog." He went without his jacket. The stars were bright as they can only be miles from any city. He stood shivering on the porch while the dog ran to the edge of the yard and squatted in the shadow of the trees. It must be nice having life so simple. Just shine or squat, whatever nature tells you.

The four of them were still sitting there when James came back in. He sat down on the fire stool. In a few minutes Grandpa stood and said good-night and went out to the privy. Keri Su got up, poured herself another cup of coffee, and sat down at the table to drink it. She waited until Grandpa had come back in and disappeared into his bedroom before she spoke. "Momma seems all right," she said. James could see Jerry Lee's head nodding yes in the shadows. "Y'all have a nice Christmas?"

"Um." Meaning yes from Jerry Lee.

Don't lie, Daddy. Tell her we know she stole our song.

"How 'bout those father–son shirts? You get a kick outta those?"

Now, Daddy. Tell her we was just putting them on when we heard the record. Go on, tell her.

"Mighty cheerful," Jerry Lee said. "Nice."

Nice? James got up, grabbed the poker, pulled open the stove door, and jabbed at the coals. "You want to hear something funny?" he heard himself asking.

"What, sugar?"

"Well, you just reminded me when you mentioned them shirts." He punched the fire a few more times, keeping his back to the room. "It's crazy, but there's this guy in Tidewater keeps calling up, says he's my daddy."

"Oh my God!" Keri Su jumped up. "I spilled the damned coffee."

Earl got a dishrag from the sink and handed it to her. "Burn yourself?"

"No. It's just lukewarm. Stupid."

"Gus said I should tell you." James had started now. He had to go on. "Sometimes this guy hangs around the school."

"You spoke to him?" Earl asked.

"Not really."

"Good," said Earl. "These people don't mean no harm, but you can't be too careful."

"What did he look like?" It was Jerry Lee from the shadows.

James turned toward him, but he couldn't see his expression. "He's tall, kinda skinny. Walks like a mountain man."

Keri Su gave her jeans a final swipe and then took the rag over to the sink and began rinsing it out. "Sugar," she began, then she cleared her throat. "Sugar, tell them what Gus told you about Dottie Pierce."

"Oh, yeah." James set the poker carefully against the wall. "That Dottie Pierce who was the regular before us? Gus said thirty-seven men claimed to be secretly married to her."

Earl snorted. "Crazy. Crazy," he said.

Jerry Lee stood up. "I think I'll turn in," he said.

Keri Su squeezed out the dishrag and hung it on the peg by the sink. "Me too. C'mon, sugar, way past bedtime. We got plenty of time to talk tomorrow."

But they didn't talk tomorrow. Even the next day when Earl took off in the Buick to "see 'bout some out-of-town business," no one asked where. It was like a fancy dance—everyone stepping all around, but never on the spot. At first James was furious, but as the week wore on, he cared less and less. Let her have the stupid song. If Jerry Lee wasn't man enough to call her on it, why should he bust a gut?

The three of them rode back on New Year's Eve so that Keri Su would be rested up for the club on Sunday night. Grandma had hugged him tight against her, but he didn't hug her back. She only loved him when Jerry Lee wasn't around for her to mother. "See ya," he said. He never thought he'd be glad to leave the farm.

He was even glad to be back at school, which didn't start again until Wednesday. That is, he was glad until he got to the playground. Before he knew it, he was surrounded by screeching kids. Will Short was trying to take charge, explaining importantly that although James was indeed a celebrity who sang on TV and had his picture in the paper, he also valued his privacy and everyone should respect that and leave him alone. He, Will Short, would be in charge of getting autographs. James wanted to choke him. To the side he could see Eleazer Jones leaning against the jungle gym. He was wearing a long wool overcoat and a felt hat that made him look like a movie gangster. The King had his hands in his pockets, grinning, not even trying to help.

Mr. Dolman smiled at him when he walked into the classroom. The teacher swept his hand toward the motto board. Ah, Who Can Tell How Hard It Is To Climb / The Steep Where Fame's Proud Temple Shines Afar? (James Beattie, 1735–1803).

James kept his face in his work all day long. He even told Mr. Dolman he was sick, so he could spend recess in the nurse's office. That was a mistake. The first thing the woman said was "Oh! You're Jimmy Jo Johnson. I saw your picture on the bulletin board."

Mr. Dolman kept him after the others, not as punishment, he explained, but to ask James if he were feeling better. Never would he be invisible again.

He went to the boys' room as soon as Mr. Dolman let him go, and he waited fifteen minutes until the corridor was silent. When he came out the school door, Eleazer Jones was waiting.

"I sent the rest on," the King said, buttoning his long overcoat.

"Thank ya."

"That dude's out there by the fence again."

James's heart bounced.

"I thought I better walk you home." They started down the walk. James tried not to look toward the fence. "He still there?"

"Uh huh."

James stopped walking. "Would you—? I want to talk to him. Would you go over there with me?"

"Sure."

They headed straight for the fence. James's heart was banging up against his chest, but he tried to keep his eyes on the man to show he wasn't scared. He was going to find out once and for all . . . but when he got there, with nothing but a chain link between their faces, he froze. It was worse than any stage fright. His stupid mouth wouldn't open.

"Whatchu want?" the King was asking.

"I just want to meet my boy," the man said, licking his lips. He was nervous, too, it seemed. "I'm the boy's daddy. I want for us to get acquainted."

"He don't know you from a light post."

"No. I left. I was in the navy. I didn't even know I had a boy 'til just lately."

"Now he's some big celebrity, you coming 'round like a dog to garbage."

"No, no," the man said. "It ain't that way." He turned toward James. "Really, son. I don't want nothing from you. I just want to see you. Make sure they're taking good care of you."

"You such a good Joe," the King interrupted, "how come you run off in the first place?"

The man wouldn't look at Eleazer Jones. "I thought her daddy was going to kill us both," he said to James.

"He don' know where you coming from, man. Anybody walk up and tell somebody he's their long-lost daddy. You got no proof."

"He'll have to ask his momma. Ask her about Flem Keeser. Tell her Flem Keeser says hello."

"You had enough?" the King asked James.

James nodded. They started away.

"Wait!" the man said, poking a piece of paper through the fence. "Here's my phone number. 'Case you want to call."

The King took it and handed it to James. "Don't call us, man. If my bro wants to rap, he call you. Got that?"

"I don't mean no trouble," the man said.

"Right." The King swung about. "Let's split." They walked the length of the playground. The man was still standing behind the fence when they turned off the schoolyard to go up the street.

"What's the matter? Your mouth froze up?"

James nodded. "You think"—he managed to whisper—"you think he's telling the truth?"

The King shrugged. "Ain't you already got a daddy?"

James didn't answer. He was seeing Jerry Lee lying on the bed staring at the ceiling.

"'Bout this high." The King indicated a height near his own eyebrow. "I seed you on TV. You got you a fine daddy. Plays a bad banjo. I think my mama gots a crush on him." He shook his head. "She love that show. I know that's your daddy. Wudn't he the one wrote that song about the bird?"

"Yeah." He let her steal it, too. But James wasn't going to say that out loud.

The King shook his head again. "Multiple-choice daddies, and me, I don' even have one." He tilted his gangster hat over his right eye. "I'd take one of yours, but I need me one in a

176

matching color." He laughed at his own joke. They had reached the corner of James's street. "You be awright, white mite?"

James nodded. "Thank ya."

"Pleasure." The King tipped his hat.

Eddie Switten was sitting in the living room with the Family when James walked in. They were all waiting for him because Eddie had rigged up another last-minute booking. It was in Suffolk, so they had to leave right away.

"I don't feel so good," James said.

"Hey, Jimmy Jo." Eddie leaned forward on the arm of the couch, his little eyes bright. "They want you special. The guy heard you in Hampton."

"Well, if he don't feel up to it—" Earl began, but James could see Keri Su trying to shut him up with a jerk of her head.

"Come on, sugar. It'll be fun. You can sing anything you like. Honest."

James turned directly to Jerry Lee, who had his banjo out and was fiddling with the pegs. "How 'bout if I sing 'Broken Bird'?" No one answered. "Awright?" James demanded, sticking his chin up. "You said *anything.*"

"Well, sugar . . ."

"Now, just wait one doggone minute," Eddie said, turning from one member of the Family to the other, as though trying to puzzle things out. "What's going on here?"

"I just wanted to sing my song," James said. He appealed to Jerry Lee. "It is my song, ain't it?" Jerry Lee looked at him, his face stretched out in pain. James felt a stirring of shame, but he plowed right on down the furrow. "Well, ain't it my song?"

Eddie Switten was standing up, staring at Keri Su. "Don't tell me these two don't know."

Keri Su rubbed her lips together. "I was gonna tell 'em. I just haven't had the chance."

"Tell us what?" James demanded.

"Well, sugar, when me and Earl was down to Nashville couple of weeks ago," she began, her voice as fluttery as a little girl's, "well, they wanted more than one song for the demo—something new. It just come to me to sing it. It was for the flip side, in case they decided to make a record. I— I had to do something on the spot. I—I—" She licked her lips and pressed them together. "Now they're playing it a lot . . . and . . ."

"We heard it," James said. "On the new radio at Grandma's."

"You never said." Her eyes shifted from James to Jerry Lee's bowed head. "How come you never said nothing?"

"The deejay said you and Earl wrote the song," James said, hammering each word.

"Well, somebody had to sign for rights." She went over to the couch and knelt down beside Jerry Lee. "You weren't there, honey. Somebody had to sign, so Eddie said . . ." She put her hand on his knee and rubbed it. "We was going to tell you, but it was just going to be the flip side. Nobody was going to play it." She laughed sharply and gave his knee a playful pat. "Earl didn't even like it all that much."

"It was my song," James said. "Daddy give it to me, didn't you? Didn't you?"

"Well, it don't mean you can't ever sing it, sugar." She twisted her head around toward James. "It's just right now, while it's hot, while it's playing a lot on the radio . . . Well, folks associate it with Earl and me, so Eddie thinks it would sound a little funny if someone else in the Family . . ."

Why didn't Jerry Lee say anything? He was just sitting there, not saying a word. "You going tonight, Jerry Lee?" James asked.

"Well, of course he is, sugar. We're all going. We can't do without you and Jerry Lee."

"You done all right in Nashville—long as you had our song, you done just fine without us."

Jerry Lee looked up now. "That's about enough, son."

"Don't you see what's happening? They're trying to squeeze us out. They don't like our style. Soon as the *Countrytime* contract runs out, we're done, right?" He looked defiantly first at Keri Su, then Earl, then Eddie. Their faces weren't telling.

"Whoa, son," Jerry Lee said softly. "Take it easy." He put his arm around Keri Su, who was still kneeling by the couch, as though he felt he ought to protect her from James. James wanted to laugh. But maybe she wouldn't push Jerry Lee out. She needed his banjo. She needed his songs. What she didn't need anymore was James. She'd never needed James. She was glad to give him to Grandma and be rid of him.

"That was my song, wasn't it, Daddy?" He would give Jerry Lee one more chance.

Jerry Lee got up from the couch and put his arm now

around James, almost whispering as he spoke. "I thought I wrote it for you, James. I know I said so. But sometimes you don't know your ownself what a song is all about. Don't make me choose between you, son. I can't do that. Can't it belong to both of you?"

James stiffened against the embrace.

"A song can have lots of meanings." Jerry Lee was begging James to understand.

James jerked out from under Jerry Lee's arm and started for his room. "Oh," he said at the door, "I 'most forgot." He took the slip of paper from his jacket pocket and shoved it at Keri Su, who was now seated on the couch. "Fellow wanted you to call. Name of Keeser. Flem Keeser."

Keri Su turned perfectly white. There was no mistaking. She knew that name. James stomped past them all into his bedroom and locked the door behind him.

Each of them came to the door and tried to talk to him, but James just sat in the middle of his mattress—his jacket still on his back, his sneakers still on his feet. He waited until he heard the sound of them collecting their instruments, going out the door, the car doors slamming, the motor starting, the car driving off down the street. The show must go on. The Family can break apart into little teeny splinters, but the stupid show must go on. He sat there on the mattress until the only light in the room came from the neighbor's back porch.

James woke long before dawn, stiff and uncomfortable from having slept crouched up with all his clothes on. He crept out of the room and washed up. The kitchen clock said five fifty-eight. He got himself a swig of milk straight from the carton and grabbed the bread bag with half a loaf left, as well as the lunch that Jerry Lee had packed the night before. Jerry Lee always packed James's lunch. *You got you a fine daddy.*

James put the lunch back into the refrigerator and took some loose baloney to slap between his slices of bread.

It was cold out by the river before the sun was up, cold and foggy. The ducks were already busy, diving bottoms up into the icy water. He threw them torn-off bits of his bread. They quacked and gobbled it down. Poor suckers—didn't take much to make them happy. The river went into the Chesapeake Bay, and the Bay went into the ocean, and the ocean water evaporated to make rain and snow that came down upon his mountains and into the streams and rivers that flowed into this river that flowed into the Bay. . . .

Everything fit. A place for everything except him. He threw the bread in his hand to the ducks and began to walk. He didn't want to get to school too early. He didn't want people nibbling at him on the playground. On the other hand, if he were even a few seconds late, Mr. Dolman was likely to do something worse than any kid would think up. He borrowed the key from the filling station—"Didn't I tell you to go at school?" the attendant hollered—and hid in the rest room as long as he dared. At Anna's Chicken House, workers were cleaning the counters, but they wouldn't open until ten. No use hoping to hide in there. He should have made friends, the kinds of friends that other kids had—the ones whose houses you could go to and it wouldn't seem weird that you had shown up too early to walk to school. He'd seen kids do that on TV. They even had breakfast at the other kid's house. Or was that just in the commercials where smiley-faced mothers gave food to all the kids in the neighborhood? He had two friends, sort of. He was sure Will Short wouldn't mind if he came by, but James didn't know where Will lived. He'd never gone there. Besides, Will had turned so strange. Will wanted to show him off—like he was a prize fish or something.

He wondered where the King lived. The Family drove through a black neighborhood on the way to the TV station. Eleazer Jones must live in Lincoln Park somewhere, but James couldn't just walk into the neighborhood at eight o'clock in the morning and figure on bumping into the King. He went back to the river and walked along it for a mile or so. There were great gray navy ships crouching at anchor far out on the water. He sat down on a rock and made two sandwiches with the baloney and the rest of the bread. Gulls were circling near the bank, occasionally diving down and squawking when they spotted food. He was sorry not to have more bread to share. The fog was lifting, and he could see for miles. The river was huge. James could hardly believe that compared to the ocean, it was just a trickle.

"Hey you!" A woman had opened her back door and was screaming out. "Get off my dock. This is private property!"

He ran all the way to school. If that woman only realized who she was yelling at. . . . But that was a Will Short kind of thought. James knew that a woman who lived in a big house on the river wouldn't watch *Countrytime*. He wasn't famous where it counted, just where it hurt.

Will had been waiting for him and saw him before anyone else. "Jimmy Jo!" He yelled so loud that half the playground turned around to see what the commotion was. Or so it felt to James. At any rate, he was being jostled by kids. "Can I have your autograph?" "What you famous for?" "Sing something so I'll know if I ever heard you before." He felt as if he were choking, drowning.

"Yo! Ease up!" Suddenly the crowd parted like the waters of the Red Sea. Then the big voice said quietly, "You awright?"

James nodded. He wasn't all right. His jacket had nearly been ripped off his back, but he knew he would be all right.

The King jerked his head. James followed him to the school step.

"Hey, the bell hasn't rung!" Will called out.

"The boy got to go to the liberry," the King announced. Pulling his felt hat on tightly and gathering his big overcoat about him, he swept James safely inside.

"I really got to go to the bathroom," James said.

"That's cool." The King walked down the hall as though he owned the building.

"What we fixing to do," the King said while James washed his hands and face at the bathroom sink, "is make you a plan. Ever'body get tired of this jive in about a week, but 'til then they make you crazy. How 'bout you just lay out sick for a while?"

"I can't stay home," James muttered.

"What you mean? You just 'splain to your daddy how things is here. He'll see."

James could feel his face burning. He ran his wet hands through his hair. He pretended to study himself in the cracked mirror above the sink.

"What's the matter, man? You got problem at home, too?"

James nodded. "I can't go back home right now."

The King spit into the sink. "C'mon," he said.

They walked out the street door of the school and then circled around the block to avoid the playground, heading toward the Lincoln Park neighborhood. At first James thought Eleazer Jones might be going home, but he led James instead to the section of the neighborhood where small restaurants and shops lined the street. Between a hardware store and a beauty parlor was a narrow alley that sneaked behind the shops to a marshy finger of the river and a rotting wharf where a small skiff was tied. "Belong to me," the King said proudly, retrieving oars from under the back stoop of the beauty parlor. "Get in the front."

He rowed, his back to James, taking them out of the reed-clogged inlet into the wide part of the river. The water was calm, but still it lapped the sides of the tiny boat. "You 'fraid?" the King asked.

James shook his head before he realized that he was shivering. "Li'l cold," he said.

The King nodded. "We go closer in," he said. "Out of the wind."

It was like a dream—like being in another world. The sun was climbing high, and James forgot to be either cold or afraid. It was going to be one of those strange winter days when the temperature climbs almost to seventy and you're lulled into thinking that spring has come. He closed his eyes and bent his head back, feeling the warmth on his face. The sound of the water against the side was like music. He was safe, suspended in a magic world far away from both home and school.

"Dag."

"What?" The sudden exclamation jolted James out of his dream world.

"I shoulda brought me a lunch."

James pulled the slapped-together baloney and bread sandwiches from his jacket pocket. They were smushed, but he gave one to Eleazer Jones and ate the other himself, pleased to have something to share with the King.

After they ate, the King rowed the boat into another inlet —one of the ones that the large houses with docks and motorboats backed onto. The King didn't act for a minute as though anyone would object. He just threw his anchor, a rope tied around a heavy piece of metal, overboard and brought both oars into the boat. He took off his overcoat and sat down in the bottom of the skiff facing James, with his head and shoulders propped against the seat and his knees jammed up to his chest. His overcoat was tucked under his chin and over his body like a blanket.

"Set down in the bottom," he said. "'Less you can sleep setting straight up."

James obeyed. Maybe you couldn't own the water—maybe that couldn't be private property. Or maybe it all belonged to the King. Anyhow, the King was soon asleep, snoring peacefully. That's what it was like when you were the King, you belonged everywhere.

James woke with a start. He was cold. The sun was going down. Eleazer Jones was already awake, his overcoat on. He was seated as before with his back to James, pulling the anchor rope hand over hand, dropping the wet rope and anchor between his feet. "Boy, you sleep like you dead," he said cheerfully over his shoulder as he steered the skiff back into the main part of the river.

"I feel like I got the rheumatiz," James said, struggling to lift his body back on the plank in the prow.

"Ain't no Beautyrest."

"I love it," James said. "I wish I could stay here forever."

"You funning, man. Whatchu gon' eat?"

"I'd get me a fishing pole," James said.

"Yeah." The King smiled over his shoulder. "But it be cold out here, tomorra, next day. Like to freeze your li'l tail off."

"What am I gonna do?" James was asking himself more than he was asking the King.

The King didn't answer. He just dug deeply and rhythmically with his oars. James watched the back of the big wool overcoat and the strong brown hands that gripped the oars. Maybe Eleazer Jones would invite him to come live at his house. James waited, half hoping he might, but the King didn't say anything. When they got to the dock behind the beauty parlor, the King hopped out lightly, deftly avoiding the holes in the dock, and tied the skiff to the post. He lifted the oars out and put them down before stretching out a hand to James.

"It's late," he said. "Your daddy be worried."

And his daddy would be. James knew that, but he couldn't help it. It wasn't his fault. It was Jerry Lee's fault, choosing Keri Su, making him, James, feel like he had no place in the Family anymore.

The King walked him most of the way home. "What you do tomorra?"

James shrugged and lowered his head. He didn't want to cry in front of Eleazer Jones. The King twisted down to see his face. "What's the matter, li'l bro?"

"I reckon I couldn't . . ."

"You need to come to Eleazer Jones's house awhile?"

But James knew he couldn't. There was no place for him at the King's house. He was already squeezing, asking the King to make a place for him on the edges of his world. "Thank ya," he said. "I loved your boat."

The King grinned, his body going easy with pleasure. "You wanta go out again, you tell me, awright?"

James tried to grin. "Thank ya," he said and then turned and ran toward the corner.

19

James climbed in through his window. He could hear the murmur of their voices coming from the kitchen. He wondered if they knew he'd been gone all day. He wondered if they cared. They were in there eating supper. He could smell the biscuits. Jerry Lee had made biscuits. James was so hungry he could chew his way straight through the wall. Besides, he had to go to the bathroom.

He opened his door, pretending not to see them there around the table as he went through to the stairs.

"James!" "Sugar!" "Hey, boy!" They all called out to him as he went past, but he closed his ears to them. When he came back through, they all tried again. The smell of the biscuits was almost more than he could stand, but he refused to weaken. He marched straight past, closing his door sharply behind and locking it with a noisy, satisfying click. When he turned back toward the mattress, there in the middle of it was a plate of food. Jerry Lee must have brought it in while he was upstairs in the bathroom. He knew he oughtn't to eat it, but he couldn't help himself. You can't make plans when you're starving to death. He began gobbling down the food.

"Son."

James hastily swallowed the bite of biscuit in his mouth.

"We have to leave for rehearsal. You ready?"

"I ain't going."

There was a minute of silence, as though Jerry Lee was trying to figure out what to say next. "We need you," he said finally.

"I don't feel good."

"I need to talk to you. Can I come in?"

"No!" His remaining biscuit bounced off the plate onto the cover. He put the biscuit back on his plate and wiped up the jelly with his finger.

"It ain't your momma's fault, boy. She wanted to tell you years ago, but I wouldn't let her. I was scared I'd lose you."

James bit his lip to keep from saying anything.

"Why don't I get Grandma on the phone? Let you talk to her?"

"No! I don't want to talk to no one."

"She's worried sick about you. She wants to talk to you."

So Jerry Lee had been tattling to Grandma, had he? They'd been chirping behind his back. What's the matter with mean, selfish little James? Worrying his sweet daddy and his poor old sick grandma to death. Suddenly, he hated them both with a blind, black fury.

"Please talk to your grandma," Jerry Lee was begging.

"She ain't my grandma and you know it!" James yelled the words at the top of his voice, tearing the seams of his throat, hurling the plate and the last jellied biscuit crashing against the door. "Tell her to leave me alone. You hear? Tell her I hope I never see her again as long as I live."

189

He could hear them conferring outside the door. Earl's voice was the loudest. He wanted to bust the door in and whack James's bottomside. Keri Su was telling Earl to shut his mouth, that it wasn't his business anyway. And Jerry Lee was trying to shut them both up so he could reason with James.

"Well, whatever you do, you better get on with it," Earl was saying. "We're gonna be late to rehearsal as it is."

There was another mumbled conference. Should someone stay? Should everyone stay? In the end, to James's relief, they all went. He waited until the sound of the wagon could no longer be heard, and then he went into the kitchen and got a rag. He cleaned up the splinters of china. The biscuit looked all right, but he was sure if he ate it he'd eat bits of the broken plate as well and die of a chopped-up belly or something awful.

Would they care if he died? Would Jerry Lee write a sad, beautiful song about his lost child, which Keri Su and Earl would put on a record down in Nashville with lots of electronic backup and— Lord, they'd probably even add a snare drum. He was furious all over again.

He got Chester and tuned it and tried to play, but everything he thought to play made him either depressed or angry. "Broken Bird," "My Momma Is a Angel Up in Heaven," "Poor Wayfaring Stranger," "Will the Circle Be Unbroken?" Broke, broke, broke. There was no fixing it.

He was asleep when they got back, and in the morning, he stole out early to eat before they were up. He was getting the milk when he heard Jerry Lee on the stairs. "James?" So he just snatched everything he could carry in one load, went back to his room, and locked himself in. He could hear Jerry Lee moving about the kitchen, starting the coffee, putting bacon on to fry. He waited for Jerry Lee to come to his door and plead with him to come out. Hungry as he was, he didn't take a bite, waiting for Jerry Lee's voice. But Jerry Lee didn't say anything else after that first "James," and then the others were there eating. No one came to his door. Oddly disappointed, James ate his cold biscuits and drank his milk and then went back to sleep. There was nothing else to do. He wasn't ready to try school again.

All afternoon he waited for them to come and plead with him to come out, but they didn't. He could tell from the noises that Keri Su and Earl had left the house during the afternoon. Jerry Lee stayed behind. James could hear him practicing the fiddle in the living room. He sounded better. Not as good as Earl, but better than he had at Thanksgiving. *Does he want me to come out and tell him how good he's getting?* James lay down and put the pillow over his head. It didn't block out the sound. Next, Jerry Lee got his banjo and went to town—almost as though he was showing off all his fancy Earl Scruggs' licks. Finally he quieted and began playing his own songs, mostly sad ones about lost love and hope. That's how he thinks he can get me, James decided, he thinks he can make me come out and try to comfort him.

Anytime now, thought James, he'll come to the door and tell me he was wrong. That it was my song and he should have stood up to Keri Su and told her off. That he should have stood up to Keri Su and Earl about everything. That he should have said they had to straighten out and be a regular part of the Family and stop acting like some kinda honky-tonk stars that sing hard, brassy music and live lives to match. Or else he should have just thrown them out. They think they're so great, just let them try to make it on their own without him—without him, Jerry Lee Johnson—who wrote half their songs and played a bad banjo, and his boy—James—who was the main reason they got their *Countrytime* contract in the first place.

They ought to be grateful. James could hear the speech Jerry Lee would give, standing tall and proud, while Keri Su wept until the mascara ran black rivers down her cheeks and Earl couldn't utter a word for shame.

But Jerry Lee didn't come creeping to his door. No one did. "Hope you feel better soon, sugar," Keri Su called, and they were gone, all three of them together, to *Countrytime,* leaving him behind.

He had no idea how long he'd sat in the dark when the phone began to ring. "I'm busy, Will," he said instead of hello.

"Jimmy Jo?" The sound of the voice was like a cold electric shock. "I called the studio, but they said you were sick tonight."

"I said I'd call you, Mr. Keeser, if I wanted to talk."

"That was your little colored friend said that." The voice at the other end chuckled. "You home by yourself. Might be a good time for me to come over and get acquainted."

"No!"

"What did they tell you 'bout me?"

"Nothing. They didn't tell me nothing 'bout you. I just don't want— I ain't got nothing to say to you."

"I know it's a surprise—me showing up like this. But I want to see you. You my flesh, boy. My own flesh."

"I don't want to see you. You stay away from here."

"Don't be scairt, boy. I ain't gonna hurt you."

"I ain't scairt. I just don't have nothing to say— I don't want to— Just stay 'way, you hear?"

"I can't b'lieve you mean that, son. I'll be there ten minutes."

James slammed the phone down and ran from front door to back, checking the locks, then all the windows and locks on the first floor, and then all the windows on the second floor. Then he turned off the lights and climbed behind the sofa out of sight. He wished he'd gotten a blanket. The rug ran out under the sofa, and he lay against the cold wood shivering. What did the man want? He didn't care what anybody said, nobody could make him believe that man was his daddy. His daddy was a little scrawny banjo player that loved everybody so much he just let them walk all over him. He was a fool for loving people—woman didn't deserve him; brother that took advantage; selfish, rotten, spoiled little kid that didn't stick by him when he needed it most. James listened for the sound of the bell, like a cornered coon on a branch. Oh, Jerry Lee, come back and get me, please. I'll never ever . . .

But Jerry Lee did not come in answer to James's prayer. Instead, as he lay there in the dark behind the sofa, he saw once more in his head a black face with a gangster hat pulled down low over the eyes. "You got multiple-choice daddies, white mite. You gets to choose."

James crawled out of his hiding place, smoothed down his hair, and leaving everything else locked, climbed out his bedroom window. When the black pickup pulled alongside the curb, he was sitting on the top porch step like a country gentleman surveying his acres. Only it was cold, and he'd forgotten to put on his jacket and his shoes. He concentrated on not shivering as he watched the door of the cab swing open.

Flem Keeser was dressed in navy blues. He wants to impress me, James thought. He wants bad for me to know he's somebody. Shame I don't know nothing about insignias. The man came up the walk, his head cocked funny to the side. "Jimmy Jo?" he asked, from the bottom of the steps, just as if he hadn't seen James up close before.

"My name is James," James said. "James Johnson." He tried to say it so it sounded firm, not mean.

Keeser took off his hat and tucked it under his arm. "Well," he said. "Well." He didn't seem to know what to say. "I guess it ain't often a man gets to meet his son like this."

"Reckon it ain't," James said, proud his mouth was working and his voice hardly trembling at all.

"Well," the man said again. "Hard to know where to begin, ain't it?" He laughed. "I could sure use a smoke." He made no move to get out a cigarette, just shifted his weight from one foot to the other.

The navy should have taught him how to stand up straight, thought James. He wouldn't be such a bad-looking guy if he stood up.

"Well." Keeser gave a crooked smile as if to admit he'd said *well* one time too often. "It was quite a surprise to see you on TV with Olive and have it dawn on me you was my son. Quite a surprise." He shook his head, remembering.

James nodded. "I guess in a matter of speaking I am your son. But"—he took a deep breath—"you ain't my daddy."

Flem Keeser took a step forward, as if to argue.

James got to his feet, so that he towered over the man on the sidewalk. "My daddy don't run off and leave my momma no matter how tough things get," he said.

"Her old man probably kill me," Keeser muttered.

James ignored this. "I don't have nothing against you, but I don't never want to see you again."

The man stood there for a minute, chewing on his bottom lip. "I ain't looking for trouble," he said. "I just thought you had a right to know. You woulda wanted to know, wouldn't you?"

"Maybe," said James. "Sometime, maybe."

Keeser shook his head and looked up at James. "Well," he

said and sighed so his body shook with it. "Is it awright if I say I'm proud to know you?"

"I reckon."

"Your daddy's a lucky man."

"No sir. I'm the lucky one."

Flem Keeser put his hat on, jerking the bill down with his right hand and using the left to adjust the back. "Well, like they say, I'll see you in the movies."

James nodded. He was shivering in the cold, but he stood on the step and watched the tall man climb into the pickup, give a military salute, and screech off down the street. Then James went around back and hauled himself up through his bedroom window. He fell onto his mattress. Well, he thought, I done it. I growed up.

Somebody was blamming on the front door. He sat up to listen. Who on earth?

"James! You open this dadburn door before I smoke you out!"

"Grandma!"

He jumped up so fast he almost tripped himself. "I'm coming! Wait! I'm coming!"

They were standing on the porch—Grandpa in his best suit and Grandma in her black Sunday dress. James threw his arms around her and hugged her until she pushed him gently away. "Could we come in, you reckon, boy? We been in that cold pickup since before dawn, and I'm about to freeze my rear end off."

He drew them both into the house and then began running about turning on lights. "You get dressed, boy," Grandpa said. "Forget them lights. We got to break the speed limit to get there before the show's over as it is."

"They ain't expecting me," he said.

"Listen, boy," Grandma said. "Jerry Lee wouldn'ta called and told us to fetch you there if they wasn't expecting you. Now move it 'fore I smack it."

He should have been terrified—walking into the lights with no rehearsal, not even knowing what he was supposed to sing. But he saw them there, turning to greet him as he came onstage—Keri Su looking a little shy, Earl grinning, and Jerry Lee with a smile that was like to break his heart. He went close to the little man, who handed him the mike to introduce the number as though James knew just what he was supposed to be singing. And he did. "Tonight, friends, I wanna sing something special for my grandma and grandpa, who come all the way down here from Blue County, West Virginia, for the show tonight." He waited for the applause. "And also 'cause I'm so happy to be here with my mom and my Uncle Earl, and my daddy, Jerry Lee Johnson. We're gonna sing 'Will the Circle Be Unbroken?' "

He could see everything so clearly that it would have frightened him, if he could have been frightened. There was an old lady on the front row, holding the hand of the young woman sitting next to her. The old lady was weeping, and James imagined that her husband had died and she was thinking of the circle in that land beyond the sky. But his circle was here: Grandma and Grandpa, standing where he had left them just off stage; foolish Keri Su, who did need him and Jerry Lee to take care of her—did it hurt her that he had always loved Grandma and Jerry Lee instead of her, his own momma?— poor old Earl acting so big, but really scared that he, too, was outside the circle; and Jerry Lee— *Oh, Jerry Lee, I done you wrong. You was trying so hard to hold us all together. I nearly broke it. Maybe it can't be held together. Maybe you're a fool to try, but I*

196

swear, Daddy, I ain't going to be the one to break it. On the Bible, I swear it.

They were in the final chorus—"By and by, Lord, by and by." He looked out again, past the lights. He had forgotten in the rush to take off his glasses, so he could see every face out there. How had he ever thought they were melons? They were so full of love, looking up at him. They were like little children on Christmas morning—waiting all full of hope for a present. And he had the gift.

About the Author

KATHERINE PATERSON's works have received wide acclaim and been published in many languages. Among them are *Jacob Have I Loved* and *Bridge to Terabithia,* winners of the 1981 and 1978 Newbery Medals; *The Great Gilly Hopkins,* a Newbery Honor Book and winner of the 1979 National Book Award; *The Master Puppeteer,* which received the 1977 National Book Award; *Gates of Excellence: On Reading and Writing Books for Children*; and *Rebels of the Heavenly Kingdom.*

Katherine Paterson was born in China, the daughter of missionary parents, and she spent her early childhood there. Educated in both China and the United States, she was graduated from King College in Bristol, Tennessee, and later received master's degrees from the Presbyterian School of Christian Education in Richmond, Virginia, and Union Theological Seminary in New York.

The parents of four children, Mrs. Paterson and her husband live in Norfolk, Virginia.